COMMITMENT
AND OPEN CROSSINGS

COMMITMENT
AND OPEN CROSSINGS

The First Circumnavigation of Britain
and Ireland by Kayak

BILL TAYLOR

DIADEM BOOKS · LONDON

[FRONTISPIECE] *Pinnacle Stack by the cliffs south of Dunbeath, Caithness*
[CONTENTS PAGE] *Seas breaking on the reef of Filey Brigg, Yorkshire*

The quote on the jacket is taken from *Sea Canoeing* by Derek Hutchinson, published by A & C Black Publishing Ltd; it is reproduced by kind permission of the publisher.

All photographs were taken by team members except for those on page 15, by Paul Newman, and on pages 114–115, by Ian Bourn.

Map artwork by Don Sargeant.

British Library Cataloguing in Publication Data

Taylor, Bill
  Commitment and open crossings: the first circumnavigation of
  Britain and Ireland by kayak
  1. Voyages around Great Britain by kayaks
  I. Title
  914.104858

  ISBN 0 906371 73 2

Published in Great Britain in 1990 by Diadem Books, London

All trade enquiries to Hodder and Stoughton
Mill Road, Dunton Green, Sevenoaks, Kent TN13 2YA.

Colour separations by Planway, London

Typeset in Linotron Sabon by
Rowland Phototypesetting Ltd, Bury St Edmunds, Suffolk

Printed and bound in Great Britain by
BPCC Hazell Books
Aylesbury, Bucks, England
Member of BPCC Ltd.

FOR ROD MITCHELL

CONTENTS

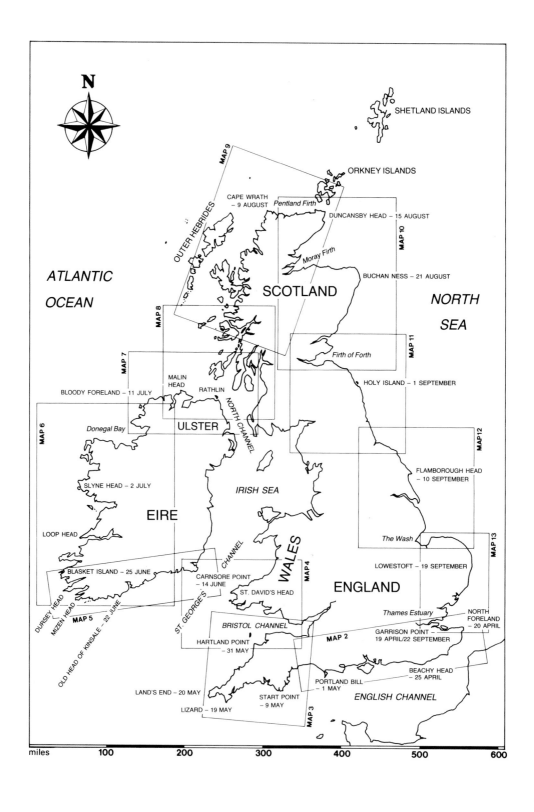

Maps in the Text

Colour Photographs in the Text

Foreword

by Jim Hargreaves

It is no coincidence that the seas around the coastlines of Britain and Ireland have spawned some of the world's great seafarers. Navigation around these shores is notoriously difficult; the coastline is rocky and precipitous and often without shelter from unexpected storms; visibility can be poor because of coastal fog, and the tidal streams are amongst the strongest anywhere. To circumnavigate Britain and Ireland the mariner has to face many areas of fierce tides and large swells. Open crossings of up to 50 miles, far from the safe, comforting embrace of land, have to be undertaken if the overall distance is to be kept to a minimum. To accept this challenge in a kayak, powered solely by will, heart and those who cheer you on, is to assume a "Tritonic" task. To have achieved this ambition in modest style is a tribute to leadership, teamwork and companionship, sheer guts and determination.

Britain and Ireland both have coastlines of incredible contrasts; from the mud flats and busy shipping of the Thames Estuary to the lonely seas of the Scottish north coast and the swirling tides of the Pentland Firth, there is a variety in the shape of the land and in the people who live there. The North Sea is threatened with sterility, and the west coast of Ireland, continuously assailed by legions of huge Atlantic swells, is as pristine an example of an unspoilt shoreline as you are ever likely to find, but these contrasts, which relate to physical and social geography, are blended by the common warmth of the human spirit. The welcome is the same from a Geordie or a Cockney as it is from a man of Clare or a Highlander. It was the people they met, as much as the places they visited and the physical challenge of completing this journey, which fashioned Bill Taylor, Mick Wibrew and Richard Elliott into an exceptional team.

In 1977 three friends and I circumnavigated Cape Horn by kayak in 23 unsupported days. This was the dawn of the era when some of the most challenging sea voyages were beginning to be tackled by kayakers. In the years that followed, the circumnavigation of New Zealand, Australia, Iceland and Japan were all achieved in quick succession in a series of daring expeditions by a small core of dedicated sea paddlers. The Irish Sea was crossed, solo, in one nineteen-hour stint. The North Sea was paddled from Felixstowe to Ostend. All of these adventures stretched the techniques, skills and equipment of the time to the extreme. As knowledge and confidence grew, each new voyage would inspire another, more audacious, exploit. It was a quest fired by competitiveness and, as each challenge was accomplished, a new one invariably presented itself.

I first met Bill Taylor when I started selling canoes out of the back of an old garage in Snowdonia in the early eighties. When he told me of his plans to circumnavigate Great Britain and Ireland, it came as no surprise. I knew him to be a bold, strong individual renowned for his good humour and explosive temperament. These qualities would surely make him a strong leader and inseparable companion during a journey such as this. The trip he planned had all the ingredients of a great expedition:

commitment, isolation and seriousness. It promised to be a formidable physical under-taking. So it proved, and with hindsight its significance has become clear as one of the most outstanding sea-kayaking passages ever completed.

It is important to realise the courage needed by any sea paddler to face the menace of being crushed against the rocks or lost far from the coast. Rigorous planning is an indispensable and effective safeguard against constantly shifting elements. However, cir-cumstances *can* combine unexpectedly to create a potentially disastrous situation, as illustrated by one episode on this expedition, between Cellardyke and Dunbar. The team was in real difficulties when, delayed by well-wishers and the press, the canoeists made a late start, the weather turned out much worse than forecast, directions proved unreliable and, simultaneously, part of the equipment failed. Conditions became so serious that the most strenuous planning was no longer enough. Then, only the determination to live "to paddle another day" and the necessary fitness could overcome the danger. This and many other occasions during the odyssey serve to remind us that sea paddlers sometimes have to face enormous risks which can, if things go wrong, be fatal.

There is, however, a lot more to expeditions than the achievement of some seemingly impossible physical goal. Anyone who has spent more than one night in a tent with someone they thought they knew well will testify to the fragility of human relationships in close proximity. The most basic domestic and social habits of your companions suddenly become the focal point of daily life. Silence can be as irritating as garrulity, fanatical energy as infuriating as slothfulness. Eating, washing, snoring or scratching can either be mildly amusing or result in complicated, obsessive murder plots hatched in the depths of a sleepless night. There seems to be no limit to human intolerance. To share each other's company, after an exhausting day, and remain agreeable, is far more taxing than it appears. To have done the same thing for 155 consecutive days – many of which involved not only gruelling physical effort but considerable commitment and risk – is in itself a remarkable achievement.

The principal piece of equipment of the modern sea kayaker still retains some of the traditional characteristics of the Eskimo seal-hunting kayak which is the forefather of the glass-reinforced plastic craft of today. It continues to be used in its original form by the Inuit tribes of Greenland and Arctic Canada where, despite the encouragement of modern technology, the time-honoured kayaking skills are handed down from generation to generation. These skills have been adopted and honed by modern sea-kayak paddlers to a much finer degree than the Inuit ever found necessary, and have enabled audacious sea voyages to be undertaken, far beyond the realms of the coastal wanderings of the Eskimos.

Many challenges remain; the vastness of the world's oceans will never be reduced by the travels of sea kayakers, but each challenge becomes that little less forbidding when you know someone has gone somewhere near the same limit before you. Bill and his two companions have set a new standard by completing their coastal tour with such good style, competence and commitment. It is an achievement which will undoubtedly inspire others to follow and accept the challenges of the oceans and lonely coastlines where commitment and adventure are certain to be found in abundance.

Author's Note

Expeditions are founded on dreams and inspiration. In my own case, the inclination to imagine myself into adventurous situations stretches back into my earliest memories. As a boy I displayed a wild and imaginative disposition which I now realise dominated both my play and taste in reading material. By the time I was ten, the pages of such authors as Defoe, Wyss, Ballantyne and Marryat had been reread many times as I shared the "desert island" existence of their characters. When the books were put aside, I created my own world of adventure on plots of derelict land around a council estate in urban Kent. With my friends from among the wildest boys in the neighbourhood, I built my own "desert island" camps, dug out caves and "secret" tunnels and was involved in all the worst forms of vandalistic behaviour that small boys can imagine. The greatest thrills always involved frightening ourselves, whether by taking on real physical risks or courting the risk of incurring the wrath of angered adults.

Most of the anti-social aspects of my behaviour were kept secret from my father. However, as I grew older, I began to appreciate his genuine empathy for the wilder side of my nature. Had he been less understanding, he would almost certainly have trained these tastes out of me and then my ambitions and aspirations would have been steered towards more materialistic goals in life. Instead, he encouraged my pursuit of adventure, which by early adolescence had begun to take on more positive outlets in a genuine love of the outdoors and the activities pursued there. My first acknowledgement is therefore to recognise the debt I owe my dad. It is one of my greatest regrets that he did not live to see this particular dream turned into reality.

Disposition accounted for, the inspiration for a sea-kayak journey to circumnavigate both Britain and Ireland rests squarely on the shoulders of one particular friend. Geoff Hunter would probably be embarrassed to read in print that I found his solo kayak voyage around the British mainland "inspirational". Notwithstanding such embarrassment, I feel obliged to acknowledge the special part Geoff played in the story that follows. Similarly, two other friends stand out as having had a major influence on my development as a canoeist. Both Dave Thomson and Ian Bourn deserve a special mention. Without their influence in my life I doubt if there would have been an expedition to write about.

The spark of inspiration was fanned into flames by many people, but there were many times between floating the idea for our journey and its actual execution when the flames dimmed to the merest glimmer. Some individuals then stood out in encouraging me to press on. The expedition may well have foundered at the "drawing-board" stage had it not been for their support and faith – which was sometimes a tonic and sometimes more akin to a kick up the pants. These people were predominantly the members of Gillingham Canoe Club, from its associated families and also from the workmates of the expedition team. Many of them were financially generous to a fault but, more importantly, their consistent interest in the expedition was a prop to our own morale. At times, when this was flagging, we were always able to pick ourselves up in the knowledge that to fail would mean letting these people down.

I was fortunate to establish contact with many individuals and companies who helped us. A number are referred to in the text, but some deserve special thanks. Foremost among such people is Jim Hargreaves who, on behalf of Wild Water, provided canoeing accessories, advice and encouragement. His reputation in the canoeing world counted for a lot when I quoted his interest and backing. Outstanding contributions were also made by John Taylor of Wavesports and Bob Palmer of Performance Sports, then Kent Watersports, who between them ensured that the expedition suffered no hardships for want of good equipment.

It took a year to turn the journals, diary notes and letters written during the expedition into the book presented here. During that time I redrafted most sections several times. My frustrations were many. Writing into the early hours after a day at work did not make me the best of company, so I must therefore thank all my friends and colleagues for being so understanding for so many months.

Particularly tolerant was my typist, Heather Barnes. Without her patience, generous allocation of time and skills with a word processor I would never have got my manuscript together before all topical interest had faded away. Apart from deciphering my hand-writing, Heather prompted me to revise several sections of the text to make it more interesting for non-canoeing readers and was an understanding preliminary editor.

At this stage, I incurred yet another debt to Ian Bourn, who gave freely of his time, expertise and dark-room facilities as we processed dozens of black and white prints from the hundreds of negatives recording the expedition. Eventually, what I had naïvely considered to be a finished manuscript underwent its true final revision as it was "test read" with great patience and understanding by Len and Lindsey Thompson. On all too many occasions I abused their generous hospitality, sitting by their lounge fire as we took the manuscript apart, word by word. These sessions gravitated between being serious, protracted debates on grammatical constructions and being extended social occasions that cost Len a small fortune in wine!

Most tolerant of all was my wife, Beverley. Knowing that it would fall upon her shoulders to pay the household expenses while I was taking unpaid leave, she still encouraged me to pursue what was obviously a personal and selfish goal. Indeed, to pay the bills she took on three evenings' work a week at an adult institute to supplement her normal teaching income. Moreover, while the expedition was away, it was Bev who undertook the unglamorous and time-consuming jobs that amounted to being both our "base camp manager" and our "expedition press-agent". She was very much an essential member of our team, even though the part she played could never be given the credit it deserved. Her only reward has been this acknowledgement and the questionable enjoyment of joining us as we traversed the coastline of Scotland's Highland Zone. It is a debt that Mick, Richard and I can never repay.

Inspiration and support aside, there would still be no tale worth telling without the months of determined effort, dedication and commitment displayed by Mick Wibrew and Richard Elliott. Living in each other's laps for 155 days, we saw each other at our best and worst on many occasions. Such relationships are a true test of comradeship. One of the greatest personal satisfactions to emerge from the expedition was to have shared the experience with such steadfast and loyal companions.

1

Setting the Scene
The Idea and a Personal View of Sea Canoeing

On the north side of the outer Thames Estuary, a few miles east of the pier, hot-dogs, amusement arcades and bingo stalls that make up Southend, lies a muddy channel in the Essex marshes which leads through to the river Roach and thence to the Crouch. This inlet is called Havengore Creek and lying athwart the channel is a triangle of reclaimed farmland, contained by a sea wall and edged by saltings, called Rushley Island. It was here, on a hot and sunny afternoon of late July 1984, that I put years of doubt behind me and casually talked Mick Wibrew (and myself) into mounting an expedition to circumnavigate both mainland Britain and Ireland as a single and unsupported kayak journey.

Any wanderer passing that way on this particular afternoon would have come across an unusual scene. A dozen or so sea kayaks were laid out in the gently blowing grass that grows on top of the sea wall, their red, yellow and orange hulls adding colour to what is generally a drab landscape. From the kayaks, partially clad figures were pulling mounds of assorted food, drink and cooking equipment. A foraging party were throwing down piles of driftwood collected from the saltings to fuel a cooking fire that was already giving off wisps of smoke that drifted out over the creek. Gillingham Canoe Club, having paddled across to Essex from Barton Point on the Isle of Sheppey, were establishing themselves for a barbecue and bivouac.

A few hours later, most of the paddlers were lying back in the grass or squatting on improvised seats drinking mugs of wine or beer, their appetites well satisfied, having demolished four legs of lamb (stuffed with anchovies), baked potatoes, baked onions and large quantities of other vegetables. Mellowed by sunshine, good food and alcohol, the various groups were intent on as many different conversations.

One discussion in particular revolved around the recall of sea-canoeing adventures in wilder and more scenic realms. West Wales, Devon and Lundy, the Isles of Scilly and, above all, the west coast of Scotland, provided the setting for most of the anecdotes. We all agreed without hesitation, "this was the life!" The only problem raised by the conversation was how to extend one's exposure to such experience. However, one of the older members of the group (who was tending to dominate the conversation) appeared to have the solution to this problem worked out already.

"Canoeists are organising expeditions all over the world when there is a trip on our own doorstep that is crying out to be done. No one has yet canoed around both mainland Britain and Ireland on a single journey. I've heard paddlers talking about it for years – usually after a few pints – but the fact remains, it hasn't been done."

"Then there must be a good reason for not doing it," interjected Sue, an attractive and extremely forthright young lady, from behind her mug of wine.

"That's obvious!" I retorted, before launching into my next monologue.

"If you think about it, there's a whole list of problems to contend with, and not all of them strictly to do with the actual canoeing," I said, before listing all the problems that would be involved and then suggesting how they might be overcome.

As we talked it through, I found myself not only convincing the others as to how it might be achieved, but myself into the bargain! After a long pause during which we all looked at each other, I added, almost as an after-thought, "I'm half-tempted to have a crack at it myself. Don't you fancy trying it, Mick?" Our expedition planning started as casually as that.

Having slept out under the stars, at 0200 the next morning we launched our boats onto the flat, calm inlet, for it required high water to get over the bar at the creek's mouth and so into the Thames for our paddle back to Gillingham, about 20 miles away on the river Medway Estuary. In the cold, clear light of a full moon, one might have expected that reason would once again prevail, and we would have dropped the project there and then. But though we were no longer inebriated, we were intoxicated by the magic beauty of the night as luminous green phosphorescence was thrown up by every paddle splash and danced like sparklers on our front decks. It would have seemed like sacrilege to laugh off our proposal in such an inspiring atmosphere, so as we paddled through the night my mind was already playing with problems of logistics, distances and the general planning that would need to be done to turn our casual conversation into the piles of equipment and specific plans that would launch our expedition in the spring of 1986.

A few days later, in the pub, following a club training session, Mick Wibrew and I agreed that having thought it over seriously we would pursue the enterprise and that we should invite one other person to take a full part in the expedition. Richard Elliott had not done anything like the amount of sea paddling that Mick and I had done, but for all that, we thought he had the right qualities and it was agreed that we should invite him. When Richard accepted our invitation with great enthusiasm, our expedition team had come into being.

Perhaps the best way to explain what followed is to begin several stages further back, and attempt a rationalisation of what canoes, kayaks and sea paddling are all about. It is the experience of most sea canoeists that the majority of the British public are ill-informed of what sea canoeing involves and this is in part due to the loose terminology paddlers apply to their sport and is also the result of misleading publicity.

Whilst the media has in general terms been kinder to canoeing in recent years, television in particular has projected a very narrow view of the sport and consequently the picture conjured up by the word "canoeist" is quite often one of two stereotypes. The first of these is what one might call the "knight of white water". Helmeted and arrayed in the brightly coloured nylon livery of his sponsors; his stiletto-bowed and saucer-hulled steed is an eye-dazzling glitter of rainbow colours; it barely supports the weight of its rider as he expertly controls its plunging and kicking through the flying spray and foam of his white-water tournament.

The alternative image is that of the soul-searching, introspective, white-water hippy. He too is helmeted, but there the resemblance to our first character ends. With unkempt beard, National Health glasses and "Tupperware" kayak, he is probably to be found seeking the ultimate challenge of wilderness canoeing in a Himalayan gorge or at the outflow of an Arctic glacier. When in action, his kayak will display disturbing, submarine-like qualities as it frequently vanishes beneath the huge waves and seething boils of a roaring cataract that will shortly disappear under a reservoir to be constructed for a hydro-electric plant! To all but paddlers from a similar mould, he will appear to be suffering from a death-wish and at the very best will be regarded as mildly insane.

So much for our stereotypes. In justice to the vast mass of mere mortal paddlers, and for the benefit of readers who are not canoeists, I must therefore straighten out a few basic points about canoeing in general and sea canoeing in particular.

The non-canoeist has probably already been confused by my loose use of terminology that interchanges the words "canoe" and "kayak" without so much as a blink. To be technically accurate, I should have made it clear that a "canoe" is propelled by a single-bladed paddle, from a variety of body positions, and has its ethnic origins in the designs used by North American forest Indians. A modern "kayak", on the other hand, is propelled by a twin-bladed paddle, usually from a sitting position, and has its origins in the designs used by the Inuit or Eskimos. Thus, when the layman here in Britain talks of "canoeists" he usually and more properly means "kayak paddlers". As far as the canoeists themselves are concerned, when they should be talking of "sea kayaking" they tend on the whole to use the term "sea canoeing". From here on, therefore, let it be made as clear as Thames mud, that our "sea canoeist" usually paddles a sea kayak!

Just to make a confusing situation even more difficult, it should be understood that not all kayaking that takes place on the sea will necessarily be thought of as sea canoeing by the specialists in that sport. There are many highly skilled kayak paddlers who only bother to venture onto the sea to enjoy the exhilaration, thrills and spills of canoeing on the surf. Whether they use a general-purpose kayak or one of the specialist surf kayaks such as a "shoe" (which one sits in) or a "ski" (which one sits on) this branch of the sport has become a specialism in its own right and is generally thought of as something separate from sea canoeing. In the eyes of his fellow paddlers, a sea canoeist is more strictly a sea *tourer*, using his kayak as a means of travelling on the sea from A to B. Specialist kayaks have been produced accordingly for extended sea expeditions; built of glass-reinforced plastic, they lean heavily on the designs used by Eskimos, but with due allowance for the larger proportions of Europeans and for the storage of the necessary tentage and other expedition equipment that civilised man relies on in wilderness situations. It therefore remains to examine the attractions of such an activity, bearing in mind that I am presenting what is essentially a subjective and self-indulgent view and remembering that one of the great appeals of the sport is that it can cater for an extremely wide range of tastes.

I can recall as if it were yesterday the sea paddle that first captured my imagination. It was a beautiful morning in early spring. The sky was clear, there was hardly a breath of wind, and after the grey days of a miserable winter, the warmth of the spring sunshine made it seem more like a summer's day. At that time, I was a barely proficient paddler and as such was part of a group of kayakers who had set out from Holyhead on Anglesey to make the classic traverse of Holy Island's North and South Stacks.

Just before midday we rounded the cliffs below North Stack to enter what to my unprepared senses appeared to be a rock cathedral; Gogarth Bay by name. The kayaks themselves made vivid splashes of colour on the emerald-green sea which sparkled and flashed in the clear sunlight. The reflected light picked out every detail of colour and shape in the wrinkled and twisted rocks which towered in wave upon wave of natural battlements above us, while in the calm sea around us inquisitive seals were swimming.

The awesome grandeur of this coastline etched itself into my memory as we took a lunch-break in the open-faced cave that lies immediately below the North Stack signal station. A little later, we explored some of the deeply tunnelled sea caves of Gogarth before paddling through the gorge-like channel which separates South Stack (with its lighthouse) from Holy Island proper. Here, the pungent odour of guano assaulted our nostrils and the air was alive to the calls of a thousand wheeling and soaring sea birds. Then we moved on again across the cliff-backed bay known as Abraham's Bosom to our campsite above a ruined slip at the bay's southern extremity.

I thought of it at that time as simply a marvellous day's paddling with something of a magical quality, but with the objectivity of hindsight, I can see now that the real impact was environmental; the canoeing itself was only a means to an end – our means of transport into an experience that swamped the senses. The creation of similar experiences has certainly remained one of my major motives for wanting to paddle on the sea.

Many years later I was running a school-based canoe club which kept a strong contingent of ex-pupils, many of whom had grown up to become keen and competent white-water canoeists. Given a good river, where I led, they would follow, but try as I might, I could not convince the adolescent males that the sea was worthy of their attention. The environmental enjoyment that meant so much to me held no attraction for them. With the aggressive assertiveness peculiar to young men, they measured the quality of their canoeing solely in terms of survival experiences, adrenalin-release and opportunities to show off their kayaking skills as they vied to impress each other. Not to be put off, I waited my opportunity to attract them to the sea on their own terms, and on a fine, warm Saturday afternoon in July, having driven from Kent to North Wales only to find the rivers so low that the lads deemed them unworthy of their attention, I saw my chance.

It was a weekend of spring tides when a greater than average volume of water would be flooding and ebbing around the headlands of Anglesey as it filled and emptied Liverpool Bay. The irregularly shaped coastline with its outlying rocks and shoals would be accelerating these rushes of water into sea rapids, properly called races, and overfalls that would produce exciting canoeing conditions, although when I explained this to the group they remained dubious as to whether it would be worth their effort. Undaunted by their scepticism, I went ahead with my plans, and being determined that their sea-canoeing début should be a memorable one, I planned a route that would take them through the overfalls of Penrhyn Mawr, off the coast of north-west Anglesey.

As we pulled away from the beach at Trearddur the sea conditions were calm and the comedians in the group were immediately making caustic jibes about finding better conditions on the flat water of our local river Medway. I kept my thoughts to myself and said no more about what to expect. The next move would be up to the tide!

A short while later, I could see that the seaward horizon was dancing in tell-tale blips, assuring me that the tide was already running hard over a shoaling sea bed and therefore forcing large masses of water into vertically rising currents to create the tidal phenomenon known as an overfall. The lads, however, appeared by their actions to be unaware of what they were in for, and from their casual manner, it was clear that they were underestimating the scale of what we were looking at.

A glance to landward would have shown them that we were being swept along at an alarming speed and it was now only a question of seconds before we were carried into the centre of the maelstrom. Suddenly, the sea surface had become an unpredictable mass of violently heaving and conical waves up to two metres in height, the crests of which were exploding skywards. Our kayaks were being tossed about like corks, forcing the paddlers to use all their skill to avoid capsizing. There was no joking or jeering now, for to stay upright needed all their concentration. Only on the bursting wave crests could they glimpse other members of the group, whilst in the troughs no other paddler could be seen. It was just as I had hoped and it was certainly what they needed. I would be most surprised if any member of that group has ever forgotten the experience. This, then, is another side of sea canoeing. Given the right combinations of wind and tide there are parts of the British coast that can produce white-water conditions that outmatch even the best of our rivers.

Another special attraction of sea canoeing is the way it offers an abundance of opportunities to carry out genuine wilderness expeditions within our own islands. British canoeists are denied access to many of our potentially good rivers, but our Atlantic coastline, particularly on the west coast of Scotland, offers seemingly endless possibilities for sea journeys. Here, the sea kayak can transport the paddler to wild and uninhabited coasts that most sea-going craft refrain from visiting, for should they dare to venture there, they would have great difficulty in landing. The total experience of such expeditions goes far beyond the enjoyment of the magnificent scenery or the physical paddling. It encompasses the pleasure of spending long winter's evenings poring over charts, maps, guidebooks and Admiralty Pilots as the idea takes shape and plans are formulated; it may include the satisfaction of visiting some remote island – Staffa perhaps – whose evocative name may have haunted the imagination for many years.

To camp in the ruins of some long-abandoned crofting settlement, cooking feather-hooked mackerel on a driftwood fire built in some ancient but long-cold hearth; to lounge by a campfire in the lingering glow of a Hebridean twilight (with perhaps just a dram of single malt whisky to enhance the Gaelic atmosphere), this too is as much sea canoeing as the battling with the elements to reach the campsite.

In this sense, the sea kayak can be a means of escape from the urban life style that most of us are forced to accept to earn a living, into a world of more ancient values. I have long been fascinated by the way Western man has progressively divorced himself from the natural world and his ancient instincts. Swamped by an obsessive worship of the work ethic in spite of the ever-decreasing job opportunities, it seems to me that society has out-distanced itself from its natural roots and by so doing is denying itself the enjoyment of much which improves the quality of life. There is much to be learned and gained by occasionally escaping from the constraints and comforts of modern life into situations where one's appreciation of weather, wind and tides becomes critical to survival. Whether one simply enjoys such experiences or finds them a vital necessity to personal fulfilment and mental well-being, sea canoeing offers an alternative to the soft life.

Lastly, sea canoeing at its best can require an exceptionally high level of commitment and gives an appropriately high level of satisfaction when the job is done. Serious sea journeys, by their very nature, do not usually offer the option of pulling out once begun. The serious coasts are those with limited possibilities for safe landings, and having set off using the wind and tide to aid the kayak's progress, it may well be impossible to turn back. By definition, the most serious trips will not offer escape routes and one has to complete the journey. This sometimes means controlling one's fear for several hours on end, when the tension can be both nerve-racking and exhausting. At the end of the day, however, the memories and rewards will match the commitment.

Perhaps all the various attractions of sea canoeing will fall into place better if I recount one particular memory that contains something of all these elements.

During dark winter's evenings, when the wind rattled window panes and it felt good to sit in an armchair by the fire, I had done a lot of research on the Outer Hebrides and there came a time when four of us were going to put some of the resulting plans into practice.

At Oban we packed our boats with all that we could foreseeably need for the next ten days, then took the ferry to Lochboisdale on South Uist. The object of the expedition was to work our way through the chain of beautiful islands that stretch southwards to culminate in the great sea cliffs of Barra Head on the tiny island of Berneray, arguably one of the most exposed headlands imaginable. The island names read like a glimpse into literature and song – Eriskay, Barra, Vatersay, Mingulay, to name but a few. So it was that on a beautiful day in late May we achieved our main objective when we rounded Barra Head and found it matched our wildest expectations.

The towering, 600-foot cliffs were being lapped by dark-blue Atlantic rollers that had swept in without hindrance from the Americas. One guidebook suggests that during the wildest storms it is possible for fish to be deposited on top of these cliffs, but on this day of only the gentlest of winds we had no such worries! The sea was alive with sea birds. Puffins, beaks dripping with sand eels, penguin-like guillemots, red-legged black guillemots and razorbills dotted the sea surface or flew clumsily over the wavetops, while graceful fulmars soared effortlessly overhead and squadrons of shags hurtled into the sea like kamikaze pilots to join the countless seals. That night we camped in the turf-grown, roofless crofters' cottages that nestle between the sand dunes and the steep grassy hill on the eastern side of Mingulay. Our campfire was built in an old fireplace and we talked late into the evening of the great day we were finishing and of trips as yet only dreams. The soft light of the fire reflected back from the squat stone walls. Overhead the stars twinkled down from a sky that refused to grow completely dark. Our bottle of Tobermory inevitably disappeared. It was a special occasion.

6

The next day dawned clear and sunny, but as the morning wore on, a fresh southerly breeze picked up until it was blowing about a Force 6 on the Beaufort wind scale. Since we now had to head north to get back to South Uist we were not unduly dismayed. We felt we could handle such a wind, for even if it produced a rough sea, it would be helping us on our way.

That the sea would be rough was a certainty. Not only was the chain of islands exposed to the full force of the wind, but the flooding tide would run hard from west to east between the islands to form races on the salient points with eddies and confused back currents behind them. After the predominantly south-westerly wind, the Atlantic swell would be running in from this direction, be forced to divide around the islands but then reconverge to the east to create dangerous and confused seas known as clapotis. Superimposed on this would be the waves kicked up by the southerly breeze. We undoubtedly had a difficult paddle ahead of us. When we first set off, the island was sheltering us from the worst of the wind and swell, but as we progressed towards the north-eastern point of Mingulay we enjoyed the exhilaration of being surfed along in flying spray and sunshine. As soon as we cleared the shelter of the island, however, the picture changed completely.

A combination of "hay-stacked" overfall waves, the wind waves on which we were being surfed, and, worst of all, the swells "clapping" together, created a frightening sea state. Our paddling strokes became an exercise in survival. At one moment we were trying to resist the forward and downward thrust of being surfed into a forward somersault known as a "loop", at the next we would be falling sideways through the air as the conical waves collapsed and then re-formed around us. A mistake could be absolutely disastrous. The outcome of an attempted roll of our fully loaded boats in such conditions could not be certain. The consequences of a swim were unthinkable, for rescuing one another would be virtually impossible in such conditions; it was nearly ten miles to outside help at Castlebay and the tide would sweep anyone in the water into the emptiness of the Minches. We were at our limits and absolutely committed, for there could be no turning back in this wind and tide.

The next hour seemed to last an eternity as we struggled to maintain control of our boats, supporting and feeling our way north-eastwards across the Sound of Mingulay towards the island of Pabbay. In fact it was the wind and tide that took us there, for we had put all our energy into keeping upright and steering the boat. It was frightening and I felt a great relief when we at last paddled into the shelter of the island.

Immediately we were out of the wind we came into a different world. The lagoon on the eastern shore of Pabbay must be one of the most beautiful in all Scotland. Tap-clear water over a shell-sand bottom combined in the sunshine to produce the pale turquoise sea more usually associated with a Pacific atoll. The small crescent of silver-sand beach is backed by a low bank of sand dunes through which a crystal-clear stream has carved a steep-sided gorge. Overlooking the bay from a turf-covered hillock is a ruined crofter's cottage, intact apart from the missing roof. We landed here to rest and eat lunch, but after the stress and exertions of the paddle we did not take long to convince each other that it would be a pity to miss an opportunity to camp in such idyllic surroundings. We carried our boats along the sandy stream bed and up onto a plateau of green sward where we pitched our tent next to the building.

The wind had been steadily veering towards the south-west and convection over Mingulay was now sending squally showers towards us. Just before the first spots of rain we ducked into the tent to sit out the shower but we somehow lost the next two hours. As soon as we stopped working, our pent-up stress got the better of us and all four of us instantly fell into a deep sleep. It must have been a reaction to the nervous strain we had just lived through. We all woke up about the same time, as the sun climbed out from behind a black shower cloud to warm the tent and create a perfect double rainbow that curved out of our lagoon.

That evening we had our campfire in the shelter of collapsed sheep pens. Later we walked westwards to the top of the sea cliffs which fall precipitously into the Atlantic on Pabbay's western shore to watch a magnificent sunset.

Such are the contrasting experiences to be encountered in only a little over one day's sea canoeing. As it happened, two of my companions on that day would be the ones who made up the team to undertake the circumnavigation of Britain and Ireland.

2

The Plans Take Shape

Preparations

In simple terms, the task we had set ourselves would require us to paddle at least 2,500 miles if the weather allowed us to cut all possible corners, but it could require well over 3,000 miles if the weather forced us to seek more sheltered options and to retreat into the larger bays that bite deep into our western seaboard. The coastline we would be traversing is among Europe's roughest, but the major constraint would be the weather. Would it allow us a sufficiently lengthy paddling season to complete such a long journey? We were determined from the outset that we would do the journey properly – as a *self-contained* expedition – or not at all, so we dismissed the idea of a land-support party or a support-boat for the extended crossings.

The outline plan which I eventually submitted to would-be sponsors and the British Canoe Union for patronage was relatively simple:

A team of three kayaks carrying full expedition equipment and without land support will leave the river Medway in mid-April and follow the coast in a clockwise direction. Weather permitting, we will cross the St. George's Channel to Ireland from Pembrokeshire to Tuskar Rock and proceed along the south and west coasts, cross to Scotland via the North Channel and continue on round the British mainland to finish back on the Medway by mid-October.

Simple as this plan may appear, it was in fact the result of considerable research. It was essentially built around the assumption that the most difficult section of the trip would be the exposed west coast of Ireland, so we would need to be there when the weather was most likely to be settled. A study of past weather records and coastal pilots demanded that we should aim to arrive here close to the summer solstice, and this in turn dictated a clockwise circumnavigation if we wanted to start from home waters. It would also give us the additional advantage of being on the south coast of England (where the weather should settle earlier in the year) during the first few weeks of the trip. My main worry, however, was the available length of paddling season.

On an assumed eight-hour paddling day, we would require up to 130 paddling sessions to complete the journey (depending upon the extent to which we had to seek shelter and avoid open crossings) and we were prepared to allow up to 200 days to accommodate this. No matter how we looked at the problem, we would have to paddle earlier in the year than was really desirable, and even then might still be forced to travel in the windy weather associated with the autumn equinox.

To put our proposal into the perspective of the development of sea canoeing, we saw ourselves as undertaking an expedition which was a logical extension of previous British sea journeys. For over a hundred years, there have been groups of Scottish sea paddlers carrying out serious sea journeys on their western seaboard. Their craft were remarkably seaworthy, built in varying combinations of timber and canvas, and included some features – like bulkheads and watertight storage compartments – that many kayakers mistakenly believe are peculiar to modern developments. Strange as it may seem, as time progressed, their designs came to be influenced more and more by Inuit (Eskimo) kayaks which had been around for thousands of years. When Ken Taylor returned from West Greenland he brought back a local Eskimo kayak of attractive lines that in 1969 was to be the inspiration for Geoff Blackford's Anas Acuta – a fibre-glass sea kayak that has proved to be a classic in concept and is still very popular today.

As long ago as 1970, Geoff Hunter had paddled his Angmagssalik (a beautiful, sleek but relatively flimsy sea kayak) on an incredible solo circumnavigation of the British mainland and by so doing, pointed the way for other great kayak journeys on the sea. Geoff is a close friend of all our expedition team and as such was an inspiration to us all, so in many ways our story starts with Geoff's marvellous achievement.

The knowledge and equipment available to Geoff was far less than what it is today. He had to make up for this with skill, resourcefulness and a great deal of guts and good humour. What he did not have, however, was adequate time or money, so after paddling northwards up the east coast, he cut through the Caledonian Canal rather than prolong his journey by taking on the wilderness areas of northern and western Scotland. It was left to other paddlers to make the first complete circumnavigation of the British mainland and that was not until 1980, when Paul Caffyn and Nigel Dennis completed the journey.

Meanwhile, the modern specialist sea kayaks were being developed, replacing canvas or thin ply with glass-reinforced plastic (fibre-glass to the layman). The best known of these early designs include the Anas, Derek Hutchinson's Baidarka and Frank Goodman's Nordkapp, designed for a journey around Norway's North Cape in 1975 and used in only slightly modified form for a journey around Cape Horn in 1977. In the same year, Geoff Hunter undertook another epic kayak voyage when with Nigel Foster he circumnavigated Iceland in the first Vynek sea kayaks. In 1978 two separate groups of sea paddlers (one from the Channel Islands and another from St. Hild and St. Bede's College, Durham) carried out the first circumnavigations of Ireland. These British paddlers were world leaders in such enterprises but, while all things seemed possible, the obvious challenge of circumnavigating our own island group as a single journey had yet to be accomplished.

Whilst I can only speculate as to why other paddlers chose not to attempt our undertaking, I can certainly explain what aspects of the project I felt were the most daunting. The trip would have a sustained level of seriousness and difficulty, giving rise to mental as well as physical stress. There are few areas of the world with bigger or more complex tides. Our islands are subject to a periodic bombardment of Atlantic depressions which sometimes queue up to produce almost permanently serious sea conditions on our western seaboard. The combination of these factors produces an abundance of taxing and technical canoeing problems. Of course, these are the very conditions that sea canoeists are usually seeking, but the scale of this journey posed the question of whether a small team could sustain its physical output, nerve and morale for the time necessary to complete the journey.

One particular technical problem overshadowed the rest and could be seen as the crux of the entire expedition. This would be the crossing from the British mainland to Ireland, which is generally seen as a major undertaking in its own right. The shortest route is across the North Channel, between Scotland's Mull of Kintyre and Rathlin Island off the Antrim coast of Ulster, which was the obvious choice of crossing-point for returning to the mainland of Britain. However, given the task we had set ourselves, the route *to* Ireland would ideally be the most aesthetic line – what mountaineers might call the *directissima* – requiring a paddle from Pembrokeshire in West Wales to Rosslare on the south-east corner of Ireland, using the Tuskar Rock Light as our Irish landfall. This line was definitely possible for it had been paddled in about 17½ hours in 1973, but it required settled weather to coincide with the right combinations of tide and available daylight. There would be no margin for error, yet an expedition making this crossing as just one part of the outer circumnavigation could ill afford to sit and wait too long for the "perfect" day. Lost time here could have serious consequences towards the end of the expedition.

Given that the biggest problems were likely to be posed by the weather (which was beyond control) and that the choice of route would be dictated by knowledge and experience, the main problem which I guess had dissuaded others was forming the right team. A collection of brilliant individualists would be unlikely to remain a cohesive unit on an expedition of this length. The "chemistry" of the personality mix would require something out of the ordinary for the team to tolerate each other's company, in what would often be adverse circumstances for an exceptional time-span.

I had been aware of these problems for a long time and had often asked myself the question, "Could I do it?" The attraction of putting together an expedition that would be a significant first was obvious, but for a long while I only toyed with the idea. It was the impulsive statement on Rushley Island that prompted turning this into a practical proposition, but in many ways the timing was no accident.

During the spring of 1984, I had been offered a secondment for the summer term. This would involve my leaving my normal teaching post as a senior teacher in a Gravesend high school, to help run the Kent Mountain Centre in North Wales, whilst Mike Petrovsky (the full-time warden) took extended leave to compete in the Solo North Atlantic Yacht Race. At the last moment, County decided that my secondment was too expensive. This personal disappointment was short-lived, however, for it was soon followed by a request to Kent from the West London Polytechnic (Borough Road College) to release me for a fortnight in June to help with a mountaineering course in the Pyrenees. Since my headmaster gave his full support to this request, I felt sure that the county would not deny it, having already let me down once. However, I underestimated the degree of bureaucratic insensitivity controlling my working life and the Divisional Education Officer refused to let me go. Consequently I finished the summer term in a sour mood which hardened my resolve to break out of my usual teaching routine, and convinced me that if I wanted to do something different, I would have to organise it myself.

Coupled with this wish to do something different was my growing awareness that the type of canoeing I had been involved in as a member of Gillingham Canoe Club over a period of several years had surrounded me with a pool of potential team members for a serious sea-canoeing expedition. It is not particularly unusual that a group of more mature paddlers should drift away from a white-water canoeing background to use their local waters more fully. In our case, this meant extensive involvement in marathon racing on the abundance of flat water in the south-east, then combining the level of endurance developed through this side of the sport with the white-water skills to become keen sea paddlers. Our trump card on many long or difficult days on the sea had often proved to be an exceptionally high level of personal fitness that we tended to take for granted, but was in fact no accident.

For many years, we had spent the winter months training hard for the world-famous Devizes–Westminster Canoe Race (usually referred to as "the D.–W.") in the hope of winning the Team Trophy. This event takes place every Easter and is sometimes described as "the toughest canoe race in the world". Even allowing for poetic licence, anyone who has tried to race a marathon doubles kayak (K2) down a 125-mile course which includes 76 portages (when the boat has to be carried for distances of up to a mile) in a time of around 20 hours, will know this is a very tough undertaking. Both the race itself and the training schedule it requires make big demands on mental as well as physical resources. Paddlers sharing this experience establish a special kind of understanding, so after racing in the D.–W. for the same club since 1982, it could be argued that Mick, Richard and myself were simply a splinter from a previously existing unit. In this sense our expedition owed a great deal to our club coach, Ian Bourn.

Both Mick and Richard had learned their paddling under Ian's watchful and demanding eye. Had it not been for Ian's personal friendship and encouragement to widen my white-water interests over many years, I would never have gained the wealth of sea-canoeing knowledge that I had picked up in Ian's company and from his circle of sea-paddling friends.

It is all very well to have an idea for an expedition and a team who want to carry it out, but it is something else to take that idea and turn it into reality. There were hundreds of hours of work ahead that had to be fitted around our normal lives. So, having made the decision to "go for it", there was no way we could get everything together before the 1986 paddling season.

From the outset, we had to come to some realistic decisions about finance. My estimated costing for the venture had to include equipment and supplies consumed en route, working out to about £9,000. This is a very modest expenditure by expedition standards but hides the true cost, for it does not show our lost earnings. We had to face the fact that there was no way any of us could get paid leave for an expedition that might keep us away from our jobs for up to half a year. Indeed, it would be difficult enough to get *unpaid* leave and ensure we had jobs to come back to. As it turned out, neither Mick nor myself had any real problem in getting leave, although Richard was asked to resign from his post as an avionics technician with Marconi-Elliott and they only rescinded this decision two days before our departure.

Mick and Richard, both living with their parents, would not have the worry of financial commitments at home during the trip. On the other hand, I had to plan ahead to cover the expenses of keeping a home together during my period without pay.

Against this background I prepared an expedition broadsheet which briefly outlined our plan. This was then sent out with hundreds of letters (followed by personal telephone calls) requesting help from possible sources of sponsorship. At the end of this time-consuming and frustrating exercise, most of the work produced only a negative reply, but some did attract interest in our venture, so that we eventually amassed the majority of the equipment at a minimal personal cost. Unfortunately, we never managed to find that elusive "financial sponsor" who would bear the day-to-day living costs of the expedition. However, at a time when dozens of serious expeditions and adventurous undertakings are competing for sponsorship, we were very grateful to the sponsors that did assist us.

I was particularly pleased when the B.C.U. Expedition Committee (then chaired by Colin Mortlock) extended B.C.U. patronage to our venture. This amounted to a testimonial from our sport's national body, acknowledging our competence to attempt the trip and gave us the air of legitimacy and respectability which would attract sponsors. Jim Hargreaves at Wild Water was the first to offer us concrete help. I had known Jim for many years and the encouragement produced by his interest went far beyond the material offer to provide us with the full range of Wild Water products relevant to our expedition. Now that I could quote backing from someone with Jim's prestige and influence, other sponsors quickly materialised. Helly Hansen U.K. Ltd. offered us all we needed in terms of their "Polar Soft", fibre-pile, thermal clothing (for we intended to use this as paddling clothing as well as for camp use) and this was supplemented by lighter thermal garments provided by Warm 'n' Dry. Mick's company – Gilletts (Faversham) Ltd – generously purchased complete suits of Gore-Tex mountaineering waterproofs from Snowdon Mouldings at a good discount on our behalf. Thanet Electronics and Cody both loaned us waterproof marine-waveband radios. Two retailers for watersports equipment were particularly helpful. John Taylor at Wavesports and Bob Palmer of Kent Watersports overwhelmed us with help and generosity. Our only financial donation from a commercial source was from AKZO Chemie U.K. Ltd, a factory on the Medway at Gillingham.

Another lucky break came when a canoeing friend working for T.V.S. put me in touch with a sports presenter, Andy Steggal, who worked on the *Coast-to-Coast* programme. When I explained to Andy what we were hoping to do he became very enthusiastic and assured me of a generous allocation of peak-viewing time exposure. It was just the type of publicity that our sponsors wanted. As it turned out, we all enjoyed working with the T.V.S. film crew when they spent two days filming a short documentary to explain our trip.

The two main items of expenditure (apart from daily food provisions) which we could not avoid were photographic film and navigational material. Kodak Ltd gave us very preferential rates for a bulk order of fifty process-paid reels of colour transparency film but we had to pay top rates for the scores of Ordnance Survey maps and Admiralty charts we needed. By the time these had been cut to a working size, annotated with pilotage information and covered with "tacky-back" to make them waterproof, it was a very costly item indeed.

The major items of equipment which we did not purchase new were the kayaks themselves. In the winter prior to our departure we had tested a prototype for a new design of sea kayak, but we eventually decided to paddle the Valley Canoe Products Nordkapps which we already owned. They were all over five years old but had been well tried and tested, with numerous minor modifications fitted to our individual requirements. It was a decision none of us were to regret, although we did intend to make another major modification by fitting a robust rudder system.

There was no doubt in our minds that a journey of this length would require us to sustain a healthy and balanced diet that precluded any reliance on specialist expedition or dehydrated products. We decided we would eat as near normally as possible, only more of it! My guess was that no matter how well we ate, our work rate over a long period would still put us on a calorie deficiency. The best we could do would be to buy several days' fresh food at a time, cook on a Primus or open fire when possible and eat in pubs and cafés where it seemed expedient. For emergency use and for our Irish Sea crossing we had been given Hot Can self-heating tins of chicken casserole by our sponsor, Pyranha.

A plan for our personal preparation was far less problematic. Our experience told us that we would be hard-pressed to improve on the level of fitness that would result from our training for the D.–W. during the Easter prior to our departure. In fact, this form of preparation would also tie down our departure date quite precisely to the first weekend after Easter when the tides would be favourable and we had given ourselves sufficient rest from the fatigue resulting from the race. We felt it only right that we should leave on a weekend to honour commitments to our sponsors who wanted the media coverage, and to our friends who wanted the opportunity to see us off.

In the last few weeks before our start date we had been overwhelmed by the support showered upon us by paddling friends and loved ones. Knowing that our personal finances had been stretched to breaking-point, they had rallied round, organised fund-raising and dug deep into their own pockets to provide us with cash to support our food kitty to the tune of over a thousand pounds. In some cases the degree of generosity was almost an embarrassment. Malcolm Gilbey, my workmate for over ten years but now setting out for a new life in Singapore, wrote out a cheque to cover the purchase of our V.C.P. C–Trim rudder systems. Ian and Bridget West, the parents of Richard's girlfriend Mandy, handed over a cheque for a hundred pounds as a "gesture" of support. It was all very moving, but while it was a great morale booster to know they all cared so much, it also put a degree of pressure on us by making it unthinkable that we should allow ourselves to let them down.

The test of our physical preparations came over Easter. Two hundred and two senior K2 crews left Devizes during Friday and the results speak for themselves. For the third year in four the club was runner-up for the Team Trophy to the Royal Engineers. Richard and his partner Dean Jordan came 6th overall in 19 hours 42 minutes, Mick and my wife Bev were 15th overall in 20 hours 04 minutes and won the Templeton Trophy for the fastest mixed crew. I put in the worst of our performances by coming 27th in a time of 21 hours 12 minutes, but I had no reason to complain. Having lost my partner Sue Phillips when she tore an ankle ligament I went on to lose my second

Departure from Gillingham Strand on 19th April. Photo: Paul Newman.

partner Mark Blatchly when he developed tenosynovitis three weeks before the race and I had eventually paddled with Simon Derham who was still a junior. We had decided to do the race with only a fortnight to go. All in all it was a most encouraging and worthwhile effort.

Saturday 19th April 1986 dawned calm and clear to produce a crisp spring morning of bright sunshine. We were due to leave Gillingham Strand on the top of the tide at 0900, so we had taken our boats to the Gillingham Water Activities Centre the previous day but we still had a few items left to stow that morning. The formidable task of packing all that we could conceivably need for a six-month journey had been abandoned at 2200 the previous evening to snatch a farewell drink at our local pub with our clubmates. Now, after so many months of preparations, it was hard to accept that our time to leave had at last arrived.

There was an awe-inspiring turn-out of family, friends and local paddlers to see us off. After all the help we had recently received, it was hardly surprising that we pushed off the beach at 0903 with croaky voices and lumps in our throats.

About a quarter to midday we beached our kayaks at Garrison Point on the Isle of Sheppey, under the great stone blockhouse that once guarded the eastern shore of the entrance to the river Medway where it enters the Thames Estuary. We had stopped to stretch our legs and eat some lunch but it was also a symbolic ritual. If we were to be successful in our adventure, this would be the very spot where we would close the circle of our circumnavigation at some unspecified time during the next autumn.

3

Style, Equipment and
Personalities

The three paddlers who set out on 19th April both looked and felt like a team. It was understood from the outset that we would carry identical personal equipment and share out the communal gear as best suited our specified responsibilities and the group needs. Having paddled together for many years, there was no doubt in our minds that this was the way that would work for us. I have on occasions come across other groups of sea paddlers where it is accepted that within the group, each individual can travel as a "self-contained" unit. This almost certainly leads to the unnecessary duplication of some equipment and denies the rest of the group a degree of manoeuvrability in adjusting their loads. To me this has always seemed unreasonable. I accept that it may suit others, but my experience over many years of mountaineering and canoeing has always suggested there are enough stresses and strains put on relationships during a prolonged exposure to arduous conditions, without building into an expedition any suspicion that someone might not be doing their rightful share of communal work.

Mick and Richard subscribed to this view with the same strength of feeling as myself. I remember a particular autumn evening in 1985 spent in a pub called The Little Gem at Aylesford, where a group of us called in after paddling from Seaford to Eastbourne – arguably the most scenic sea paddle in south-eastern England. The conversation after a few beers had inevitably got round to our expedition planning and one of our club members insisted on dreaming up all conceivable scenarios to test our preparedness to meet all circumstances.

"What will you do if . . . and supposing . . .?" The conversation dragged wearily on.

Eventually, my two expedition companions were asked what they would do in the event of my suffering an injury that would prevent me from continuing the trip. They found the whole situation highly amusing, for, without waiting for their answer, the inquisitor went on to say what *he* would do in such circumstances. At last I could stand it no longer and had to intervene.

"As far as I am concerned, either we all finish or none of us finish." The other two echoed my sentiments and that killed the conversation.

To some readers, this might sound like a soft option which would offer an easy way out of a tight situation. Yet this was certainly not our intention. Having come to this agreement, it put the greatest possible pressure on each of us not to let the other two down under any circumstances. That is the degree to which we felt like a team.

The pages that follow explain our choice of equipment in detail. My hope is that this great mass of technical information will be of interest on at least two counts. Whilst it is primarily directed towards satisfying the curiosity of fellow paddlers, it is also essential information for the general reader who wishes to gain a more enlightened insight into our daily routine and general life style.

We were not going to use neoprene wet suits. Even the best of them would be too restricting on body movement for the number of hours we would be paddling each day. They would probably cause chafing, then sores, and become so smelly as to become unbearable. Dry suits would be far too hot. Our needs would be best met by varying combinations of thermal clothing. Admittedly they would not do the same job as a wet suit if one were fully immersed in the water, but then we would be doing everything to avoid that possibility! However, providing a paddler is not in the water and is wearing a wind-proof cagoule, water quickly drains through soaked fibre-pile thermals and one stays not only warm but more comfortable than in a wet suit.

A typical outfit for a day's paddling would therefore consist of thermal long-john underpants, over which we would wear chest-high salopette trousers of fibre-pile. To keep the upper body warm, we would wear thermal long-sleeved vests. The loop-stitch construction, incorporating wool, made them as warm as a medium-weight pullover but they were much lighter and more comfortable. In extreme conditions we could easily wear a further *thermal* vest underneath, although this rarely proved necessary. Over these garments would go a normal nylon canoeing cagoule. On our feet would be ordinary socks and neoprene bootees. Whilst our headgear was left to individual taste, for very wet conditions we tended to wear traditional sou'westers, or woollen ski hats if it were cold.

In camp we had duplicate sets of thermal clothing so that all our gear was interchangeable. In chilly conditions we could ensure that we stayed warm by using crew-neck, military-style pullovers and zipped cardigans, both made of fibre-pile. To cope with wet camps we carried full suits of Gore-Tex waterproofs – a mountain jacket, salopette trousers and a pair of sailing wellies. This last item we felt to be invaluable. It was the only way we could guarantee having dry feet at some stage in the working day. Ordinary training shoes were our normal camp wear and a traditional fisherman's smock proved to be an excellent garment for keeping thermal gear clean (like a camping overall). Our concession to luxury was to carry two T-shirts and a pair of jeans.

The boats and paddling accessories require a much fuller account. We had chosen to use our Nordkapp kayaks in spite of their age. This was partly due to the number of tested modifications we had fitted over the years and which we felt would make our life that much easier. The basic boat is an excellent sea kayak for extended expedition use. It is over 17 feet long, handles well, is relatively fast, has a good load-carrying capacity and manages to do all these things whilst retaining beautiful lines.

This last consideration must not be overlooked if a reader wishes to understand how we treated our boats. Slalom and general-purpose kayaks just come and go over the years. It is accepted that they get smashed up as part of the sport for which they are designed, and to a lesser extent, our marathon racing K2s are eventually condemned to a boat-smashing race like the annual Exe Descent. But a sea kayak is different. It *looks* like a real boat and when personalised it takes on a unique character, like much larger craft. Accordingly, one treats it with love and care. Carry it carefully and the boat becomes like an old friend. Look after it and it will not let you down.

The Nordkapp would carry most of our gear dry because it has bulkheads and watertight hatches in the deck to give access to the storage areas. A standard production model can be purchased that has a bulkhead fitted in front of the footrest with access to the forward compartment via a seven-inch hatch on the front deck, fitted with a rubber cover. Similarly, there is a bulkhead about ten inches behind the seat and another seven-inch hatch on the rear deck gives access to this storage area. Because these hatches are absolutely watertight, it means the storage areas also supply buoyancy to make the boat unsinkable.

We needed to utilise every available cubic inch of potential storage space so we had ourselves fitted a third bulkhead immediately behind the cockpit area, with a large, oval hatch-cover in the bulkhead itself, working on the strong-back principle. Through this large hatch could be pushed those items such as eight-inch cooking billies and a frying-pan that would not go through other hatches. The last area of fixed storage was a "knee-tube" – rather like a piece of half-guttering – that we had built in fibre-glass and then fixed into place on the underside of the front deck, inside the cockpit, so that it would take odd items that we might need to get at quickly during a day's paddle and also double as a knee-brace.

So far, all the storage mentioned would hold the equivalent of two large rucksacks of gear and also keep it dry. Other items would have to be stowed where they would probably get wet. Tent poles would jam between the sides of the seat and the sides of the hull. Two-litre plastic beer bottles holding paraffin would jam between the footrest and the front bulkhead. A small marine radio in a waterproof case would be kept close at hand for emergency use. This would be held beneath elastic shock-cords on my rear deck, immediately behind the seat. A spare pair of split paddles (carried in two halves that joined by a quick-fit ferrule) would be carried under shock-cords on the rear deck, along with a cooking grill for open fires. To stop the steel mesh of the grill from chafing the spare paddles, it would be carried in a hinged "book cover" of closed-cell foam. Further shock-cords would hold two-litre plastic lemonade bottles filled with drinking water and the buoyancy aid (which we generally only wore when we anticipated extreme sea or weather conditions).

Beneath shock-cords on the front deck would sit the maps and charts for the day, sometimes a fishing line with mackerel feathers, a stainless-steel knife and odd pieces of cord and rope that might serve a dozen purposes. For example, on the curved deck, my ruler for measuring distances on a chart is a piece of nylon cord which gives a straight line when stretched. Forward of this "chart-table" area is the bubble compass, for at sea we would need to be able to execute all the navigating procedures usually carried out by a passage-making yachtsman. Around the edge of the deck and secured in place by built-in, recessed runners, is a continuous deck-line which provides a means of holding on to the boat at sea or when in the water.

To seal off the cockpit when sitting in the boat we would be wearing Twin-Seal spray-decks, rather like nylon body-tubes with an elasticated skirt that would grip into place around the cockpit rim. To remove water that still managed to get inside the cockpit area (by trickling down through our clothing, or if a spray-deck came off, or if the boat had to be emptied after a capsize) a small, hand-operated bilge-pump is fitted.

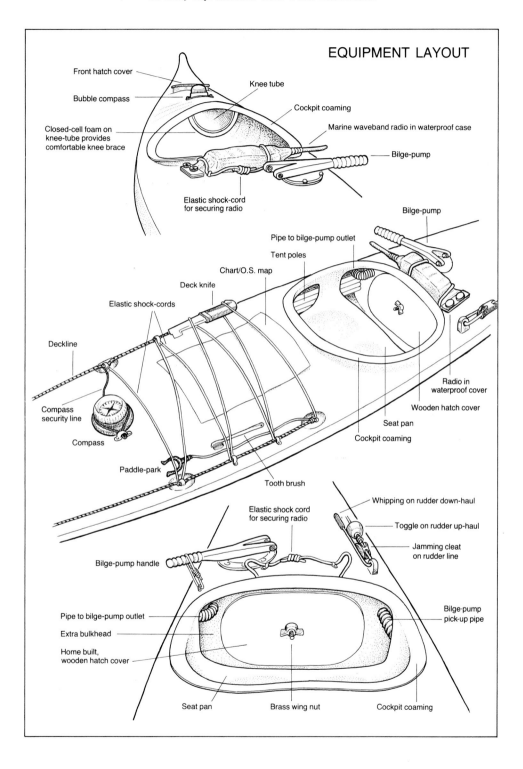

EQUIPMENT LAYOUT

Front hatch cover

Knee tube

Bubble compass

Cockpit coaming

Marine waveband radio in waterproof case

Closed-cell foam on knee-tube provides comfortable knee brace

Bilge-pump

Bilge-pump

Elastic shock-cord for securing radio

Pipe to bilge-pump outlet

Tent poles

Chart/O.S. map

Deck knife

Elastic shock-cords

Deckline

Radio in waterproof cover

Compass security line

Wooden hatch cover

Seat pan

Compass

Cockpit coaming

Paddle-park

Tooth brush

Whipping on rudder down-haul

Elastic shock cord for securing radio

Toggle on rudder up-haul

Jamming cleat on rudder line

Bilge-pump handle

Pipe to bilge-pump outlet

Bilge-pump pick-up pipe

Extra bulkhead

Home built, wooden hatch cover

Seat pan

Brass wing nut

Cockpit coaming

To propel this unit through the water, we were to use Wild Water "Laser" paddles. These have asymmetric glass blades set at right angles to each other and a strong, glass loom, making the paddles efficient, light, durable and maintenance-free. Some sea canoeists advocate the use of paddles with long, flat blades (more akin to the traditional Eskimo type) as opposed to our paddles which were little more than "beefed-up" racing blades. The arguments over which type is better for sea use are ongoing. The Eskimo-type advocates claim their long, thin blades enable them to maintain a low-arm, low-gear paddling action, keeping the paddles low so that they are not snatched by the wind. There is truth in this view, but it ignores the scientific fact that all marathon paddlers have to accept – namely that for an efficient paddling action the paddles must be carried with high arms and with a pull close to the boat's keel line. This demands the light asymmetric paddles produced by modern technology. Could it be that Eskimos would have used the same if their available materials and knowledge of fluid mechanics had been the same as ours, instead of building their paddles from what scarce pieces of driftwood they could find?

For our safety equipment at sea we carried a range of flares including red "parachutes" and red "hand-held". These were supplemented by mini-flare packs that could be carried in the pockets of our buoyancy aids. Thanet Electronics of Herne Bay had given us an I.C.M. 12 radio which they had waterproofed with an Aquaman sealed bag. This first-class little radio has a good selection of marine-band channels but its great appeal to us was its power source. It does have a rechargeable battery unit but we liked its alternative – a unit which takes normal pen-cell batteries. Since we would be unable to guarantee recharging a battery, the pen-cells were immediately appealing. Lastly, our T.V.S. coverage had generated some useful spin-off. No sooner had their first filming of our expedition been screened than we had been contacted by Cody Electronics who loaned us three of their F.C.900 waterproof, marine-band radios, as used by inshore lifeboats and rescue helicopter winchmen.

The V.C.P. C-Trim rudder of a sea kayak.

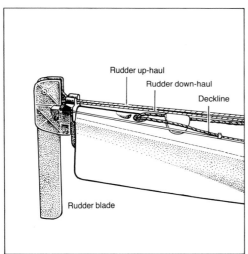
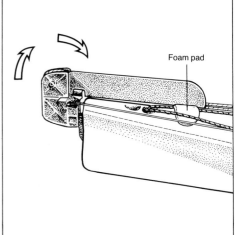

Our home and shelter for most of the trip was going to be a Vango Force 10 Mk 4 tent. With a cotton inner and a nylon fly-sheet, this three-man tent has been around for many years. Its traditional design was of particular use to us, for it has a strong system of double "A" poles connected by a ridge-pole, which lends the tent to being put up on unorthodox surfaces such as harbour walls, car-parks or loose pebble beaches – all sites where tent pegs cannot be used. In such situations the tent can be erected between two kayaks. After placing the fly-sheet over the pole framework, hooked shock-cords can be attached to the corner-rubbers of the fly-sheet and the bottom of the poles passed through these elastics. The shock-cord is then passed *under* the heavy kayaks and stretched to be secured in place on the deck-lines. In this way the weight of the kayaks holds the tent rigid on any sort of camping surface. The rear bell of the tent could be pulled to the third kayak laid across the ends of the other two. We had sewn two extra guy-lines onto the main panels on each side of the fly-sheet which could then tie down directly to the deck-lines.

On a journey as long as ours, we had to face the possibility that the poles might be fatigued and collapse in a high wind or that we might irreparably tear the fly-sheet. We therefore carried a complete set of spare poles, a set of pegs and a spare and modified fly-sheet, giving us both a full set of spares and the option of using an extra shelter during prolonged delays.

Since we were prepared to put up a tent on almost any surface, we had to make sure we would be comfortable for sleeping. Our answer to this problem was to use Therm-a-rest mattresses. These are a compromise between a traditional air-bed and the closed-cell foam insulating mat, commonly used by back-packers. By opening a valve in one corner, the mattress self-inflates to become about 3cm thick, giving excellent insulation and a fair degree of comfort. The mattresses were also useful because they can be rolled to expel the air and they then pack down to less than half the size of equivalent closed-cell mats. They were an obvious choice when our needs demanded that we should ruthlessly conserve all available stowage space.

For bedding we had experimental sleeping-bags from the Brett Harris "Snug-Pack" range. Instead of being fitted with bulky insulating materials, these had a heat-reflecting sheet (developed from N.A.S.A. space research) between the lining and the outer. These bags packed down to about half the size of a normal sleeping-bag and so were once again immediately attractive to us. For unseasonably cold weather, we carried a Warm 'n' Dry thermal sleeping-bag liner, which could also be used by itself on hot nights.

Our cooking system was based on using a one-pint paraffin pressure stove, plus a spare stove and up to ten litres of paraffin carried in two-litre plastic beer bottles. We also had a complete set of non-stick nesting billies with an extra eight-inch billie can. We carried Army canteens to eat from and a complete set of cooking utensils. Whenever possible, we intended to cook on open fires, and to make this easier we carried a hatchet, a supply of fire-lighters, a cooking grill of one-inch steel mesh about 18 x 12 inches and a roll of cooking foil.

As the story unfolds, many readers may be surprised at the quality of food that is mentioned from time to time. Because of the types of expedition that receive most media coverage, the general public have been conditioned to believe that all expedition food has to be bland, dehydrated or tinned. In such situations, food is simply a fuel to power the body. But it does not have to be that way – at least as far as sea kayaking in British waters is concerned.

Joints of meat baked with herbs and spices can be served with fresh baked vegetables as the "norm" where open-fire cooking is available. Rich, spicy stews can easily be made over a single burner of a paraffin pressure stove. To make such a style of eating possible, we would be carrying about five or six days' fresh food in our kayaks and keep the supplies topped-up to this level wherever convenient. I am not advocating this idea as the only way or the best way of feeding a sea kayak expedition. It is simply the way we like to do it. Most of my journeys have been in the company of paddlers who enjoy gourmet food. Some of them would regard good eating on an expedition as an end in itself – a glorified and extended picnic in wild surroundings – and have been known to become competitively obsessive in their creation of several courses of top-quality food. It is certainly a very pleasant way to fill in the long summer evenings of a camp in high latitudes. In fairness, however, it must also be said that I know sea paddlers who would rather set out with the bare minimum of simple, "fuel-type" food and part of their enjoyment is in having to "live off the land", relying on catching fish and collecting shellfish and berries.

Space also had to be found for a large number of other essential items. Our first aid kit had to be comprehensive, enabling us to cope with anything from midge-bites to major bowel upsets and cuts that would require sutures. Similarly our repair kits had to enable us to sew up tents, clothes, shoes; make major engineering adjustments to rudder systems and, in the event of a real disaster, rebuild large sections of the kayak hulls in fibre-glass.

Most of the navigational information we needed had been written onto the Ordnance Survey maps and charts, but there were far too many maps for us to be able to carry all of them at once. We therefore proposed to carry about six weeks of maps at a time and had to arrange the delivery of the next sections of coast at points where we knew we would see people from home. This fitted the major legs of the journey nicely, for we knew we would be met in Pembrokeshire by Geoff Hunter, since he was going to make the crossing to Ireland with us – it was the only piece of navigational work planned in detail before the expedition set off. Geoff's delivery would see us round Ireland and into south-west Scotland, where our clubmates would meet us for their holiday paddling. Their delivery would see us to Northumberland, where I had an old friend living at Whitley Bay and all the east coast of England maps could be picked up there. Because we needed detailed tidal information for the entire journey, I had pruned down a *Macmillan & Silk Cut Nautical Almanac* to take with us. It was a sizeable volume even then, but this luxury also gave me a summary of pilotage information and a complete set of tidal flow charts. It was well worth its weight.

I had used a Nikonos IV A diver's camera for many years and Richard purchased the latest Nikonos V model just before we set off. These cameras are very robust and need to be when living on the deck of a kayak. The fact that salt water is alternately allowed to splash and dry out on them poses problems that go beyond the camera's designed diving function. We had to rinse the cameras in fresh water as often as possible to reduce salt corrosion and keep them working. Richard and I used Kodachrome 64 colour film, while Mick took black and white shots on his new Fujica DM.

We carried the cameras in nylon bum-bags. These are like a small rucksack built into a waist-belt and are usually worn round a skier's waist with the zipped carrying compartment at the back. We would simply wear the bum-bag reversed so that the compartment holding the camera was sitting on the spray-deck in front of us. However, we found that this method (which I had always used on shorter canoe journeys) caused aggravated chafing of the spray-deck during extended use, particularly when worn in conjunction with a buoyancy aid. For this reason, the bum-bags were eventually carried on the front deck of the kayak as part of what normally serves as the chart-table, the belt being adjusted to fit tightly under the deck-lines. This system functioned very well and made it easier to get the cameras in and out of the bags.

Having expounded the rationale of our plans and equipment, I must now explain my thinking on the choice of team. In the previous chapter I suggested that my main concern was to find a group with complementary skills, rather than find a group of brilliant individuals. However, I first had to decide on the size of the team that I was hoping to form.

My experience urged me to believe that for what we were attempting, "small is beautiful". This narrowed the choice to a three- or four-man team. Any less than three would be straining safety factors; any more than four would strain logistics. Whilst a camping unit of three can fit into one tent, use one stove, one set of cooking gear, etc., it makes life more difficult in other ways. Anyone who has experienced extended sea-canoeing expeditions will know that one of the hardest physical jobs each day (and also one of the most hazardous jobs so far as minor personal injury or boat-damage are concerned) is that of carrying the loaded kayaks to and from the water. A badly carried boat can lead to a crippling muscle-strain; a badly dropped boat could spell disaster for the whole expedition. Four people can certainly carry a heavily laden boat with greater ease, with more balance and with less chance of harming the carriers or the kayaks.

It was not an easy decision. Three men in one tent were more likely to feel like a team and would *have* to get on with each other. A four-man unit would need two tents and therefore had the potential to split the expedition's unity into two twos. Yet, some of my best sea paddling had been in a group of four. At the end of my deliberations I was prepared to keep an open mind, with the important condition that the team of three already identified should unanimously agree on who the fourth member should be. This proviso eventually kept the team to a basic unit of three, although it would be expanded to four during two important stages of the expedition.

I must stress at this point that I did not see our team as being a group of what some would describe as "aces". None of us had ever won a major race, been up for international selection or previously attempted to canoe something no one else had done. We were just a group of club paddlers with a determination to work for each other and with a broader-than-average all-round experience of canoeing.

Mick Wibrew, at thirty-three, was almost perfect "cannon fodder" for what I had in mind. I knew from the hundreds of occasions we had paddled in each other's company that he could be relied upon to do his best in all circumstances. Our expedition would require what might be called a "head-banging" attitude. The fact that Mick had only missed one D.–W. in eight years bears testimony that he has more than his share of this quality. Lean and sinewy, he would never complain (even in the most miserable or painful situations) and could be relied upon to sustain his special sense of humour that thrives on setting himself up as a butt for other people's jokes. His humour would be a pillar to our morale.

He would be the first person to laugh at his own misfortunes and limitations. In a club which has several "Micks", he is affectionately identified as "Mick Mate" or "Mick-the-Chin" because of his facial features. He has a notorious reputation for allowing himself to be put upon, particularly at work, so he is frequently very late for social and canoeing appointments. A popular club joke says that Mick is great to have along on a trip – once he has bothered to turn up!

He is almost as famous for his navigational skills, or rather the lack of them. During an expedition to south-west Scotland some years ago, we had paddled from a camp on Gigha Island to Islay. We had made the crossing in dreadful weather on a compass bearing and the next morning we sat round our breakfast campfire, amusing ourselves by poking fun at each other. Mick had already been dragged round the camp by his chin (it is the easiest way to get hold of him) and the same feature had been smeared with porridge by Ian. The latter knowingly asked Mick if he could point out on the horizon the spot he thought we had paddled from. This question focused all attention on Mick, who rose to the occasion in classic style. Grinning from ear to ear, he stood up, held out his arms as if crucified, faced the eastern horizon and simply nodded.

For all his jokes, Mick is a very experienced sea paddler and he would happily take on the mundane jobs around camp that most people don't want. It was no coincidence that when Geoff Hunter had attempted to make a 70-mile crossing of the English Channel from Poole to the Channel Islands he had included Mick in his team.

It was Mick who first suggested that we invite Richard Elliott to join the expedition. Richard was only twenty-two at the time, his experience of sea paddling was limited, but he was an obvious choice for all that. One could almost say that he had been trained for the task, for Ian had spotted Richard's canoeing potential when he was still a young lad and nurtured him along very carefully.

Ian achieved this by assigning Richard to the care of Rob Catchlove, who is a widely experienced canoeist with some very good sea expeditions to his credit. Rob had himself been selected for special attention when a lad by John Ramwell (author and publisher of the B.C.U. manual, *Sea Touring*, London 1977) and so is jokingly referred to within our group as "Ramwell's Boy". Richard had now become "Rob's Boy".

This name has obvious connotations of derision. Indeed, to be a "boy" means to turn up reliably in all situations, to make the tea, to wash up, to be a dog's-body and to be a target for everyone else's humour. It is an uncompromising apprenticeship which can be very tough. The humour of those who train "boys" can often be cruel and jokes often go too far. Driving a "boy" to the point of tears (and sometimes beyond) has not been unheard of when the trainer has unwittingly been too insensitive.

But just as the stakes are high, so are the rewards. "Boys" trained in this hard school get taken to all the best canoeing venues, get special attention, brought into the inner circle of canoe-socialising and usually end up as the best canoeists. Their training is well rounded, thorough and deep. At twenty-two, Richard owed a great deal to Ian and Rob, for his eight years of canoeing had all been purposeful and properly thought out, and what Ian and Rob did not teach him he had picked up within the circle of white-water fanatics to whom I had introduced him.

Like Mick, Richard has a sense of humour. I suspect this is largely inherited from his dad, developed by his own instincts for social survival and finely tuned during his canoeing apprenticeship. This was essential for Richard to graduate from being a "boy". Even now he is often baited for his boyish looks and "clean-cut" image – he looks the sort of lad that mums want their daughters to bring home! However, his appearance belies his maturity and level-headedness. He may be a quality-control technician in the avionics industry by training, but by inclination he is a natural craftsman who can be relied upon to carry out all types of craft work and minor engineering jobs with care and precision. It was perfectly natural that during the expedition he should assume responsibility for keeping all the equipment in working order.

Responsibility for the main decisions on the expedition would rest on my shoulders. By training and by experience it was natural that this should be the case, for my outdoor background stretched back twenty-five years.

I had first used a kayak on the sea when I was fourteen. It was an old two-seater design, built of canvas and lathe and known as a P.B.K. double. The venue had been a section of rocky coast near Bloody Bridge in County Down, literally, "where the mountains of Mourne sweep down to the sea". Thrilled by this experience, during the next winter I helped build a single kayak in a similar construction but from the drawings of a traditional Eskimo design. The finished craft looked elegant but proved to be a disappointment. On its maiden voyage, I realised the kayak had a warped keel so that I had unwittingly built in a wonderful but frustrating safety device – the boat was best suited to running in circles! Moreover, it was so unstable that it needed the skills of a tightrope walker to keep it upright. My interest became dampened in every sense!

By this time, however, I was beginning a lifelong love affair with the mountains. For almost a decade I largely neglected my embryonic interest in kayaks to seek adventure in high places and high latitudes. It was an interest that became a key factor in my choice of university (Manchester) where I soon made friends with a group of dedicated climbers. Wednesday afternoons and Sundays were often spent on the local gritstone edges of Derbyshire and the West Riding. When we could afford it, North Wales and the Lakes were within easy reach. We made winter visits to the Cairngorms and Ben Nevis.

One day, a climbing friend dropped a casual remark which was to change my whole life. He told me how another friend of his was going to a recruiting lecture given by the British Antarctic Survey. My interest was immediate. Ever since I had seen the newsreels showing the first crossing of Antarctica in 1957, I had nursed an ambition to visit the South Polar Regions. Suddenly, it had become a realistic possibility. I went to the lecture and by the time I left the hall I knew I was never going to put the Law Degree for which I was studying to any practical use. The result was that when I graduated in 1967, I joined B.A.S.

After a three-month training course at the Meteorological Office, I sailed from Southampton in October, kitted-out in the Falkland Islands and was on base by mid-November. The next two years made a great impact on my life. The existence was hard but enjoyable. Survival, mountaineering, skiing, boating, and eventually, dog-sledging, became part of my everyday existence. It also taught me a lot about human nature, particularly on such issues as leadership style, that has stood the test of time. It was February of 1970 before I got back to the Falklands, but rather than return home on one of the Survey's research ships, I spent the next seven months making my own way home through South America.

By now, the "outdoor experience" was in my blood. It had contributed so much to my own personal development that it gave my life a clear direction. I had to become a teacher so that I could share what I had learned with others, selling the idea of outdoor education with an evangelical fervour at a time when the idea was just getting a toe-hold in educational circles. My superiors soon realised that my background was more sound than many who were paying lip-service to the subject and in 1973 I was seconded on a one-term course in Outdoor Education at Plas-y-Brenin – the Sports Council's most prestigious centre south of the Border. A large part of the course was dedicated to canoeing. It reawakened my old interest and I became acutely aware of what I had been missing. Once back at work, I did all I could to make up for this neglect, and over the next few years the canoeing began to compete for time with my mountaineering interests. Slowly, the canoeing pushed the climbing into second place and almost without realising, the mountaineer-canoeist had become a canoeist-mountaineer.

As far as Mick and Richard were concerned, I knew they would happily let me make the decisions. In turn they knew I would never ask them to do what I was not prepared to do myself and I would keep them fully informed of why we would be doing things in a certain way.

4

The South Coast is Easy

Gillingham Strand – Seaton: 19th April – 4th May

19th April. Noon. Sitting on the concrete apron of the sea defences below the blockhouse at Garrison Point we finished the last of our sandwiches. From where we sat we could look out over the grey-brown waters of the Thames Estuary with our three kayaks pulled up on the shingle in front of us. The excitement we had experienced on at last getting under way had now subsided. Alone with our private thoughts, our chatter had died into a protracted silence.

In spite of the sunshine which picked out the colours of the buoys stretching off to seaward, the view was hardly inspiring. The main characteristic of the outer Thames Estuary and North Kent coast is its very lack of outstanding natural features. It is the absence of natural relief that gives the area a special quality – an openness of horizons that appears to enlarge the sky and suggest a sense of space – now sadly despoiled by man-made horrors, like the huge concrete chimney of Grain Power Station, the distant tower blocks of Southend and the intrusive network of power cables with their ugly pylons.

It was Mick who broke the silence. Always quick to inject his personal brand of homespun philosophy into the most poignant of moments, he captured our awareness of having isolated ourselves from the routine of our normal lives by one, simple statement,

"Then there were three."

By late afternoon we had used up the full run of ebbing tide to put the Isle of Sheppey behind us to reach Swalecliffe, just to the east of the ancient port of Whitstable, famous since Roman times for the oysters which live on the offshore shoals. Twenty-five miles was a respectable distance for a first day, but the main accomplishment was simply getting started.

In a strange way, the physical workload of nearly seven hours of paddling was positively relaxing compared to the rushing around and pressures of the previous few days. Like most expeditions, we had found the number of tasks we had put off to the last moment almost overwhelming. There had simply been too few hours in the day. Sleep had been minimal. Richard had only managed to finish fitting the C–Trim rudder to my kayak on the previous Tuesday. There had been no time to test it. The worst last-minute crisis occurred because our order for O.S. maps mysteriously failed to materialise. After some stormy telephone calls it became only too clear that the agent with whom we were dealing had never, in fact, placed the order! Richard had to drop

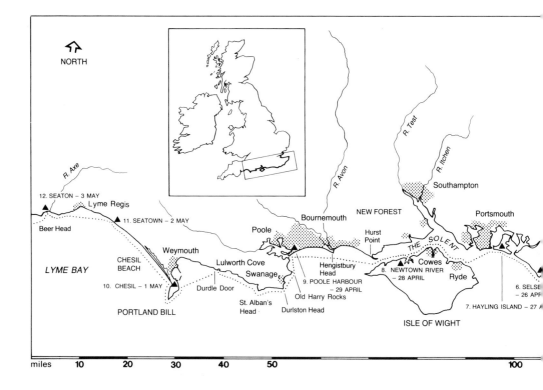

NORTH

12. SEATON – 3 MAY
Lyme Regis
Beer Head
11. SEATOWN – 2 MAY
R. Axe
LYME BAY
CHESIL BEACH
Weymouth
10. CHESIL – 1 MAY
Durdle Door
Lulworth Cove
Swanage
PORTLAND BILL
St. Alban's Head
Durlston Head
Poole
Bournemouth
Hengistbury Head
9. POOLE HARBOUR – 29 APRIL
Old Harry Rocks
NEW FOREST
Hurst Point
R. Avon
THE SOLENT
8. NEWTOWN RIVER – 28 APRIL
Cowes
Ryde
ISLE OF WIGHT
R. Test
R. Itchen
Southampton
Portsmouth
6. SELSE – 26 APR
7. HAYLING ISLAND – 27 A

miles   10   20   30   40   50   100

everything and drive to Southampton to collect the maps direct from Ordnance Survey. As a result, for the rest of the week we had to work into the early hours in a vain attempt to get all the maps cut down and properly prepared for the journey. It was hardly surprising that this degree of pressure would lead us into some problems which would have to be sorted out after we got going.

The first of these became evident as soon as we had arrived at Swalecliffe. We carried our boats, each weighing over 2cwts, across a short section of mud flats and over the two systems of sea walls into the "Sea View" caravan site (where one of our friends had previously gained permission for us to camp). On removing the cover from my rear hatch, I was alarmed to find there had been considerable leaking, soon tracked down to where the new rudder fitting was attached to the stern. Our first job was therefore to get the Primus stove going to dry the boat out. We then secured the boat vertically to a nearby contractor's cabin, broke out our repair kit and poured into the aft storage area a heavily catalysed quantity of resin to make a supplementary end-block, hopefully sealing the leak.

We woke up the next morning to the drumming of heavy rain on the fly-sheet. It was unthinkable to break camp in such a downpour, but the forecast was for an improvement later. This gave us a late start that lost us the first part of the favourable tide that we had planned to take us round the North Foreland of Thanet, and so into the Dover Straits. It was a delay that was to have serious implications later in the day.

We had always anticipated that the early part of the trip, taking on what in theory

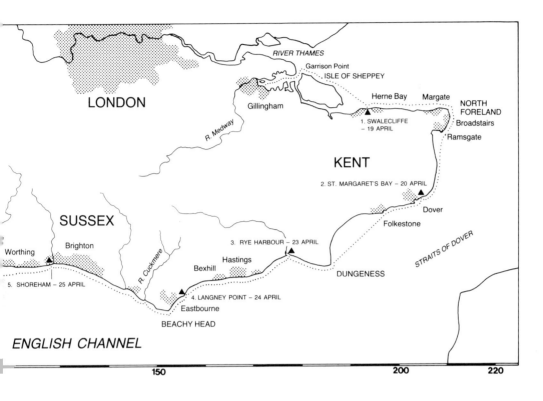

was a relatively straightforward coast, would be a shakedown period as we established a routine. Consequently, we felt it important that we push ourselves very hard to identify the problems at an early stage and so enable us to adjust both our equipment and our ideas before getting too far from home. Therefore in spite of not getting away until just after noon, we set ourselves the target of reaching St. Margaret's Bay (just north of Dover, and about 35 miles away) by the end of the day.

All went well at first. A fresh westerly wind assisted the tide in speeding us past the North Foreland. The morning rain had given way to bright sunshine. The scenery was nothing special. Low, brown-yellow cliffs of London clay had eventually given way to the chalk cliffs of Thanet, although we were having to stand out to sea to clear the apron of rock platforms exposed by the falling tide. Our interest in the surroundings picked up when we ran into the rescue boats and leading K2s completing the Round Thanet Canoe Race. About 1600 we stopped briefly at Broadstairs. It was pleasantly warm in the sun once we were out of the wind, for this had become both stronger and more gusty as the day had worn on. A cheeseburger and hot drink later, we were off again to pass Ramsgate and the open expanse of Pegwell Bay. Here the wind was blowing straight off shore to whip up a short, choppy cross-sea to give our rudders their first real test. Without them, progress would have been problematic. As it was, when we reached more sheltered waters off Deal we were tired and soaked through. But more worrying was the fact that we were about to lose the tide.

Slowly but surely we were putting ourselves under a number of pressures that would eventually compound into a tricky situation. The first mistake was in phoning home from Broadstairs to say we would reach St. Margaret's that evening. This meant if we did not arrive we would probably cause some alarm. The second and more fundamental mistake was in setting ourselves too unrealistic a goal, given that we had started late. The other factors that now emerged were not within our control but would combine to guarantee us our first scare.

When we reached the steep pebbles of Walmer the tide had turned against us. There was no obvious place to camp and even if we could see one, landing would have been a problem because a groundswell was now working in from the south to cause a vicious "dump" on the steep shingle. Such waves are more properly called "plunging breakers". They are caused when waves hit a steeply shelving beach so that they form swiftly and over-topple in one great crash, rather than break slowly from one end as would happen on a gently shelving beach. There was also the problem of having only limited daylight left.

As we reached Kingsdown and the beginning of the chalk cliffs for which the Dover Strait is famous, progress became even slower. The swells were reflecting back from the sea defences to form a confused sea which stopped us moving close to the shore to get out of the strongest tide. It was also near high water, so the rock ledges which would normally provide protection to the beach where we intended to land would now be covered, allowing the swells to run in without interruption.

At 2045 we arrived off the low point in the cliff-line known as St. Margaret's Bay. The other two kayaks had become colourless, vague shapes on the general greyness of the heaving swells that were running beneath us to dump in a deep-throated boom and swish on the steepest section of the stone storm beach, we guessed about 200m to our right. In five minutes it would be completely dark. My journal takes up the story.

It had to be inspired guesswork to choose a place to attempt a safe landing from our blind, seaward side of the breakline. I called over to Mick and Richard and we paddled back out to sea a little way to give us thinking space. The conversation was very brief. The landing had to be made very quickly and we would only get one chance to get it right. We checked that all the "junk" on our decks was properly secure beneath the deck-lines and shock-cords as we talked. I would go in first, followed by Richard, then Mick.

We edged towards the beach, eyes straining into the gloom to detect any let-up in the surf. There was a chance that Bev and Mandy might have driven down to see us so I let out a loud "Whoop!" that we often used in our canoe club to signal to each other in the darkness. It was more for self-assurance than in any real hope that it would be answered, but we all thought we could hear a response and a few moments later we could just make out two figures waving and shouting. They were signalling to us to move left and we had no choice but to trust their judgement.

Not wishing to lose my hat and paddle-mitts, I tucked them inside my cag and pulled up the rudder. Tense and anxious, I eased towards the beach on the back of the swells, avoiding as far as possible any attempts of the larger waves to surf me in.

Let the biggest waves roll on under the boat, choose a smaller wave and time it so that I could dash in behind the break. Now for it. A flurry of paddle strokes at full power and the kayak was surging up the beach. A moment later and welcome hands were grabbing the bow-loop to hold the weight of the boat against the powerful pull of the backwash and effects of gravity on the steep shingle. The next wave exploded around my ears and threw me a metre further up the beach. Tugging off the spray-deck, I made as quick an exit from the cockpit as my stiffened legs would allow to help drag the boat to the security of the upper ledge of shingle. At least I was ashore.

Meanwhile, Mick and Richard were barely visible. After a quick exchange of shouts, Richard's boat came hurtling in but at an angle, causing it to be pulled sideways to the waves in the backwash. The next wave hit almost immediately so that it was broad-side on. Richard half-fell and half-scrambled out just as the third wave washed over him to fill his cockpit. With maximum effort we could just manage to drag the boat up the beach. While Bev began pumping the water out, Richard and I stumbled around in the surf to retrieve the paraffin bottles which had been torn from their deck lashings.

It was now Mick's turn and he too came in at less than a right angle. This time the kayak was pulled back beneath the next dumper by the full force of the backwash. About 5 feet of vertical water collapsed in one huge thump over Mick's boat, spinning it over so that Mick was flipped onto his head in the shallows while his paddle was sent spinning through the air and up the beach. Floundering into the water, Richard and I leant over the up-turned bottom of the kayak, fumbled for Mick's body and turned him up the right way.

Much to our relief, we could just see that Mick was smiling so was presumably no worse for wear.

"Good job you landed on your head!" was all the comfort he received for his ordeal. Within seconds, we had pulled him from his boat and both he and it were dragged to the upper beach. Then we fell about laughing.

The swell that gave us our landing problem was the forerunner of very strong south-south-westerly winds that were to keep us gale-bound at St. Margaret's Bay for two days. It was frustrating to encounter this hitch at such an early stage but it turned out to be as good a place as any to get stuck. Overlooking the beach is an attractive pub of knapped flint called The Coastguard. Not only were we given permission to camp on the grass adjoining their car-park, we were spoiled with hospitality and it was soon arranged that we could move into a nearby lock-up hut belonging to the local sea-angling club. The access to a dry building meant that Richard could make a lasting repair to my rudder fitting (it never leaked again) and on the second day we walked south along the cliff path to visit H.M. Coastguard Maritime Rescue Co-ordination Centre that stands on the cliff-tops just north of Dover.

Like most sea paddlers, we were apprehensive about the reception we would receive. It is common to hear stories of the Coastguard being unsympathetic to sea canoeing and one gains the impression that they will always try to dissuade paddlers from undertaking serious journeys. This, however, was not to be our experience.

Cooking and kayak repairs in the sea-angling club hut at St. Margaret's Bay.

The personal contact we made on this day marked the beginning of a rewarding working relationship which lasted throughout the trip. Not once were they to try and talk us out of the plans we put before them. On the other hand, we went out of our way to keep them informed of our intentions so they were assured of the sea-worthiness of our equipment and our ability to use it. It also guaranteed that any good impressions we made were being passed on ahead of us. The most immediate benefit of our visit to the M.R.C.C. at Dover was that they arranged for us to contact the Dover Port Control on our radio so that our progress past the busy entrances to Dover Harbour could be properly monitored.

When we did get away at 0715 on Wednesday, the weather was fine, the rough seas in the Straits were dropping off fast but they were still big enough to give us a tense passage past Dover Harbour. The tide runs very hard here and with waves clapping back off the breakwater of the outer-arm, a very confused sea state of peaked waves kept our adrenalin pumping. We had contacted the Port Control on our radio as soon as we were clear of the wave-cut platforms that guard St. Margaret's Bay and it turned out to be a wise precaution. Because of the sea state, the Port Control were unable to see us off the Eastern Entrance, so they sent out a patrol boat to locate and circle our kayaks, thus enabling the bigger harbour traffic to avoid us.

We had left on the last of the south-west flowing ebb to avoid the worst effects of wind against tide but the nasty sea had slowed us more than I had expected. The tide was flowing hard against us when we put into the inner harbour at Folkestone for a rest, where we waited for the tide to turn in our favour and were off again at 1445. By now the sun was out and the winds had become very light. We set a compass course for Dungeness, since the coast skirting the levels of Romney Marsh is devoid of interest and it would take three hours to turn the prominent headland of pebbles overlooked by the power station. Meanwhile, the weather worsened. Lightning flashed and thunder grumbled on all sides of us. Out of sight of land for the first time in the trip, we paddled in an eerie atmosphere until we were at last hit by a fierce, gusty wind and the torrential rain of a thundery squall, about two miles short of the ness. This we rounded in choppy seas set up by the tide ripping off the point. Our bouncing ride through the race ensured that we were soaked through to the parts that the rain had been unable to reach!

A long, dull trudge of a paddle now saw us past the uninteresting beach which protects the southern shore of Romney Marsh. We would have been happy to stop, but this is a Ministry of Defence "Danger Area" so we paddled on to the sand dunes of Camber. The prospect of carrying our heavy boats over the vast area of dry sands dissuaded us from stopping and we kept going.

We were heading for the mouth of the river Rother where the tide was already beginning to flood up the straight man-made cut towards Rye. Having paddled about 25 miles since leaving Folkestone, we were growing weary. It was 2045 and almost dark when we reached the concrete slip by Rye Harbour Sailing Club.

I was glad to see lights on in the clubhouse, where a committee meeting was in progress. Caked in salt, I entered the club. Standing in a fast-growing puddle that drained from my clothes I asked if they could oblige us with a place in their dinghy park where we could put up a tent. Taken unawares, they must have found it difficult to refuse the strange being before them that appealed to their maritime instincts. A few minutes later we had used their changing rooms, changed into dry clothes and had rushed over the road to the William the Conqueror to buy some "pub grub".

We were still there an hour later when we were sought out by members of the Sailing Club committee. In our absence, they had given more thought to our predicament and

"The seas were still big enough to give us a tense passage past Dover Harbour."

welfare, and now offered us their company, beer and the key to their premises so that we would not have to put up our tent. Therefore we were showered, warm and well fed when we pulled on our sleeping-bags, just before midnight. I fell asleep instantly.

While at St. Margaret's we had decided to make every possible effort to reach Hayling Island (at the eastern entrance to the Solent) by the following weekend. This would give us over 180 miles in our first week of paddling, but now, having lost two complete days in the gales, the chances of achieving this objective looked remote.

During the morning of Thursday it was pointless leaving our "luxury" accommodation at the Sailing Club because a strong south-westerly wind was blowing and a very powerful tide flooding up the Rother cut. To kill time, I amused myself studying the nautical almanac and charts, realising as I did so that we could only reach Hayling on time if we produced a canoeing equivalent of a magician pulling a rabbit from a hat. In the meantime, we had heard a very promising weather forecast that would keep us in settled weather until after the weekend. It gave me plenty to think about until we finally launched at 1315 that afternoon.

Clearing the light surf that was still running off the river entrance, we paddled west in fast improving weather. By mid-afternoon there was bright sunshine and a very light southerly breeze. The coast was changing in character too now that we were in East Sussex and the cliffs of Fairlight ran on to Hastings, where we stopped to stretch our legs before pushing on to cross Pevensey Bay. As the light began to fade, it grew increasingly chilly, so when the tide began to flow against us we decided to land at Langney Point, which is overlooked by one of the many Martello towers that are to be found on the low sections of the south-east coast and were built to defend these shores against the possibility of a Napoleonic invasion.

This was the first of many occasions when conventional siting and pitching of the tent was out of the question. We had to establish a camp on large stones above the groynes and set up the fly-sheet as a bivvy, securing its base to some old railway sleepers we found among the fishing-boats at the top of the beach. It was nearly dark by the time this was done, so we cooked our evening meal on the Primus by the fluorescent green light of a device known as a light stick. These are one-off chemical lights in a small plastic tube (little larger than a thick-barrelled fountain pen) and activated by bending the tube so that an inner, rigid tube breaks, thus allowing the chemicals to mix and produce a yellow-green glow lasting several hours.

As we settled down into our sleeping-bags I presented to Mick and Richard an idea that I had been turning over in my mind all day. If we were prepared to make a very early start on Friday and accept paddling against some tide, and providing the weather remained good enough to do some paddling in the hours of darkness, we could yet reach Hayling Island on Saturday. They agreed that we would give it a try. Extracts from my log for Friday give some idea of what followed from this casual agreement.

Richard's wrist alarm went off at 0400. We got up with some reluctance, knowing we would have to put on paddling gear that was still wet from yesterday.
Outside the fly-sheet it was cold. A full moon shone down from a clear sky to throw the long shadow of the Martello tower over our boats. The sea was calm but

the lightest of breezes chilled us to the bone as we got changed. Forgoing breakfast,
we were off the beach by 0530.

The tide was already going slack and had turned against us as we cleared the
rocks beneath the chalk cliffs of Beachy Head. Our arrival here coincided with the
dawn, which was reflected in the calm sea and made a magnificent backdrop for
some photographs. Because of the spring tide, the red-and-white tower of the
lighthouse was standing on a dry ledge.

Passing the succession of white cliffs and hanging dry valleys known as the Seven Sisters,
we reached Cuckmere Haven at exactly 0800. To my taste, this idyllic spot is the most
scenic on the south-east coast, for it is here that the river Cuckmere cuts through the
South Downs in a valley of text-book meanders and breaches the shingle bar of an
unspoiled beach to reach the sea. We planned to stop here for an extended breakfast
and await the tide to turn in our favour.

In warm sunshine we collected driftwood, built a fire and with watering mouths
watched our pork chops sizzling on the cooking grill. They made a welcome
change from our usual breakfast of porridge. This was more like it!

Breakfast at Cuckmere.

We were ready to move off again just after midday and picked up a good tide off the
clay-stained chalk of Seaford Head. The light glared back at us from the mirror-calm
sea and it was too hot to paddle in our cags as we pushed on past Seaford and
Newhaven. At Brighton Marina, we stopped briefly to refill our water bottles and by
1730 we were landing in the entrance to Shoreham Harbour, so that we could listen
to the 1750 shipping forecast. This clinched the decision to press on again when the
tide turned at midnight.

We boiled a joint of bacon in the shelter of the harbour wall and used the last of the evening sun to take the worst of the wetness from our paddling clothes. Then we snuggled down into the lee of the wall to snatch some sleep beneath the stars. It was cold and I had little enthusiasm to leave the comfort of my sleeping-bag when the alarm sounded at 2345. Pulling on damp clothes never gets any easier and I resorted to running up and down the harbour wall to try and get warm before finishing my packing. As we slipped beneath the lines of the anglers on the breakwater and out of the harbour it was exactly half past midnight.

Paddling in darkness was in itself not unusual. During the winter months we frequently paddle our K2s in the Medway Estuary at night. Having stated that, it is only fair to add that paddling on a calm sea by the light of a full moon has always retained a sensual quality for me and this occasion was no exception. The moonlight was sufficiently bright to cause distinct shadows, but because we intended to lie off shore to get the full benefit of the tide, I had taken the precaution of securing a taped-up light stick under my chart elastics which cast a directed glow onto the compass. It was an unspoken understanding that we would paddle within easy talking distance from each other.

Within an hour of leaving we had covered over 5 miles to reach a point about 2 miles off Worthing Pier, easily identified in the mass of promenade lights. A little over one more hour and we had separated ourselves from Shoreham by almost 13 miles to pick up the buoy off Littlehampton Harbour. A north-easterly breeze had sprung up by this time and we checked the strength and direction of the tide running off the buoy before pressing on by compass heading to hit the next one.

So the night passed on to another clear dawn. Exactly five hours after getting into our boats we beached by the lifeboat station which stands on stilts about half a mile north of the low, stony headland of Selsey Bill. We were wet, cold, hungry and tired. Richard in particular was suffering. A washing-line was quickly strung out between the struts of the lifeboat slip to hang out our wet gear before laying our sleeping-bags between our boats to keep the wind off us, crawling inside and falling into the sleep of the dead.

I awoke suddenly to the rhythmic thump of a donkey engine. As I pulled my sleeping-bag back from over my head the bright sunlight stung my eyes which were sore from the salt and the lack of sleep. Blinking to clear them and identify the cause of the disturbance I could see that a fishing-boat was being winched up the beach, with the cable running a few inches from Mick's head. He, however, remained unaware and blissfully continued snoring! I looked at my watch to see that it was still only 0830 . . .

Later . . . we cooked some porridge and changed into dry but salt-hardened paddling gear. We were back on the water at noon precisely . . . The tide race sped us past the point of the Bill so that to the north-west we could at last see Hayling, now less than half a day's paddle away.

At Wittering we were intercepted by a lone sail-boarder. This was Dave Thomson, whom I had phoned from Shoreham on the previous evening to arrange accommodation on Hayling. Dave now escorted us across the busy waters of the entrance to Chichester Harbour and to the sail-board club at Langston – the western end of Hayling sea-front. It was 1420. There were plenty of interested helpers to assist in carrying our boats to the car-park and we were now assured of a carefree weekend with a comfort-able roof over our heads. Dave was one of the few people who would appreciate the effort involved in covering the 67½ miles from Langney Point since the previous morning.

There was some irony in the situation that Dave should now be in a position of helping our expedition, since it was he who had nurtured my enthusiasm for canoeing. Before he had moved to Hayling we had shared a house and enjoyed numerous memorable expeditions together, both in the mountains and in kayaks. It was a relationship based on trust and respect. He had taught me most of what I know about white-water canoeing and I had in return passed on all I knew about the mountain environment. We had pulled each other out of numerous scrapes and I was confident we would enjoy our stay with Dave and his wife Dawn.

Bev and Mandy were at the Thomson household when we arrived. Our tiredness was soon forgotten as we began an extended feast and excitedly relived our adventures of the previous week. We already knew that paddling on Sunday would be impossible. I had put a large stress-fracture and hole in the bottom of my boat (beneath the seat) and this would require a tricky repair that we could not afford to rush or bodge.

Our wild campsite near Newtown River, Isle of Wight.

We spent the morning of Monday 28th April buying supplies for the next leg of the journey and waiting for the afternoon tide. This condemned us to waste the last of the fine weather, for the forecast was a poor one. A fresh south-westerly was already blowing when we thanked Dave for his hospitality and bade him farewell. Crossing the area of breaking waves on the sand spit off Langston ensured we were instantly soaked.

The spire of Ryde church gave us our heading to cross the busy shipping lanes of the Eastern Solent and so to the more sheltered waters of the Isle of Wight shore. When we reached Cowes it was raining hard and the wind had become strong. The wind-against-tide conditions were kicking up choppy seas that frequently ran "green" along our decks to slap us in the chest. It was cold, wet and very hard work paddling into what was now a dead head wind.

We had set out hoping to reach Yarmouth that evening but the steadily worsening conditions forced us to rethink. We were still only off Newtown River by 1715 so we tucked inshore to study the O.S. map for an alternative stopping place. This identified a "wild" campsite behind the shingle bank to the west of the river mouth where we now sat. We landed just as the rain eased and were very pleased with our find. The neighbouring oakwoods provided complete shelter from the wind and a plentiful supply of dead wood for a fire. With the tent pitched we warmed ourselves by the fire before letting it die down to cook on.

The next day dawned clear and sunny. We took our time in packing for we wanted a chance to dry out our gear. When we launched at midday we had decided to fight the tide so that if sea conditions permitted, we would be able to use the period of slack tide to visit the Needles. The seas in the Hurst Castle narrows (where a great spit narrows the Western Solent to form a tide race) dampened our enthusiasm for this option so we crossed the race to the fort and took a direct heading for Poole, about 18 miles away across Christchurch and Poole Bays, so beginning a five-hour slog into the wind with a moderate sea running against us. In the places where our now favourable tide might have offered most assistance – such as off the ledges of Hengistbury Head – it only served to increase the size of the waves to about two metres and guarantee us a soaking. The whole paddle was extremely strenuous. When we eventually came to the narrows of the Haven to enter Poole's natural harbour, the tide was running out at about 3 knots. We could only progress by a series of short sprints from one obstacle to another.

Eric and Jo Bird – members of Poole Harbour Canoe Club – had kindly invited us to stay with them when we reached Poole, so we edged our way to Parkstone Marina where the Birds owned a house that overlooked the saltings. Had we arrived half an hour earlier we could have paddled to their back door, but now the mud was showing and we were forced to leave our boats to be picked up later. Once again we were overwhelmed with hospitality; once again we were about to miss a day of fine weather, this time because of Richard's boat.

He had landed with his cockpit awash but for no obvious reason. During Wednesday we worked in the Birds' back garden subjecting the boat to a thorough test for leaks – but without success. As a last resort, Richard checked the bilge-pump and discovered the non-return valves were not closing properly. Our minds at rest, we returned to the pleasant task of being spoiled.

Passing Old Harry, one of the finest features on the Dorset coast.

May 1st. Overslept until 0630, putting us an hour behind schedule. It was a mad rush to get packed in the early morning fog and we narrowly avoided being stranded on the mud. We were finally clear of Parkstone at 0800. So my diary notes begin the entry for what still stands out in my mind as an exceptionally fine paddle.

As we left the Haven the fog was burning off quickly to give a calm, fine morning for the start of our traverse of the Dorset coast. The narrow steep-sided cliffs and chalk stack of Old Harry were soon astern to put us on Swanage Bay. Rounding the Purbeck limestone cliff of Durlston Head we met our first puffin of the trip, along with hundreds of guillemots and a few razorbills. I was not expecting to meet them so far east.

West of St. Alban's Head lies the Lulworth Gunnery Range and we reached it to find the red warning flag flying. It was time to test our I.C.M. 12 radio which we had kept handy in anticipation of this problem. I called up the Coastguard and was surprised to be answered from the distant Portland station. After a short pause whilst they contacted the Range Officer, we were cleared from noon onwards, but since it was now only 1140, we paddled into Chapman's Pool (a cove just west of the head) to land and cook the breakfast we had missed in our rush to get away.

There was no wind and the cove acted as a suntrap. Stripped off in the sun, we had to force ourselves to move on after a most pleasant two-hour break. The scenery was by far the best we had so far encountered and we discussed the possibility of returning at a later date to walk the coastal footpath.

When we stopped again, at Lulworth Cove, we had come as far as we had planned for the day, but we felt guilty about wasting such conditions and decided to eat a quick snack so that we could paddle on into the evening. We were approaching Portland Bill – the first major technical problem of the expedition. Jutting into the tidal streams of the English Channel, it is famous for its great tide race which runs up to 10 knots on spring tides and so had to be treated with great respect. We had perfect weather conditions (i.e. no wind) and a look at the tide tables showed we had just enough time to paddle there in order to find the best tidal conditions for a west-going passage.

Leaving Lulworth, we paddled along the foot of the cliffs as far as the symmetrical limestone arch of Durdle Door. Here we headed out to sea towards the hazy, wedge-shaped outline of the Portland Peninsula. Such is the power of the tide flowing across the tip of the Bill, a south-going eddy flows along its eastern flank for 10 hours of the 12 in a tidal sequence. We used this to good advantage and met the first turbulence off the eastern point of the peninsula. When at Cave Hole, with a mile to go before the Bill proper, we were only a paddle's length off the foot of the low cliff and being swept south at about 4–5 knots. It is here that the eddy suddenly sets off shore to join the turbulence of the main race so we broke out of the flow into the relatively calm "inner passage" that provides the softest option to small craft wishing to traverse this notorious headland. At 1930, with the sun setting, we sat in the calm water on the very tip and watched the dancing, broken water of the main race that almost encircled us.

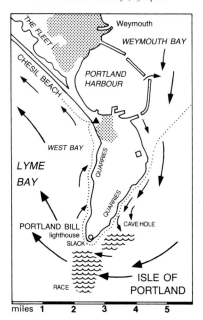

Tidal streams 1st May 7.30 p.m.

Two hours later we were setting up a bivvy on the north-west flank of the peninsula at Chesil. We had good reason to feel pleased. Since leaving Poole that morning we had covered about 40 miles and enjoyed the most rewarding paddling so far.

The forlorn blast of the horn on the Portland light boomed out through the fog to wake us early the next morning. The sea-fret obscured the sun until late in the morning and refused to be burned off. To kill time, we wandered round the shops, waiting for the afternoon tide.

We set off at 1400 and began a tedious paddle along the featureless and seemingly endless miles of Chesil Beach. The thin mist limited our vision, veiled our progress and every mile was like the one before. After about 16 miles we reached Burton Bradstock and the stone beach at last gave way to low sandstone cliffs. We finally stopped for the night at the Anchor Inn, Seatown, with little more than half the previous day's mileage covered.

Our shingle camp near Seatown.

Camping on the shingle, we found just enough wood to make a small cooking fire and then retired to the pub to rebuild our sagging morale. This was duly achieved, thanks to David Miles and his wife Sadie (they owned the pub), who did everything possible to make us welcome and comfortable. When we set off just after midday on Saturday 3rd May we were on the point of talking ourselves into staying.

The day had in fact started badly. When I woke at 0550 to listen to the weather forecast, rain was beating heavily on the tent in a fresh south-easterly breeze and the forecast promised it would strengthen. Already a short, steep sea was dumping on the shingle where we had made an easy landing the previous evening and we prepared ourselves to declare the day a write-off. Later, when the rain eased, I phoned the Portland Coastguard for an inshore forecast and was surprised to hear that they were not expecting the wind to exceed F3−4. This was puzzling but encouraging, prompting us to pack and prepare to leave.

Launching proved difficult. Our first attempt washed us back up the beach, virtually on top of each other and embarrassingly at the feet of the spectators. Our second try was more successful and saw us drenched but afloat. Mick's diary was kept in the form of brief notes but it creates a vivid impression:

After goodbyes it was back to the boats and an entry which guaranteed a ducking to start the day's paddle. Seas dumping on the beach. Bill off first, only to be pushed broadside, but eventually landing upright but under the front of Richard's boat. Not the done thing for a couple of aces? I decided to push off and just about got it right. After a couple of waves had blocked out the sun I was clear of the break. A little damp but relieved . . .

Now that we were off the beach we accepted the occasional soakings of breaking waves and set our course off shore to head for Beer and glorious Devon. In the open water of Lyme Bay we could detect that there were two seas running – south-east wind-waves over a southerly swell that sometimes seemed uncomfortably large. It looked as if the original forecast was the more accurate and we began to wonder what we had let ourselves in for. To make matters worse, my cockpit was awash with water above the seat-pan. I had suspected my bilge-pump valves were leaking before I set off so I had blocked off both the inlet and the outlet as a stop-gap repair. Now I was regretting it, for the boat had developed an increasing tendency to wallow. I needed to land and sort things out but the nature of the coast made this impossible. Meanwhile the seas got bigger.

The first place I could see on the map where we might get in was at Seaton, where the river Axe flows into the sea, protected by a sand-bar. By the time we were half a mile off our intended goal we regretted ever leaving our friendly pub back at Seatown. We could see even at this range that the surf sets were big as they creamed in towards Axmouth, where we could see concrete breakwaters forming a proper harbour entrance.

When a commercial fishing-boat came in from seaward we stopped paddling to watch the line he took to cross the bar and enter the harbour. It left a sickly feeling in the pit of my stomach when the fishing-boat was caught in the bar-break and thrown sideways up the eastern breakwater. We had no choice but to follow and risk similar treatment. The next few minutes were very anxious as we struggled to stay in control of a deteriorating situation and run the surf in one piece. It was a great relief to eventually find ourselves safely into the river but we were only just in time. By evening a full gale was blowing and creating a frightening sea.

The local Harbour Master proved most helpful. He arranged for us to stay in a chalet belonging to the Axe Yacht Club and to use all their facilities. As we enjoyed the hospitality of the bar that evening, we reviewed the progress we had made reaching Devon and amused ourselves recalling the glib forecast of one of our clubmates. In total ignorance of what was involved, he had dismissed the sum total of our achievements in the simple statement, "the South Coast is easy!"

5

Testing Ground

Seaton – St. Ives: 5th – 20th May

We were looking forward to reaching the scenic coastline of South Devon; but then we were not to know that the south-west peninsula would prove to be our testing ground. The weather pattern was about to degenerate, producing almost a month of high winds and unseasonably cold weather. As our journey became bogged in a series of frustrating halts, we responded by embarking on gruelling paddles in marginal conditions to make up lost time. All too often we came dangerously close to pushing too hard; on occasions it was only luck that allowed us to escape with nothing worse than chastening frights and bruised egos. Our fitness, stamina and courage were to be stretched, almost to breaking-point.

When we left Seaton on Monday 5th May, the wind was a fresh onshore southerly but the sea had dropped off. Even so, we had to take care to recross the bar in the mouth of the Axe that had given us such a scare when we arrived. The leak which had forced us in had turned out to be nothing more than a badly chafed spray-deck, so from this point on we invariably wore two spray-decks to ensure there would be no repetitions of the problem. The sun was breaking through the dispersing cloud by the time we had crossed the bay to pass Sidmouth, leaving the last of the chalk cliffs of Lowland Britain and so to the distinctive red sandstone of Devon. Turning a rocky headland, we came ashore at Budleigh Salterton to eat lunch and stretch our legs before setting off across the wide estuary of the river Exe. In spite of the sunshine, the wind made it too cold to hang around and we were on our way again as soon as possible.

As the afternoon wore on the wind was slowly strengthening. We were also crossing the tide that was flooding into the Exe Estuary, so when we were a couple of miles off Dawlish and began to turn towards the south, the combined forces of wind and tide reduced our progress to a tortuous crawl. At first we were prepared to slog it out, punching into the wind and waves until we were so wet, cold and weary that we gave up the plan of paddling straight to Teignmouth. Instead, we made an unscheduled landing beneath the coastal railway at Horse Cove, where a breakwater sheltered a small stony beach backed by steep bluffs.

There was some time before the tide would slacken. We kept active by collecting driftwood and building a huge bonfire which warmed us up and got most of our soaked clothing dry. Towards high water, as the flood slackened, we moved on again, fighting the wind to reach the river Teign. Turning the point on the north side of the river entrance, we at last came into the lee of the hills on the south shore and so escaped from the wind. From here it was a short and easy paddle to the Shaldon road bridge, beside which we found a small plot of land where we could erect the fly-sheet and bivvy down for the evening.

During the night we experienced torrential rain. A fine spray beat through the fly-sheet and we realised that whatever the forecast, we had little choice but to move on. When the day dawned clear we spread out our wet gear to dry in the early sun. The river at our feet was calm and peaceful but we knew from the forecast that once out of the estuary it would be a different story. It was essential that we utilise the tide in such conditions, so after a cup of tea we moved off at 0800 on the tide ebbing from the Teign, bouncing through a little race where it entered the sea.

There followed a hard battle with the wind to make 10 miles to the fishing port of Brixham. The sun was shining again but the wind was a strong southerly, ensuring we worked hard for every metre of progress and keeping us cold and wet into the bargain. Crossing Babbacombe Bay we came to Torquay and Hope's Nose, the headland demarking the northern limits of Tor Bay. Off this point set a brown, slimy and foul-smelling slick from a sewer outfall, contrasting sharply with the dark green waters on either side. It was all of 250 metres across and flecked with suds and foam. We had no choice but to paddle through the neat sewage as it sloshed onto decks and clothing in the chop set up by the wind. This was a sickening way to be reminded of the inability of water authorities to tackle a major problem and the lack of government resolve to conserve our coastal environment. Quite unusually, our conversation took on a distinctly political tone until we emerged from the waste to find ourselves by Thatcher's Rock!

At last we paddled into the shelter of picturesque Brixham. Suddenly finding ourselves out of the wind, we had paddled into summer, the sunshine accentuating the colourful array of brightly painted fishing-boats. We landed on the slip below the lifeboat station, spread out our wet gear to dry and walked towards the town. Our first stop was a visit to the Coastguard and then on to the Royal Mission for Deep Sea Fishermen (where we felt confident we would get a cheap meal). Later in the afternoon, having restocked on supplies, we went back to the Coastguard Station to get an updated weather forecast. We were watching the anemometer when the wind backed into the south-east.

After the morning's efforts we had become preoccupied with the problems of fighting a head wind to the exclusion of almost all other considerations. Consequently, the wind shift prompted us to hurry off, pack and get away. This would prove to be a mistake; we had grossly underestimated the change in the sea state caused by the wind shift.

South of Brixham is a seven-mile section of committing coastline which stretches unbroken to Dartmouth. The sea cliffs and jagged rocks make for spectacular scenery but create demanding sea conditions in onshore winds – which is what the wind shift had produced. Such were the problems that it took us nearly 3½ hours to cover those seven miles.

Leaving the harbour, it took only a few minutes to reach the towering precipice of Berry Head, which had been keeping the wind off us and was where we would be running into the full flow of the tide. The character of our paddle now took on a sudden and dramatic change. The south-easterly wind-waves were reflecting back off the rock face and across the morning's residual southerly swell. It resulted in a frightening confusion of steep, pyramidal waves up to four metres in height. Full concentration was required to stay upright and there was no let-up for long periods at a time. The

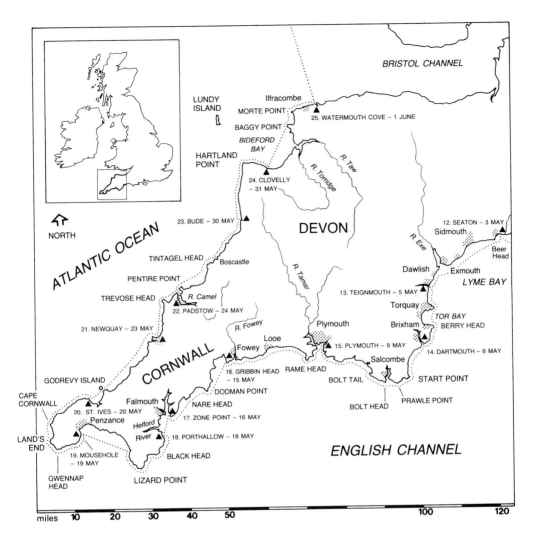

paddle became a mental more than a physical strain. In contrast, the scenery was magnificent. Steep reefs thrust up through the wild seas; high, steep cliffs plunged into the sea.

For the first hour or so the sun continued to shine but as we paddled on into early evening, the fine weather gave way to a thickening pall of cloud that threatened rain. Just short of Dartmouth is a rocky islet called the Mew Stone where the seas were again very confused. Once past this problem we could enter the Dart but now the tide had turned and was running out to create long, roller-coaster standing waves, on which we could sit the entire length of our kayaks. By the time we had entered the narrows between the castles which once guarded the anchorage, we felt totally drained.

The town of Dartmouth stands on the western flank of the beautiful, steep-sided valley cut by the river Dart. The sea has flooded this valley to provide a first-class haven for small boats, so moorings and marinas abound, both around Dartmouth itself and the settlement of Kingswear, standing on the opposite bank. As we paddled into this setting on this miserable evening, the immediate prospects of finding somewhere to stay looked to be very poor, but a combination of luck and coincidence was to improve our circumstances considerably. Some dinghy sailors suggested we made enquiries at the Darthaven Marina, on the Kingswear shore. The marina office had been left in the charge of Bob Barton, a canoeist that Richard had met the year before on a white-water trip in the Austrian Alps. We were subsequently offered a free site in their car-park and a key to their shower-block so that we could get cleaned up. Fortune had smiled upon us. We were to be stuck here in strong winds for the next two days.

During this time we contacted Chris Woods, an old friend of both Mick's and Richard's. He had been instrumental in introducing both to the outdoors and had been a radiographer in the Royal Dockyard at Chatham. When the dockyard on the Medway had started to run down he had moved down to the Devonport yard and so was living at Plymstock. We had arranged to stay with Chris and his family when we reached Plymouth and on the third evening of our enforced incarceration at Kingswear he drove over to Dartmouth and we took the ferry across the river to meet him. On a dull, blowy evening of poor visibility with a driving, heavy drizzle, we were driven out to Start Point in order to inspect the problems we might encounter.

This headland is the western limit of Lyme Bay, where the coast again takes a turn to the west. The pilotage information suggested this point might be a serious technical problem, particularly since we would be tackling it on a spring tide. Our visit meant that when we got away on Friday 9th May, we thought we were well prepared for what the day might have in store.

We left the Dart at 0805, about half an hour after high water, to give ourselves a full span of ebbing tide to continue the journey. It was another day of thick cloud and the fresh wind had shifted a little to blow from just west of south, thus providing some shelter once south of Torcross and the trapped lagoons of Slapton Sands. Where the old village of Hallsands is slowly collapsing into the sea, we took a short break in case it would be difficult to land later. Then wondering what was in store, we paddled on to Start Point.

It was an anti-climax. The tide was running at about four knots and the race working well, but we found we could paddle round the head inside the worst of the turbulence. In fact, Prawle Point, just a short distance to the west, created a much bigger tide race. Once this too was behind us, we felt confident of our ability to handle the three-metre groundswell which was running in from the south. We were going so well that we abandoned our original plan of putting into the deep inlet of Salcombe to press on and turn the cliffs of Bolt Head, requiring us to cross an area of shoals and submerged reefs. The combination of turbulence and "clapping" waves reflecting from the cliffs once again set up a scary sea, similar in size and appearance to the one we had encountered on Berry Head. We eased to seaward to escape from the clapotis but as we drew close to Bolt Tail, we began to encounter fog. Thus, when we turned the Tail at about 1400 we were keen to take a break in the sheltered bay of Hope Cove.

A break for hot pasties in a deserted tea-room put new vigour into us. With a pained expression, the proprietor quietly accepted the puddles of water that drained onto her floor and as warmth returned, the 13 miles left to Plymouth somehow became an attractive option. If we could get there that evening we knew Chris would be there to meet us and put us up. More important, it would offer us a chance to take the whole weekend off, allowing Richard to take a train home and put in a surprise appearance at the 21st birthday party of his girlfriend Mandy. It was easy to talk ourselves into going on and this decision resulted in a paddle that would be difficult to forget.

Having phoned to alert our contacts in Plymouth of our pending arrival, we left Hope Cove. While we crossed Bigbury Bay towards the rocks of Burgh Island, the fog thickened until visibility was down to about 500 metres and I was forced to resort to compass navigation. At intervals of estimated distance we aimed off towards the coast to get an accurate fix on our position, risking a real danger of getting caught inside the breakline of the surf. It also began to rain.

When we met two sailing cruisers entering the natural haven of the Yealm we began to appreciate that the seas were increasing in size, for at close range we were frequently losing sight of the mast tops in the swells. When the craggy outline of the Great Mew Stone islet loomed out of the fog we became afraid that the seas would break in the inside channel, forcing us to pass on the swell-battered western flank of the rock. Here the sea was being kicked up into a wild mass of peaks and tottering wave crests in which I lost contact with the other two kayaks. Only when well clear of the area was I prepared to ease up and find them, but, wherever I peered in the swirling fog, I could see nothing but the on-rushing swells. When my companions finally came into view it gave me a new fright and I had to rapidly rethink my sense of scale. Both boats were paddling towards me, down the face of the same huge swell, one kayak in front of the other with plenty of room to spare! Thus we entered the approaches to Plymouth Sound: in fog, on house-sized swells, eyes straining into the murk to find the narrow gap between Fort Bovisand on the mainland and the Plymouth Breakwater. We found ourselves through the gap before sighting the fort and never did see the Breakwater on this particular evening.

Thanks to Chris, some paddlers from the Port of Plymouth Canoe Club were out to meet us. They were sheltering in the lee of the fort and, because we were not expecting them, only realised they were there when a torch flashed at us out of the gloom. It had just turned 2000 and we had paddled for almost eleven of the last twelve hours. As soon as the seas calmed and the pressure came off us, we became suddenly aware of our weariness and aching bums – the price of a 37-mile day.

Chris's organisation meant that our arrival at the Phoenix Wharf was hassle-free. He had arranged for us to leave our kayaks at the Canoe Club; there were hot drinks waiting for us and within a short time we were being bundled into cars to be taken to his home. I shudder to think what the story might have been had we arrived without support in such an exhausted state, in the middle of a major city.

Thanks to the weather, our plans for a "weekend off" were hopelessly optimistic and we were to be guests in the Woods household for a total of six nights. It has to be admitted that it was a particularly hospitable and comfortable place to be stuck. We owe Chris a lot for using up his valuable leave to look after us.

When Richard returned to Plymouth from his flying visit to see Mandy, we had plenty of time to overhaul our equipment and research the next leg of the journey. This still left time to look at places of local interest. Frustrating though the protracted halt may have been, it was enjoyable in other ways. On one windy and rainy afternoon the three of us went for a walk with Chris, trudging over the hills from Plymstock to Fort Bovisand. During the conversation I mentioned that I had seen a television programme advertised that I thought we would all be interested in. We almost ran back to the house to see *Portland Bill; a storm at sea*.

The title conjured up a pictorial epic based on the notorious headland we had so recently paddled round. Just two minutes after the programme's start time we arrived panting in the lounge and turned on the tele. Chris's young son Andrew seemed highly amused at our concern when we could not "find" the channel showing the programme we were hoping to see. On the advertised channel, all we could see were some animated puppets. Frustrated, I searched out a newspaper.

"Look, it's advertised here!" I persisted with some annoyance. Andrew, by this time, was rocking on the floor, holding his sides in half-suppressed mirth. It took some time before we came to realise what he found so funny. He thought we were really stupid. After all, doesn't everyone know that Portland Bill is the lighthouse-keeper in a children's television programme?

The period of strong southerly winds finally came to an end in the early hours of Thursday, 15th May, enabling us to escape from Plymouth. Chris's wife, Mary, drove us down to the wharf, close to where the *Mayflower* had set out for the New World. Just before 1100 we waved goodbye.

Although the sun was shining, conditions were still far from ideal. The wind had become a fresh westerly, easing the sea state but giving us a head wind. Crossing Plymouth Sound to pass Drake's Island we remained in shelter and had the tide to help us reach the open sea at Penlee Point. From here on there was no escaping the wind, so having passed the heights of Rame Head just after 1230 we had a long slog over the open expanse of Whitsand Bay towards distant Looe. Seeking a sheltered course along the shore's edge was out of the question. Apart from the surf, the area extending from the cliffs on this fine coast is a gunnery range, so we had to paddle off shore. It took until 1600 to reach a sheltered cove opposite the western side of Looe Island, where we came ashore for a rest and some lunch.

On our way again, the difficulties eased because we could paddle along the rock-ends, just outside the breakline. This was Cornwall and the scenery had become ruggedly pretty in a way quite unique to this coast – rocky headlands, cliffs and caves and quaint fishing villages perched on the sides of winding green combs. With so much to keep our interest the hard work went unnoticed. Polperro and the inlet of Fowey were put behind us, but as the time approached 2000, we had to abandon our intention of reaching Mevagissey. Almost immediately we were presented with an opportunity to land in a wooded and sheltered cove, just east of Gribbin Head. Above the beach was a low dam wall concealing a fine campsite. An area of level grass overlooked a large lake, which we later learned had been constructed as a decoy to draw German bombers away from the munitions port of Fowey. The owner of the stone cottage by the lake

The two extremes of sea kayaking: a forward loop in surf and dead calm conditions with kayaks propelled by a helpful tide. During our trip we tried to avoid the former and seek out the latter.

The kayak, equipped for long distance sea travel, can also be used to support the tent.

The team members: Richard Elliott, Bill Taylor and Mick Wibrew.

One of the delights of sea kayaking is being able to explore the impressive cave

Passing below Beachy Head at dawn on 25th April. In the low 'spring' tide the lighthouse stands clear of the sea on its plinth of rocks.

*The magnificent chalk formations by Old Harry,
one of Dorset's most impressive coastal stacks.*

[ABOVE] *Chalk cliffs west of Old Harry, Dorset.*
[BELOW] *Passing the limestone arch at Durdle Door, west of Lulworth Cove.*

*South Cornwall: watching the surf gather strength during a lunch stop at Hemmick Beach [ABOVE]
and passing a rocky headland to the west of Looe [BELOW].*

[ABOVE] *Approaching St Ives after our day rounding Land's End.* [BELOW] *The flotilla is haloed in a fog bow in the afternoon mists we encountered in the St. George's Channel.*

was happy to allow us to stay and we quickly set up camp, but it was nearly 2300 before we had finished eating. We were so tired that the washing-up got left for the following morning.

The new day began at 0550, when the alarm went off so that we could take the early shipping forecast. The weather sounded promising, for a fresh to strong easterly wind was expected with a gale later. The level sheet of cloud showed signs of lifting so we packed in good spirits, expecting to have a relatively easy, wind-assisted day.

Shortly after 1000 we were clear of Gribbin Head and on a south-westerly course to cross the wide bay to Dodman Point. Within an hour the sun had dispersed the cloud and about 1230 we arrived off the rugged headland of Dodman. The seas had been building up steadily throughout the paddle and were already larger than we might have expected for the actual wind strength. It was a warning sign that we had already learned to take seriously and confirmed the forecast's prediction of a blow later.

Just west of the point we were able to take shelter in the lee of the head, landing in the corner between the cliffs that make up the promontory and the sands of Hemmick Beach. The swell was refracting round the headland to create regular lines of perfect surf but it was easily run and we spent a pleasant hour over lunch, taking the opportunity to strip off in the rocks and soak up the sun. During this break, the surf was steadily growing and we could see the ranks of white horses increasing out to sea. With growing unease, we cut short our stop.

Launching now proved quite awkward and we eventually picked our way through the rocks near the head, where the surf was more broken. Once we were clear, the wind blew us out into the bay, helping us along so that we ate up the first few miles. This took us well off shore to clear the craggy towers of Gull Rock. Meanwhile, the wind continued to strengthen and the seas grew in size. Blowing a steady F6, the easterly wind was occasionally producing much stronger gusts which snatched at the paddle blades and caused them to slice rather than bite the water; the odd wave crests were being blown off and all too often we were using the paddles to support our balance, rather than for forward propulsion. The frequency of these happenings increased. During the course of half an hour our easy paddle had turned into another survival epic. The seas were about three to four metres in height, broken and confused by the tide and running close together. There was a real danger of being blown over on the crests but there was no shelter available before the Falmouth Estuary.

An hour and a half of sweaty tension followed before we at last reached St. Anthony Head and rounded Zone Point to enter the shelter of Falmouth's Carrick Roads. It was all too obvious that the gale was arriving ahead of schedule and our best shelter was to be had on the eastern side of the ria, on the wooded inlets of the beautiful Roseland Peninsula. So, turning into the narrows between St. Anthony and St. Mawes, at 1800 we paddled into the tiny bay at Place, overlooked by woodland and the gothic-style residence of the High Sheriff of Cornwall.

A slip provided a landing with access to a level area of grass, tucked beneath a hedge and bank. The sheriff's gamekeeper gave us permission to camp here, where we would get maximum protection from the pending gale. No sooner had we established ourselves than the sky clouded over. We stayed dry for the evening but were woken in the early hours of Saturday by the drumming of heavy rain.

49

It continued to rain hard and blow throughout Saturday. The local radio station was reporting a southerly F7 at Falmouth, but by lunchtime we were tired of being bottled up, so donning full waterproofs, we set off in the driving rain on an hour's walk into the village of Portscatho. After a pint in The Plume of Feathers, life looked less grim. We bought further supplies and sat out another cloudburst in a hotel tea-room. When we set off back to Place, the rain had stopped and the low pall of scudding cloud suddenly began to break up. Within a few minutes we were enjoying bright sunshine but the wind had picked up to blow a full gale again.

Walking back to the tent by the shores of the Percuil River, we were struck by the beauty of the local woods, where some of the plants were semi-tropical. These, however, only served to accentuate a more significant factor. Here, in mid-May, in what is clearly one of the mildest areas of Britain, the trees were not yet in leaf.

Late that evening, as we lay on our sleeping-bags chatting, reading and listening to the mournful wind in the tree tops, we noticed an unfamiliar sound in the woods across the little bay. It sounded like the grunting and squealing of pigs. On Sunday, we brought this to the attention of the gamekeeper, who told us we had been listening to the local badgers.

This was a bright and sunny Sunday morning but we were still unable to get away, because the wind remained too strong. We decided to walk around the coastal footpath towards Zone Point, where we were able to observe what the sea conditions were like in open water. Paddling plans were temporarily abandoned but when the wind began to ease in mid-afternoon, Mick walked back for another look. He returned with good news and we packed for a late start at 1600, setting off on the ebbing tide towards Helford River in an attempt to put ourselves within easy striking distance of the Lizard.

Two hours later we were off a grey, shaly beach that led to an equally drab and seedy-looking village. This was Porthallow. Bleak and uninviting as a quarry working, it was none the less well sheltered. It was also our last chance to get ashore on the Lizard's eastern flank, before getting caught up in the fast-running tides around the rocks of the Manacles – the graveyard of countless sailing vessels. We landed.

Wandering into the main village, we found a cheap place to eat in a little café. The elderly owner was friendly and turned out to be chairman of the village Beach Committee. He told us not to worry about the "no camping" signs we had seen around the beach, so when we returned to our boats, we set up camp where the beach merged with the car-park of a pub called The Five Pilchards. This was an interesting place to fill in a long evening, for almost every piece of bric-à-brac in the bar had been salvaged from wrecks on the Manacles.

The Lizard is a rocky and rugged headland forming the most southerly point of mainland Britain and around it the tide sets hard. Turning this head was the problem we faced when we woke at dawn to thick sea fog. To clear the Manacles we wanted an early start, so without bothering with breakfast, we were away at 0700. The rocks have emotive and apt names – like "The Shark's Fin" – and had a particularly evocative atmosphere as we paddled through them in the fog, for we had all read the pilot reference to over 700 mariners who lie buried in local churchyards, victims of the wrecks, as well as hundreds more who had not been washed ashore.

At 0815, with the fog showing no sign of thinning, we put in at the little harbour of Coverack for breakfast. A hot pasty and pint of milk from a local grocer warded off hunger and by 0900 we were off again. As a fresh south-easterly wind began to pick up, the fog started to disperse and we were treated to glimpses of the sun and blue sky. The weather was clearly improving but we were now behind schedule and had lost our opportunity of carrying a fair tide round the Lizard itself. This would complicate sea conditions to an extent we did not foresee.

As the head grew closer, the forlorn booming of the lighthouse fog-warning grew louder and louder. Just as we arrived at the south-eastern point to turn west, the fog cleared dramatically and we could see the problems. A tide race was working against us. Sprinting hard, we surfed across the face of the waves to come into more settled conditions off the main and most southerly point, but the next problem was not so easily tackled. Being low water, we could see a wide expanse of reefs extending from the cliffs, a long way out to sea. After the recent south-westerly blows, the main groundswell was running in from this direction to be channelled between the reefs and steepened to form nasty-looking breaks. To progress, we had to choose a channel and then time it so that we cleared it between the bigger swell sets. First we picked our route, then we studied the wave pattern and made our move. We got it wrong.

Richard's journal describes what happened.

Bill was 20–30 metres in front of me, with Mick about the same distance behind. The foghorn was still deafening, making verbal communication difficult. I remember thinking: Just a few hundred metres and we're in the clear.

No sooner had the thought passed through my mind than a huge wall of water could be seen rushing towards us, growing and steepening. It was almost transparent and was completely blocking the channel. There was nothing to be said. We all knew that for the next few moments it would be everyone for himself.

We all sprinted towards the wave. Bill's boat picked up speed, climbed steeply and burst through the crest just before it broke. I could just see Mick pulling up on

my right, then the wave was on us. It seemed to catch Mick first and his bow rose
to the vertical but ceased to climb as the boat stalled. The crest was now breaking
and crashed into my chest. I tottered on the top, was airborne then smashed
down on the reverse side in a crash that shook the whole boat, but Mick had not
fared so well. He had executed a "reverse loop", as the kayak stood on its stem
and the bow had continued to arch backwards over Mick's head before being swept
shoreward in the breaking wave.

Bill was now looking back but past me, and over my shoulder I could see why,
for the bottom of Mick's capsized boat had just emerged on the back of the wave.
His paddle was pushed to the surface as he set himself up to Eskimo-roll but
what Mick did not know was that a second wave was already forcing Bill and
me into a second sprint. It broke right on top of Mick and he disappeared from
sight as the wave surfed him upside down towards the very foot of the cliffs.
Roll! Roll! I was praying.

The next time we saw Mick he was swimming and trying to hang onto his boat
and paddle in the white water and foam, just a few metres from the rocks. He was
in real trouble.

These were anxious moments. There was a very real danger that another big wave
would smash both Mick and his kayak on the rocks, while both Richard and I could
easily be put into a similar situation. Although instinct shouted to rush in and pluck
Mick out of his predicament, good sense urged caution. The guilt and frustration
evoked by this dilemma showed in Richard's face as we looked helplessly on.

In such circumstances, conventional methods of emptying and righting Mick's kayak
were hopelessly inadequate. They would take too long. Making a quick decision, I sent
Richard to find a landing-place and steeled my own resolve to make a dash for Mick.
For a few seconds I attempted to tow him and his swamped boat away from the rocks.
In the sloppy seas it was a useless effort. There was no telling how long it would be
before the next set of big waves would arrive so I simply righted the kayak and pulled

Mick Wibrew's capsize at the Lizard.

Passing Land's End on the long paddle to St. Ives.

Mick into his cockpit with the boat still full of water. This meant it was wallowing and unstable but Mick had the skill to paddle it like this out of the danger zone. In reality and in retrospect there was no other choice. I escorted him with encouraging words but no physical help to where Richard had found a kelp-covered shelf at the foot of the old lifeboat ramp where we landed to sort things out. Mick was very shaken but we had in fact paid very lightly for our mistake. The only equipment loss was a piece of foam that Mick had been using to pad his seat. We had all learned a valuable and chastening lesson.

No one could have blamed Mick if he had declined to move any further for the day but a couple of hours later we had paddled through the reefs again and were heading north up the Lizard's west flank to Mullion Cove. Here a large rock protects the little harbour from the worst of the swell and allowed us to land for a lunch break. Then we were off again with the intention of spending the night at Porthleven, only to find on our arrival that the surf was breaking right across the harbour entrance. It forced on us a decision that was already tempting us. The wind had almost disappeared, it was a fine afternoon and the conditions ideal for crossing Mount's Bay. We paddled on into the early evening, arriving in the tiny harbour of Mousehole at 1915.

Several local people watched our arrival and were keen to help. The Harbour Master allowed us to camp out on his car-park. Local cottagers brought down biscuits and hot drinks. The local rowing club were out training in their racing gigs and Leon Pezzack [their coach] invited us to meet him for a drink and to come home with him for supper. Mick and Richard ended up staying the night while I returned to the tent so that our gear was not left unattended.

The morning following the incident on the Lizard we had to mentally prepare ourselves to go round Land's End, where the main tidal flood moving in from the Atlantic divides. Moreover, the tides are further complicated in so far as the inshore and offshore streams are quite different. This posed us the problem of careful timing if we were to carry a fair tide west from Mousehole and up the North Cornish coast beyond Cape Cornwall itself. Exposure to wind from almost all directions, the possibility of big seas and lack of landing-places are all factors that combine to make this leg serious. We were therefore fortunate to have a reasonable weather forecast, enabling us to complete most of the section along the southern shore in bright sunshine with the granite sea cliffs making a fine spectacle.

On the final approach to Gwennap Head we moved off shore and did not turn north until we were well to the west. This was a significant moment in the expedition. With the Longships Light and the distant bulk of Cape Cornwall now to the north, we had put the south coast of England behind us.

Meanwhile, a lazy swell of some size was rolling in from the south west and we were probably being over-cautious in staying so far out. Such an approach denied us both a possible bum-rest at Sennen and a seaward inspection of the famous granite headland and rugged skerries of Land's End, but in any case we were reluctant to stop and give away the last of our tidal assistance. As it was, we were just off the dark cliffs of Cape Cornwall when the inshore ebb tide began to flow against us and the weather changed with the tide. Cloud, which until then had been thickening slowly, now darkened quickly. A south-westerly breeze sprang up and it began to rain.

A fierce tide race forms off Pendeen Point when the ebb tide meets a south-westerly wind and sea. We managed to avoid the worst turbulence by sneaking through, close to the point's rock-ends and, having put this possible hazard behind us, we now had nothing to lose if we looked for a landing-place to take a short rest.

On the north side of Pendeen, a cove bites into the cliffs. On its southern shore we came to a steep slip used by mackerel fishermen who work from shanty-like cabins on the hillside above. The fishermen had just finished winching out one of their boats when we arrived and we would have had problems in landing had they not been at hand to grab our kayaks as they surged up and down the slip on the swell. Once ashore, they took us up to one of the shacks for some tea. Inside it was dark and musty and we found ourselves looking at a way of life from the distant past with little to remind us that this was the twentieth century.

When we moved north towards St. Ives an hour or so later, the wind had become quite fresh. But while it assisted us against the tide, it also ensured that a minor race was working off every set of rock-ends. In all respects this section of coast was a good one. Rugged sea cliffs are topped by rolling moorland. In some places, abandoned mine workings dominate the skyline to lend the area a special character. When the cloud began to break up to give us periods of sunshine between showers, we could see it at its best.

Around 1900 the town of St. Ives came into view and half an hour later we were ashore in the dried-out harbour, but our search for a spot to erect a tent forced us back into our boats to return to the "new" pier. Here we set up the tent between our boats on the concrete sea defences. If it blew from a northern quarter we would be in trouble, but the forecast was for a south-westerly gale and we did not have the energy or inclination to look any further. Mick summed up the situation nicely.

"We're cream-crackered. This will do!"

6

Beyond Our Limits

St. Ives – Watermouth Cove: 21st May – 1st June

The Atlantic coast of North Cornwall and North Devon is very exposed and seafarers who wish to experience its beauty need to treat it with a healthy respect. Cliffs alternate with surf beaches, making landings serious or impossible. The harbours are well spaced and generally only safe to enter or leave at certain stages of the tide. Our experience here was to prove particularly arduous, almost to the point of destruction as our limitations were hammered home to us in moments when the future of the expedition hung on a very fine thread.

During our first night at St. Ives the expected gale arrived. With it came sheets of rain. When we woke in the morning, the downpour was keeping visibility down to a few hundred metres. All thought of travel was abandoned even though by midday the sun was shining. Our corner was sheltered and we sat around sunning ourselves while protecting our gear from curious tourists. They appeared fascinated by our concrete campsite and the goulash I was cooking on the Primus. Almost all the holiday-makers appeared to be pensioners at this time of year and I suppose much of our modern camping gear was beyond their experience.

By the next morning the blue skies had been replaced by a blanket of grey cloud but the wind had dropped to become a F5–6 south-westerly. We decided to try to get to Newquay and just before 1100, as the spring tide began flooding north, we launched.

With a tail wind and a fair tide we took only a few minutes to clear the bay, but once we had lost the shelter of the land it was obvious that this would be no easy passage. We estimated the groundswell that was rolling in from the west as being something between five and six metres. Over this the south-westerly wind was generating its own sizeable waves. The sea state was generally frightening with moments of near-terror as, from time to time, a wavetop would get blown off, making us think it was going to become a full break. Yet, in spite of the sea conditions, we were travelling fast and could soon see the detail of Godrevy Island, a rocky islet which lies off the point of the same name and is separated from the mainland by a narrow channel. The island held our gaze like a magnet because the seas were making such spectacular breaks over it. In the channel a submerged ledge was causing the waves over it to peak. With the seas running away from us it was not clear whether they were reaching their breaking-point. Our route would take us through this and the idea became increasingly distasteful the closer we got.

With about a mile to go Mick shouted over. He did not want to go on. This sort of situation had been foreseen and we had agreed that when one of the team wanted to abort, we would all respect that decision. Now that I was being called upon to honour that agreement I did not like it. Mick was asking for a safer, but not softer, option. It had taken us about forty minutes to paddle to where we now were and it would take more than twice that to get back, fighting wind and tide. The situation might be likened to walking down a hill and then being asked to run back up it.

My initial annoyance was about to flare into anger. Mick had been lagging behind when we were surfing off the waves but now we had turned, he shot off ahead, did not look back and was soon about 400m ahead. He was breaking the basic rules of safety – a group must stay within communication distance. Richard shared my annoyance but was on the whole more forgiving and said he thought Mick was probably feeling sore at himself for letting us down. Richard was probably right. There was also Mick's close shave – or "Lizard factor" to be taken into account. At the time, however, I listened to what Richard had to say before voicing a reply that was none the less harsh.

"I can accept Mick losing his nerve but not his *-*-* head!" This was the first time in the expedition I had got angry with one of my companions.

We did not catch Mick up until we got back to St. Ives. I wasted no time in telling him what I thought but he said nothing. He knew what he had done and was not going to try to defend it. Still feeling angry, I walked off to be on my own to cool off and the incident was never discussed again.

One good thing came out of my anger. When off by myself I got into conversation with the Harbour Master – a black-bearded Cornish giant. To save us camping, he offered us accommodation in the old lighthouse which stands on the harbour's main breakwater. Once we had moved in we used the light gallery as a kitchen/bedroom and the railings around the balcony made a first-class washing-line.

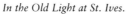

In the Old Light at St. Ives.

This unusual home also brought us face-to-face with the sad realities of the Cornish fishing industry. The fishermen (who knew better) had not gone out, so the quay was a bustle of activity as they used the time to repair their nets. Talking to them was an enlightening experience. One skipper patiently explained the cold-blooded efficiency of his modern equipment. He knew he was destroying the fisheries and with it his future livelihood and this hurt his conscience, but he was unable to see how he could afford to live if he did not use the technology available to him. I asked him what he thought the answer to this dilemma was. The simple wisdom of his reply took me by surprise. He quoted at me a statement made by a Scottish Fisheries spokesman.

"There are enough fish in the sea to feed everyone but not enough to satisfy man's greed."

The next day was sunny and the wind had decreased in strength from strong to fresh. But while we were anxious to get away, after the previous day's sobering lesson we were less keen to make mistakes, so having got to know the fishermen better, I gathered as much information as I could, only to find much of their advice contradictory. One old skipper was adamant that the swell was still too heavy to let us pass Godrevy. Some hedged their bets. The fisherman–philosopher who had put us straight on the economics of fishing had spent some time looking at our gear. Stressing that he did not wish to tell us our business, he said that if we were careful we would be O.K. I already liked and respected him and happily accepted his assessment of the situation.

The sea conditions at Godrevy would be less daunting during the period of slack water, so this time we set off at 1040 – while the tide was still running against us – so that we would arrive off the island just as the tide turned. The groundswell was still a heavy one but with less wind than the previous day it was far less intimidating. The result was that we cleared Godrevy without problems and, with the tide under us, closed quickly with St. Agnes Head. Three hours on from St. Ives saw us in bright sunshine off Man and His Man Rocks and about half an hour later we noticed a fishing-boat ahead. We frequently lost sight of it in the troughs between swells so it was by no means certain that the crew had seen us. When our courses appeared to be converging, we changed our heading. Still the boat bore down on us. Eventually we realised the manoeuvre was deliberate and she was trying to intercept us.

As Mick began a conversation with crew members leaning over the stern, I watched fascinated as the kayak and fishing-boat took their turns to hang high above each other on the sloppy swell. When Mick broke away to join me he told me that *Guiding Lights* of Padstow had received a radio message to look out for us because another fishing-boat was coming from Newquay with a news cameraman from Television South West. Because *Guiding Lights* had time to kill before she would have sufficient water to enter Newquay harbour, the skipper had offered to shepherd us along and make it easy for the other vessel to find us. This arrived on the scene a little later, circling us several times as the cameraman was thrown around in his attempts to film us.

Newquay and its harbour are partially protected by the rocky promontory of Towan Head and its associated reefs which jut north into the Atlantic and delimit the southern end of Watergate Bay. As the headland drew near we were treated to a magnificent display of thundering, breaking seas. We needed little urging from *Guiding Lights* to stay in her wake to take the safest line to turn the head. Because of the sea conditions, a great deal of froth and foam had been generated on the headland (presumably from some local sewer outfall) and we paddled through long streaks of head-high suds before turning south into the sheltered area of bay which eventually led into the tiny harbour. The Harbour Master was there to meet us and offer us a sheltered corner to put up our tent – such are the wonders of a television film camera and the celebrity status it can confer on those on the lens end! We thanked the fishermen for their help and interest and accepted their offer to join them for a beer or two later in the evening at the Newquay Rowing Club.

The morning of Saturday 24th May was exceptionally fine although the Radio Devon inshore forecast was a poor one. South-south-westerly winds of F4–5 (with F6 on exposed headlands) were expected to increase as the day progressed to give gales later. The outlook was for more strong to gale force winds, so if we were not to have a long stay in Newquay we were under pressure to move as early as possible. Unfortunately the decision could not be quite that simple. We were on top of spring tides, giving us three separate problems to be taken into consideration. Firstly, to use the tidal stream to assist us north, we needed to set off around low water – yet this would be so low on a spring tide that the harbour entrance would be close to drying out and the surf working into the bay would break across the entrance. Secondly, we had to get past Trevose Head, where the fierceness of the tide would create difficult sea conditions in high winds. Thirdly, the big seas running on the west-facing coast north of Newquay would deny us any opportunity for a reliable landing for over 12 miles, when we could turn south into Padstow, but this would require us to cross a notorious sand bank known as the Doom Bar, where seas would break heavily for all but the period around high water.

These factors persuaded me to adopt a plan involving a mid-morning start and try to make Port Isaac about 20 miles up the coast. This would take us past Trevose before the flood tide had gathered its full strength and hopefully have us off the water long before the gale arrived. When 1030 (our start time) arrived we found ourselves watching surf break inside the harbour entrance and we accepted the Harbour Master's advice to delay our start until mid-afternoon. It was 1430 when we got away and once into Watergate Bay found ourselves in a heavy Atlantic swell that would inevitably pick up as the flood tide progressed and the waves generated by the coming gale began to work in. Our fast progress was no consolation in the frightening seas that were rushing in from the south-west. Some of the crests began to tumble and I began to feel more than a little uncomfortable. Before long, however, I became more concerned for Mick's obvious unease.

From my diary . . .

We had covered about 5 miles and were off Park Head when Mick had the misfortune to be on a crest as it collapsed, giving all of us a shot of adrenalin. For Mick it was one shot too many. His distress was obvious as he apologetically said he couldn't go on. The point was not argued or discussed but turning our bows back towards Newquay was an awesome experience. Because the wind had been increasing on our backs it had not been noticed, but now that we had it on our faces the paddling up the face of the swells was like trying to paddle uphill. For about twenty minutes we pulled at our best rate to make little more than half a mile's progress. We were in trouble – again!

I faced the situation with mixed emotions. My sympathy for what I guessed was going on inside Mick's mind helped me contain my own fear and concern. I also appreciated that he had pushed himself to his personal breaking point to get as far as we had, but I resented the fact that he had left it so long before saying anything. His late decision had inflicted what, at best, would be several hours of frightening toil and drudgery and, at worst, was the impossible task of getting

*back to Newquay before the gale. The thought of this scenario became increasingly
unthinkable as the minutes ticked by and I shouted above the wind to turn and
regroup.*

Regardless of Mick's wishes our only real chance of survival without a rescue was to
run with the wind and tide. Mick stoically accepted this judgement as we headed north
once more. We all knew we had to get past Trevose Head and into the shelter of the
land where the coast kicked to the east, and our course would require us to run through
the mile-wide gap between the headland and the rocks known as the Quies. In the gap
we would almost certainly encounter overfalls as well as the confusion of swells caused
by reflections around the Quies and back off the head.

All too soon we were into the gap. I suddenly realised I was talking to myself –
"Please don't let there be any breaks!" No doubt similar sentiments were being thought
(if not uttered) by Mick and Richard when, quite suddenly, the sea state changed in
character. The giant, steep-faced waves that had been running in regularly from behind
and on our left were replaced by smaller, pyramidal and "stack" waves with dancing
and bursting crests. The overfall was killing the wind-waves. Thank God we had not
met wind-against-tide conditions! Even now we were picking our way forward on
supportive rather than propulsive strokes and in a short time the swift tidal stream had
borne us past the head.

No sooner had we paused on the far side of the overfall to regroup and take stock
of our improved position than we experienced several great gusts of wind as it backed
to just west of south and began to blow steadily at near-gale strength, whipping the
tops of the waves in sheets of fine spray. The tide and wind continued to sweep us
north as we pulled for the east and fought to steer the boats. Without rudders it would
have been even more difficult, for they were kicked hard over to balance the boats on
the wind. The gale was arriving ahead of time and it was imperative to land at the first
opportunity. Once inside Gulland Rock we abandoned all hope of going on to Port
Isaac and headed south of east to gain the shelter of Stepper Point to enter Padstow
Bay and the great inlet of the Camel River. High water spared us the problem of
breaking seas on the Doom Bar as we inched our way south into the teeth of the wind
towards the harbour. Every paddle stroke that took us in was a great effort, although
the full extent of our labours only became fully appreciated when the dangerous seas
were left well astern.

Meanwhile the weather had degenerated swiftly with the change in wind and it was
a grey, miserable evening by the time we landed on the slip inside the fishing harbour.
The quayside was crowded with tourists who had arrived for the Whit Bank Holiday
and we immediately abandoned hope of finding a local bivvy site. Minutes later we
were back in our boats to paddle a few hundred metres further up the estuary to camp
on a patch of grass in the main town car-park, adjacent to Padstow Canoe Club.
Unbeknown to us, we would be forced to stay for six nights.

Next morning, with the wind buffeting the tent, we lay listening to the early shipping
forecast. It simply confirmed what we already knew. A gale warning was in operation
for the local sea areas of Lundy and Fastnet. The outlook was for no change so we lay

in and ate a late breakfast. Meanwhile, the car-park attendant in charge of the area where we had camped was panicking about our presence, so I walked to the Town Clerk's office, in what had once been part of the closed-down railway station. When ushered into the office I regretted not tidying myself up, for I was not expecting to meet a lady, but she was most sympathetic and consented to let us stay put.

This allowed me to phone home and tell Bev our whereabouts. It was her half-term holiday so she was planning to drive down to the West Country to see us, bringing her teenage brother Darren, "Boy" (our springer spaniel) and a couple of general-purpose kayaks to do some surfing. Richard's Mandy had organised a few days off work and would catch a train down to join us later in the week. This news was some consolation so that our unwanted rest would take on something of a holiday atmosphere, beginning with a good pub meal when Bev and Darren arrived that evening.

On Monday, the south-westerly continued to blow hard with further gale warnings and it was more of the same for Tuesday. It was Wednesday before the wind veered to the west and began to slacken off, but after such a prolonged period of high winds the sea was still too rough to consider moving. Apart from the wind, the weather was reasonable enough. Cloudy mornings gave way to sunny afternoons but it remained exceptionally cold. We kept ourselves amused by eating a succession of huge meals which Bev cooked and did nothing more strenuous than walk the dog along the coastal footpath to watch the seas breaking on the Doom Bar. At other times we could always watch the windsurfers getting themselves into trouble on the estuary. Being almost land-locked, it has the appearance of an innocuous piece of inland water but in fact the tide runs exceptionally fast. Time and again, the windsurfers who knew no better would find themselves unable to return to their point of embarkation and have to be towed home.

This prolonged halt also provided us with some useful information for our proposed crossing to Ireland. When members of the local canoe club arrived for their usual Wednesday evening meeting the group included Ian Tatum, who was able to describe to us his own experience of a kayak crossing of the St. George's Channel in the early seventies. The conversation was not entirely beneficial, however, for it focused our minds on the job ahead and reawakened our impatience to get away. We were determined to make a try the next morning.

When the late-night shipping forecast mentioned moderate north-westerlies we felt sure we would be spending no further nights in Padstow. We arranged for Bev, Mandy and Darren to meet us at Boscastle for a lunch stop on our way north to Bude and were up at 0540 to launch for 0700, just as the tide began flooding the channel by our camp. Once out in the estuary it was immediately apparent that there was more wind than had been forecast. It was hard work paddling out into Padstow Bay and took nearly 1½ hours to reach Pentire Point, where the waves were "clapping" up to an ugly and confused sea as it reflected back off the head and refracted around the cliffs of Newland Rock. Our recent experiences had done little to improve our appetite for such adventures, disproving (for the time being at least) that "familiarity breeds contempt", for in this instance it had increased both our caution and respect for the sea. We all agreed on this occasion that we would "chicken out" and retreated back to Padstow. Bude would still be there on Friday.

We were lucky to get back to where we had camped before the girls had set off for Boscastle. As we recounted why we had come back I became increasingly conscious of the gulf in understanding that had developed between us. Only those that have actually experienced for themselves a prolonged exposure to big seas could really understand what we were saying. The three of us discussed this later and we shared the same view. It is a much-recorded and familiar phenomenon in wartime, when the gap develops between front-line soldiers and civilians at home. After a short while we lost the inclination to explain our fear, knowing it would almost certainly invite further frustration in communication.

After a second breakfast we still had most of the day in front of us and were keen to use it to some purpose. The result was that Bev drove us to Bude so that we could see for ourselves the problems of landing through the surf. While on the beach we met some instructors with a rock-climbing group from the Waterfront Centre. One of the partners who runs "Adventure Days" was with them and he offered us accommodation at the centre whenever we should arrive. On the drive back to Padstow we also checked out the beautiful little harbour of Boscastle. Set in a flooded gorge, it provides a natural haven that is almost invisible from the sea. More important to us, however, was that it would be a relatively easy landing, providing it did not blow hard again.

On Friday 30th May we repeated our plan to leave Padstow, but this time without problems or mishaps – other than my rudder becoming inoperable when the tiller bar's copper pivot sheared. The swell was dropping off fast on the light north-west breeze and with the sun shining, the temperature at last came up to its seasonal norm. By 0800, in company with a flock of puffins, we had cleared Pentire Point and the rocks known as the Mouls. Our confidence increased with every mile paddled. In a talkative mood, we recalled how the old coxswain of the Padstow lifeboat had put himself out to talk to us on the dreadful Saturday evening of our arrival. In his broad Cornish brogue he had advised us that we would not get weather conditions to let us north until the neap tides the following weekend, "But perhaps on Friday if you're lucky." His prophecy was no doubt based on a lifetime's experience and had proved to be spot on, denying all scientific explanation.

The headland of Tintagel, with its tall cliffs and associations with Camelot and the Arthurian legend, retained something of its glamour and atmosphere from the vantage point of our kayaks, for the highly commercialised village which despoils it from landward remained hidden from view. At 1050 we paddled into Boscastle and found the girls waiting with hot pasties which we ate in a rush because we did not want to waste the tide. Away once more, we came across the carcass of a dead whale. It had been stripped bare of its skin and the vertebrae protruded through the grey-white blubber as hordes of gulls ripped and tore at it.

We finally arrived off Bude Haven at 1415. Darren was out surfing but we were able to slip around the end of the breakwater where Bev signalled us in. From the beach below the lock gates holding back the Bude Canal, we made a long portage onto the canal, for the Waterfront Centre occupies a canal-side warehouse and we were about to take up the accommodation offer. The showers, meals and use of their tools to mend my rudder completed what had been a good day. The hospitality was appreciated even more when the weather closed in to give a damp and dreary evening.

Entering Boscastle harbour after harrowing adventures along the Cornish coast.

We were about to start our seventh week away, it was the last day of May and still we were waiting for the weather to settle down. After the fine day that had got us to Bude it was another discouraging forecast. Rain and sea fog on a fresh north-westerly air stream was hardly ideal for our journey north through the fierce tides of Hartland Point, which we now had to turn to reach the great bite into the coast of North Devon which is Bideford Bay and so reach Clovelly. This intention really required us to make an early start to ensure that the tide carried us round Hartland Point, but to avoid offending such kind hosts, we delayed to eat the breakfast that had been prepared for us. As a result it was 1030 before we had got our boats onto the beach.

Looking out to sea was most depressing. Visibility was down to around half a mile and the surf was quite sizeable. Waving goodbye to Bev and one of the Centre's partners who had come down to video our departure, I set off in the rip running down the edge of the breakwater. It required full power and timing to get through the surf. Several times the kayak was momentarily airborne as it broke through the breaking crests and crashed onto the back of the wave with a shuddering thump. Five minutes later we were all through and regrouped beyond the breakline, having suffered nothing worse than a good soaking.

Fighting the head wind, we set off northwards to put Cornwall behind us. We declined to land at Hartland Quay, where Bev, Mandy and Darren waved down to us from the hotel, for we were fast running out of tide. Shortly afterwards it turned against us and, as so often happens, this brought about a change in the weather. Visibility improved and the wind began to drop off.

The rugged cliffs between Hartland Quay and Hartland Point are punctuated at regular intervals by long and jagged reefs which extend seaward at right angles to the shoreline, rather like natural groynes. These provided some measure of protection from the tide as we eddy-hopped towards the point proper. Here the tide was flowing around the rock-ends at about 4 knots and a turbulent race was working off shore, for although the wind-waves were with the ebbing tide, the residual, south-westerly groundswell was still against it. Our only possible way forward was to stay as close to the rocks as we could. Normal paddling only allowed us to mark time and we progressed by short sprints whenever the main swell assisted us with a surge.

As soon as we had turned the point and could head east, we sought out a landing on a patch of steep shingle in a small, north-facing cove. The object was to stretch our legs but my timing was dreadful. Hesitating to release my spray-deck and jump out I was caught by the next wave and dumped up the beach. Soaked through, my cockpit swamped, I made a most undignified exit. My overreaction and annoyance kept Mick and Richard amused for the rest of the day.

The tidal streams on this southern extremity of Bideford Bay are not necessarily what one would expect. Therefore we fought the tide east as expected as far as Chapman Rock, but then picked up an east-going eddy that carried us past Black Church Rock to Clovelly, where the inshore lifeboat sped over to us for a chat which proved very useful. They saved us a job by reporting our position to the Hartland Coastguard and then made contact with the lifeboat station at Clovelly. This was manned by Jim Conibear, one of the full-time crew operating from the Clovelly Station, which shares the distinction with Spurn Point (on the Humber) of being the only lifeboats with full-time crew members.

Consequently when we paddled into the harbour, Jim was at hand to see us in and immediately offered us the use of the station to store our boats, as well as accommodation for two of us in his own cottage. There was nowhere to camp and since this was the last evening of Bev and Mandy's holiday we were disinclined to bivvy. So it was Mick and Darren who took up Jim's offer of a bed while the rest of us walked up the steep, narrow high street (which is famous for its stepped cobbles and ancient cottages) and found bed-and-breakfast accommodation in a 400-year-old cottage.

The light north-westerly winds were still with us the next morning, with the same unbroken canopy of low cloud and visibility of around four miles. The weather matched the party's sombre mood and we had an unusually quiet breakfast. There were no plans for a further visit until we got to Scotland and that seemed a lifetime away. We had said our goodbyes by 0915 and, having left the harbour, headed straight out to sea. Richard in particular seemed to feel the strain of parting from Mandy and it was soon clear to Mick and me that he was determined not to look back. Indeed, he paddled apart from us and did not speak for about two hours.

In the meantime we had lost sight of land in our crossing of Bideford Bay, for to follow the coast of surf beaches and across the estuary of the Taw and Torridge would only add distance without interest. In fact, the course we had chosen was still not quite direct, even though it was the fastest. For the first hour we headed a little west of a direct line so that we could be more certain of picking up the main flood tide streaming north-eastward from Hartland Point. Then we paddled on a compass heading that took us to the Baggy Leap Buoy that lies off the rocky headland separating Croyde Bay from Woolacombe, its northern neighbour. The 12 miles from Clovelly to the Buoy took only 2¼ hours on the good tide that was running and we were quickly across Woolacombe Bay to the Morte Point Buoy.

Bouncing through the impressive race that forms where the tidal streams accelerate as they fill and empty the Bristol Channel, we were soon on Devon's north-facing coast. Having paddled it before, I knew it to be one of the most scenic sections of English coastline – at its best where Exmoor plunges into the Severn Sea – but there was little to see or enjoy on such a dismal day.

Almost as soon as we began heading east we found that the tide close inshore had turned against us so we put into the sheltered cove of Lee Bay where we stopped to rest and brew tea. When we set off again about an hour later, we paddled close to the rocky shoreline to try to keep out of the strong tides that flow all along this coast. We would have been quite happy to call a halt for the day when we reached the resort of Ilfracombe but in such built-up surroundings there was no clear place to set up a bivvy, let alone a proper camp. In the end we pressed on along the cliffs to Watermouth, where a lovely little cove makes a deep, narrow inlet forming a natural harbour with a gently shelving beach.

Having landed, we had to carry our boats a long way among the many vessels dried out on the bed of the anchorage to reach the slip at the head of the cove. Here we sought out a real "old salt" of a Harbour Master called Bill Watkins, who found us a corner of his boatyard adjacent to the local yacht club. We had just put up our tent when a family working on their boat took pity on our salt-encrusted condition and offered us the use of the club showers. Then we met Alf – a colourful character who was determined to be of use to our enterprise. In late middle years, Alf was a heavyweight in both appearance and personality. Although living locally, he had retained both the manner and speech of Billingsgate Fish Market (where he had once worked) and he made it his personal business to ensure that our stay should be as comfortable as he could make it. This included giving us the mackerel he had just caught for his own tea.

During the evening that followed we had to make some important decisions, for our position required us to think more than one move ahead. One option was to continue to paddle east along the North Devon coast, below the cliffs of Exmoor to reach Porlock, where we could then turn north to cross the Bristol Channel where it narrows. We would then have at least two days' paddling west on the South Wales coast to put us north of our present position. The alternative was to make a direct, longer but more serious crossing of the Bristol Channel from where we were now camped to put us on the Gower Peninsula in just one day instead of at least three. The latter course would require a settled weather forecast but would be a good practice run for the Irish Sea crossing we would soon be required to undertake. With the matter still unresolved and my brain churning over the relative merits of each option, we eventually agreed to let the weather choose for us. The decision would then rest on what the early-morning shipping forecast had to say.

7

Commitment and Open Crossings
Watermouth Cove – Rosslare: 2nd – 14th June

Although it was good to be making progress again, we were still anxious about the time we had lost. Nagged by a sense of urgency, we wanted to get to Whitesands Bay in Pembrokeshire* for the neap tides that would occur over the weekend of 14th/15th June, when we would also be assured of long hours of daylight to improve our chances of making our crossing to Ireland. To give ourselves a safety margin, we set ourselves the target of getting to Whitesands for the weekend before, ensuring we would be well rested. But first we had to cross the Bristol Channel.

The B.B.C. shipping forecast at 0555 on Monday 2nd June was as good as we could hope for to make our crossing of about 22 miles to the Gower Peninsula in South Wales. The plan was to angle our boats in a ferry glide to cross the last 2¾ hours of the flood tide, hit slack water in the middle and then, having angled off in the opposite direction, ferry-glide the ebb into Port Eynon. With this in mind, we launched shortly after midday and took comfort in the weather developing exactly as forecast. The wind was north-westerly F2–3, visibility had been poor all morning but was improving, and the sun was threatening to pierce the veil of cloud. The hills and cliffs of the Exmoor coast receded into the haze but by the time we were in the middle, visibility was moderate, so that for the last two hours of the paddle we could see the cliffs of the Gower.

We hit the sandy beach of Port Eynon at 1900, having taken about half an hour longer than planned because the flood tide had run stronger than anticipated on the Devon coast. We were pleased at how the crossing had gone, for this was the longest open crossing we had so far undertaken in the expedition. However, no sooner had we carried our boats up the endless expanse of beach than fog came in. A ridiculously long carry to the official campsite was out of the question, so we settled down to a dreary and gritty bivvy by the car-park wall at the top of the beach.

We now had another choice: we could spend two days creeping round the edge of Carmarthen Bay, on a relatively dull coast with mud flats and firing ranges to contend with, or we could take on another open crossing of about 15 miles, across the mouth of the bay from Worms Head to Caldey Island on the Pembrokeshire coast, about 22 miles from where we were now bivvied at Port Eynon. We decided on the latter option and were up at 0350 the next morning to get the best from the tide. It was only just

_____
* Old county names have been used in this book.

getting light and it was still foggy, so as we pulled on our wet gear it was difficult to be enthusiastic. We managed to be on the water for 0530 and once clear of the bay's shelter we were paddling into a chilling F3–4 north-westerly wind. Visibility was about half a mile. We could see nothing of the fine limestone cliffs that characterise the coastline of the south-western Gower, so we were glad of a temporary lifting of the fog that gave us an accurate fix on our position when due south of the jagged ridge of rock that is Worms Head. In spite of the moderate sea and fog we managed to pick up all the buoys as we crossed Carmarthen Bay on compass bearings. The fog eventually began to clear, but only to give way to squally rain that closed the visibility in to less than it had been in the fog! Then with about six miles to go, the rain eased and we could discern the smudged outline of Caldey and a trace of the Pembrokeshire cliffs. The wind increased, however, giving us a miserable and wet time and slowing us sufficiently to make us lose the tide.

It was 1115 when we landed on Caldey. We were cold, wet and hungry and busied ourselves building a roaring fire from driftwood to dry out. Large helpings of porridge warmed us up and we decided to press on. Afloat once more, we ferry-glided the fiercely running tide in Caldey Roads to get back to the more sheltered mainland shore, then, all through the afternoon, we fought a foul tide and a north-westerly F4–5 head wind, creeping along the edge of the spectacular cliffs of South Pembrokeshire, where rock climbers looked down at us from the precipitous limestone buttress of Lydstep Head. It was too physical to be enjoyable and we were glad to land on the sandy beach at Freshwater East for a bum-rest and more food. However, we were very reluctant to spend another night camped in sand and, although it was 1700, we decided to use the tide that was about to turn in our favour and push on through the tide races off Stackpole and St. Govan's Head. There seemed no reason why we should not reach Milford Haven comfortably before nightfall.

In fact we were being too ambitious and I had failed to apply common sense to my reading of the tidal stream charts. They had shown we would get a favourable tide all the way to Milford Haven (which would have been true if we had remained off shore) but they did not show (although I should have realised) that since it would be high water in Milford Haven long before the tide finished flooding north, the tide would be rushing *out* of Milford by the time we got there. Thus, after a relatively straightforward passage to Linney Head, as we turned north we found ourselves in an awkward situation. The elements combined against us and we could hardly make headway into the fresh north-westerly head wind, a heavy sea and over 2 knots of tide. The swells were too big to risk trying to land on the beach at Freshwater West; indeed the local fishermen at Freshwater East had specifically warned us to watch for offshore breaks on this section. The best we could do was to paddle flat out for about three quarters of an hour to get close to the cliffs north of Freshwater, where the tide would be running less hard. Progress was still very slow and when we finally got to the wide entrance of the natural harbour, it was gone 2300 and completely dark.

With no moon, we picked our way round the coast to East Angle and ran our boats ashore into the pitch blackness. Our first attempts put us onto soft mud, but eventually we found an area of sand and rock which we cursed profoundly as we stumbled around in the darkness to find the top of the beach. I was absolutely exhausted. With buckling

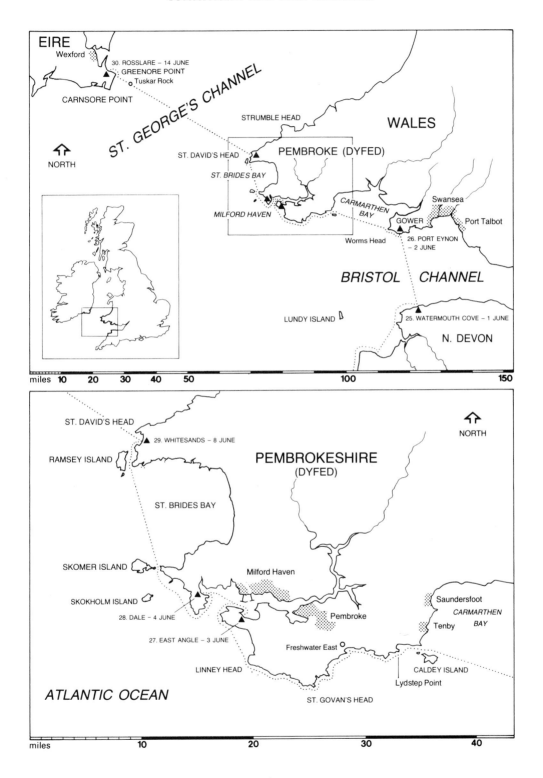

and stiff legs we could barely carry the boats, eventually settling down to sleep where we were, far too tired and cold to cook a proper meal. There was nowhere to put a tent. Shivering, we changed into dry clothes and disappeared into our sleeping-bags with chocolate bars and hunks of fruit cake. I was still angry with myself at making such a dangerous error of judgement and in our semi-exhausted state our morale hit an all-time low. We were certainly convinced at the time that our 15 hours of paddling to make 52 miles had taken a bigger physical toll than the D.–W.

Fortunately, when we woke at 0500 it was a beautiful clear dawn. We had slept like babies and were sheltered from the wind, which we could see blowing smoke horizontally from the chimneys across the harbour. With the sun to warm us, we were soon joking about the previous day's misery and were ready to push on again. When I managed to call up the Coastguard by radio through a relaying station, the forecast was for north-westerly F4–5. Whether we were still tired from the previous day or the wind was stronger than forecast I am not sure; the fact was we were making very slow progress and we cut our losses by putting into Dale, camping out in a boatyard. We were to be trapped here for several days, unable to make progress while the fresh-to-strong northerly winds stacked up the seas in the strong-running streams of Jack Sound.

A good forecast for Saturday 7th June failed to materialise, but there was to be a lull in the wind strength (before it turned south-westerly) in the early hours and morning of the 8th. Raring to go, we were up for 0340 and paddling by 0500. Our timing had to be exact if the spring tide was going to take us through both Jack Sound and Ramsey Sound in one paddle.

This coast is pure delight to sea paddlers, and now the sun shone, winds were light and the paddling went like clockwork. Looking down on aquamarine rock pools, we had walked the cliff-tops to Wooltack Point (opposite Skomer Island) to watch the breaking seas in the spectacular tide race of Jack Sound, when the north-flowing tide was stacked up by the north wind. Today it was more like a river of fast-running glides and oily boils. The hazy outline of Ramsey Island could just be seen far off to the north across St. Brides Bay. The island is exposed to the full fury of Atlantic storms, has a sensational south-western shoreline of stacks with towering cliffs, and possesses some of the most impressive sea caverns to be seen. The sanctity of its wild beauty is protected by very intimidating tide races and overfalls, and as we arrived off the toothed reef of the Bitches in Ramsey Sound, we enjoyed a half-mile ride on standing waves that would have been more at home on grade 2–3 river rapids. We were on the beach at Whitesands, 21 miles from Dale, in under 3¾ hours and were at last in position for our Irish Sea crossing.

During the next few days we rested, made a special point of eating well and refurbished our equipment. On Wednesday 11th June, Geoff Hunter joined us, for he too was going to make the crossing. Every few hours we telephoned the Cardiff Weather Centre for the latest developments and on Thursday we managed to wangle our way into the

[LEFT] *Below the spectacular limestone cliffs of Lydstep Point, Pembroke, during our 15-hour paddle from the Gower to Milford Haven.*

met. office at R.A.F. Brawdy and saw the weather outlook was most promising –
an anticyclone was slowly establishing itself from the south-west. Armed with this
information, we presented our plans to the Coastguard at Dale, and they gave me a
land-line contact with the Harbour Authority at Rosslare in Eire, so that they too knew
what we were intending. In an atmosphere of mounting excitement we now waited for
the right combination of weather and tidal sequence.

At twenty to eight in the morning of Saturday 14th June, no one would have noticed
the departure of the one Vyneck and our three Nordkapps from the beach at Whitesands.
Not only was it too early for the usual contingent of the malibu surf-board brotherhood
to be about, the visibility was only 150 metres in the thick fog and light drizzle that
condensed in the breathlessly calm air. We could not even see the end of The Ram –
the low, rocky headland that forms the northern end of the beach.

For those who have never stopped to consider the technical problems of crossing the
southern end of the St. George's Channel which separates Wales from Ireland, it should
be understood that the departure point and landfall are notorious for their tidal
problems. Tide races and overfalls abound as the main tidal flood from the Atlantic is
constricted into the gap between West Pembrokeshire and Carnsore Point (on the
south-eastern tip of Ireland) to fill the Irish Sea. To reduce the problems of negotiating
these potentially hazardous tidal conditions around Ramsey Island and the Bishops and
Clerks on the Welsh side, and around Tuskar Rock on the Irish side, it is best to move
through them when the tidal movements are at their least – near slack water on neap
tides. The timing of our crossing would therefore need to be built around the times of
slack water at our point of departure, and our landfall. Paddling at a speed of 4 knots,
we would therefore encounter another period of tidal slack in mid-channel, half-way
in time through the journey. Clearly, we wanted as little wind and sea as possible, for
this would throw our water speed calculations into the factor of the unknown as well
as making the trip uncomfortably wet, more tiring and consequently more dangerous.
Speed is a great safety factor in a sea area famous for its fickle weather. The weather
forecast we wanted was therefore a period of predictably little wind, regardless of the
increased likelihood of sea fog. This would introduce an element of danger in crossing
the major shipping lanes but was not a serious navigational factor in our view, for we
would be out of sight of land for most of the crossing anyway.

The last factor to be decided was whether we should build a night-crossing into the
trip. The advantage of this would be that any serious problems causing a delay would
then be sorted out in daylight, rather than in darkness, as would be the case if things
went wrong in a daylight crossing. In the event, we were prepared to paddle it either
way, as long as the weather pattern was right, for there would only be about four hours
of proper darkness at this time of year anyway.

Geoff and I had talked through all these points of general principle during the
previous winter. We had then gone off and worked out the navigational detail quite
independently, before coming together and comparing notes. Reassuringly, our conclusions were exactly the same and we had laid our final plans accordingly.

Throughout Friday 13th June we had regularly phoned for meteorological forecasts.
Looking at the weather from our campsite at Whitesands beach it was hardly a

promising prospect in the usual sense. Fog thickened and thinned throughout the day. Sometimes we could make out the dark cliffs on the north end of Ramsey Island about two miles away. Occasionally we could see the outline of the South Bishop and its lighthouse which is much further. At other times we could see neither. If we were going to leave that evening, we had to set out about seven o'clock, so when the visibility closed right in around five o'clock it forced a decision. We would wait until morning.

Later that evening we all went off with Geoff to drop his car at the newly opened Twr-y-Felin Outdoor Centre, above the main town of St. David's. Looking out from the lighthouse-like top of the old mill tower of the centre, we could see that visibility had improved to give outstandingly clear views of far-off Grassholme and Skomer Island. Such is life. Philosophically we downed our ale to ensure a good night's sleep, then walked back to Whitesands, taking some comfort in the fact that perhaps we had done the right thing after all, for the fog was down again.

My alarm was set for 0430, but as is so often the case in such circumstances, I woke with a start just before it was due to go off. Outside the tent, the fog was the thickest it had been so far and a very fine drizzle did little to cheer us as we hastily breakfasted and broke camp. In an atmosphere of nervous apprehension, little was said and a lot got done more quickly than usual. By ten past seven the loaded boats had been carried down to the beach and I had phoned the Coastguard at Dale to say we would be away in half an hour. Without stops, our navigational sums said we could do the trip in 12 hours. We would need between one and two hours for breaks, so to be safe, and not cause undue alarm, we gave Rosslare E.T.A. as 2230, allowing up to 15 hours for the crossing.

Only a slight surf was running as we launched, so we hoped to get off fairly dry. In thick fog, however, this was easier said than done, for the bigger sets only showed when they were on top of us. The result was that both Richard and myself started with wet heads, but beyond the surf line, the sea was oily calm.

We then paddled north to pick up the south-facing cliffs at St. David's Head in an eerie atmosphere. Only the splash of our paddles and the sinister honk of the South Bishop horn broke the silence. It was a grey atmosphere and a grey morning, and our brightly coloured boats and accessories also became grey and drab if we paddled as much as 20 metres apart. Even the sea birds were strangely silent.

Once on the tip of the headland, we stopped paddling and sat to observe the effect of the tide on our boats. Because it was approaching slack water at the end of the tide's southerly set, we were being pushed slowly south, to our left. We no doubt made a strange sight for the two fishermen who looked at us in some dismay as their boat slowly emerged out of the mist and chugged by. For canoeists to be out at all on such a morning would have been bad enough, but to be sitting still, drifting on the tide, was ridiculous!

So this was it. We angled our boats in a ferry glide to compensate for the south-going tide and struck out to pick up a small rock known as Careg Trai, about one mile off to the west. In the 200-metre visibility we could hear the breaking sea long before we could see the rock, and took comfort in it appearing in the right place at the right time. Similarly the North Bishop Rock came up on schedule at 0830, confirming our calculations for the tide were right.

The mist clears during the St. George's Channel crossing.

This was very important of course, not just because we wanted to be exact, but because a confidence booster was psychologically right at this very moment, when we were about to lose sight of land for possibly 12 hours. Personally, I was feeling more than my usual sense of responsibility that morning. Mick and Richard had put absolute and unquestioning faith in my calculations on which their very lives could depend. I took great comfort in having such a seasoned and experienced paddler as Geoff with us, knowing he had double-checked everything.

For the next three hours we paddled through the fog over gentle, oily swells which ran in from the south-west. The horn of the South Bishop slowly receded on our left and was eventually lost to hearing. Occasionally, the sun made a valiant effort to break through the foggy canopy shrouding us. Every hour, on the hour, we made adjustments to our compass heading, angling the boat to compensate for the differing rates of tidal flow and thus staying on an imaginary line of about 37 sea miles connecting North Bishop with Tuskar Rock. Every second hour we stopped for a few minutes to eat, drink and sometimes carry out that most awkward sea-canoeing manoeuvre – "the rafted pee". This latter task was a constant source of amusement and lewd banter. Whilst Richard persisted in making intimate and personal gyrations within the dark confines of his cockpit, occasionally producing an old condensed-milk can full of wee, Geoff preferred a more aggressively extrovert approach involving a "bum-shuffle" onto his rear deck and an arched cascade "à la Brussels Cherub" onto Mick's rear deck! It is situations like this that make or break canoeing friendships.

Around noon the fog dispersed, revealing a strange world of bright sun, blue sky and limitless horizons of oily swells. A gannet might wheel above us and cast a fierce eye over our intrusion into his domain. The odd puffin would attempt to ignore our presence completely, suddenly slapping off with a staccato of wing beats in comic and ridiculous panic at the very last moment. We saw more storm petrels than I have ever seen in British waters. At one stage a female porpoise with her youngster executed a few graceful arches about our boats before disappearing.

Now that the fog had gone it was very hot. We removed our cags and drank plenty. The direction of movement of the ships now visible in the shipping separation lanes confirmed our estimated position. Only once did we have to alter course and eventually stop to avoid a possible collision.

By four in the afternoon, when our morale was very high, the conversation suddenly took a turn for the worse as the fog banks began to close in again. It was not the thick grey fog of the morning, but thin, white and very bright. We were paddling as in a dream world of blinding light. The sea was as burnished as polished bronze, merging indiscernibly into the brightness of the fog and sky. The sun continued to beat through to create stifling heat. Had we entered some "other world" for sinner canoeists, condemned for ever to paddle in an eternity of glaring light? Suddenly there was a partial clearance and behind us appeared a strange vision. A perfect arch of white light – a fog bow – which dogged our progress for endless miles.

Just before the visibility had closed in we had witnessed another strange sight. In the distance, on our position line ahead, we could see a stationary tall object on the horizon that we assumed was the lighthouse on Tuskar Rock. As we stared hard, across our line of vision passed a perfectly rectangular object, possibly two miles off. We presumed afterwards that it must have been the conning-tower of a submarine.

From five o'clock onwards we were straining our ears, hoping to hear the horn of

The calm conditions allowed us to make a brief meal stop.

the Tuskar. For a long time, however, the only sirens were those of shipping. It was nerve-racking to hear the Fishguard ferry bear down on us in the fog, getting closer and closer. First the blast of her horn, growing louder and louder, then the throb of her engines. Please let the sound diminish and pass away!

Then, very, very faint, we could hear a distant horn where Tuskar Rock *should* be. It grew more distinct and was getting closer. Like a magnet, the sound kept pulling us off our compass heading and towards itself. We had to resist this temptation, for to give in to it would cause our boats to be swept south of the light on the strong race that sets off the rock and so require us to fight straight into the tide to gain the lighthouse.

As we focused our senses on the horn we could almost feel the air vibrate. We were so close. Then, quite dramatically, we burst out of the fog bank into an island of blue sky and bright colour. Dominating the scene was a tall tower, less than half a mile away. Decked in bright paintwork of red and white, there stood the Tuskar light with the tiny silhouettes of the two keepers coming down to greet us.

A short ferry glide across the tide race, still breaking and boiling in spite of the generally calm conditions, and we were into the sheltered water of a great tidal eddy that led us to the rock itself. It was exactly quarter past seven, just fifteen minutes later than our armchair navigational sums had predicted.

All feelings of relief were eclipsed by our satisfaction and elation at things going so well. It was difficult to decline the warm hospitality and cups of tea offered by the lighthouse-keepers who had been alerted to watch out for us by Rosslare Harbour. But decline we did, for we had to press on; the fog, having been kind enough to clear and allow us our photographs, was closing in again fast.

About a mile out from the rock I called up Rosslare on our radio to confirm our position and warn them to expect us. The last few miles to Rosslare were the longest two hours of the trip. An easterly wind sprang up making the fog suddenly become cold. Until then it had not seemed threatening. But now we wanted to be out of it. We were also becoming aware that the tide was running much harder than we had anticipated between Tuskar and the Irish mainland, pushing us south more than we would have liked and eventually causing us to aim-off further left to get a more certain landfall. When it came up, it was quite unexpected. The coastline on this south-eastern tip of Ireland is flat and featureless with long sandy beaches backed by low cliffs. I thought I was looking at a change in density of the fog bank when the sea suddenly changed colour from grey to turquoise-green and I could see small wave breaks. The beach was less than 100 metres away.

After a short slog along the coast we rounded Greenore Point and could soon see the breakwater of Rosslare Harbour. As we turned into its shelter below the ferry terminal, it was twenty minutes to ten, exactly 14 hours since leaving Whitesands.

With big grins and a great feeling of satisfaction, we paddled over to the lifeboat station. Figures were waiting to meet us and they greeted us like old friends. As Lifeboat Hon. Sec., Buddy Miller (whom I had spoken to from Dale) had set aside their old shed to accommodate us and he patiently waited for us to get changed before taking us off in his van to buy our first pint of real Irish Guinness.

8

The South Coast of Ireland

Rosslare – Crookhaven: June 15th – June 23rd

In spite of our exertions in crossing the St. George's Channel, force of habit had me awake for the 0555 shipping forecast the next day. It was a beautiful summer morning and we were soon up and about, for Geoff had to catch the 9 o'clock ferry to Fishguard and we began receiving a string of visitors who turned up to inspect our equipment – news of our crossing having spread very quickly round the port.

We said a sad farewell to Geoff, gained a customs clearance and then walked into the town to change our currency, for we were determined to get away and not waste the fine weather. It was early afternoon before we eventually set off, by which time a fresh north-easterly breeze did something to ease our efforts in fighting the tide to turn Carnsore Point, so putting us on the south coast proper. The shoreline generally lacked interest and was a succession of sandy beaches, interspersed with rock ledges and backed by low cliffs. We made slow progress and the low outline of the Saltee Islands took a long time to draw closer. When we paddled out to the inner of the two islands we failed to find a reasonable landing-point and set off back to the mainland at Kilmore Quay, meeting a group of Dublin canoeists in mid-channel as they returned from a weekend camp on the outer Saltee, where they reported an excellent campsite! Sod's law had triumphed again.

Landing inside the harbour, we suffered a muddy portage to set up a camp by the breakwater but there were many willing hands to help us from the Dublin group and we attracted a large group of tourists who were fascinated by our equipment. As the sun set in a thick haze, we retired to the local pub, ate a meal from the nearby chip shop and turned into our sleeping-bags earlier than usual, for weariness had at last caught up with us.

When the alarm went at 0400 the next morning the haze had thickened further to produce an oppressive dark sky. It was hot, very humid and a thunderstorm seemed imminent. By the time we launched at 0540 to catch the tide west, we could barely see the Saltees and it had started to rain. Navigating by compass, the only points of interest were the hundreds of gannets wheeling overhead (visitors from the colony on the outer Saltee) and the sinister horn of the lightship off to the south. Eventually, after nearly three hours of paddling, the outline of the lighthouse on Hook Head loomed out of the murk and slowly took on detail, its black and white paintwork dominating the entrance to Waterford Harbour. All around us were numerous small fishing craft, making the best of the calm conditions as they drift-netted for salmon.

We were in fact making for the seaside resort of Tramore, but it was not the funfair

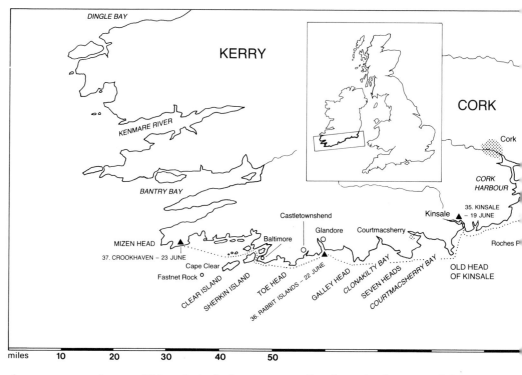

that was attracting us. This relatively large town offered us the best possibility to reprovision our boats on a major scale, before arriving on the wilder and less populated sections of coast. Fortunately, by the time we had completed our shopping it was early afternoon and the sultry cloud was dispersing to give hazy sunshine. It grew very hot and we were able to paddle in bare tops along the next section, which was one of dramatic cliffs, jagged pinnacles of rocks and numerous stacks and caves. With the sea mirror-calm we were content to paddle at a leisurely rate and enjoy the scenery. By early evening, with over 30 miles behind us, we camped on large pebbles at Kilmurrin Cove, having been forced to backtrack two miles when Bunmahon Bay (which looked an ideal campsite on the Irish half-inch O.S. map) proved to be an unacceptable combination of sand dunes and muddy saltings.

When we got up at 0600 the next morning, the stormy atmosphere of the previous day had given way to a fresher, cooler air stream, and the weather forecast was for an offshore F2–F3 north-westerly breeze, tempting me to plan a direct route across the bay to Mine Head, about 14 miles off. It would be like paddling the diameter of a circle as opposed to its circumference and would put us up to four miles off shore.

For the first hour or so, all went well. We were making good speed on the tide and had fine views of the mountains overlooking Waterford. But then events took a turn for the worse. A much bigger sea began to work in from the west and what had been a gentle north-westerly breeze steadily freshened until it was blowing a good F4–F5. We were at the centre of our "circle" and since the forecast was clearly going wrong,

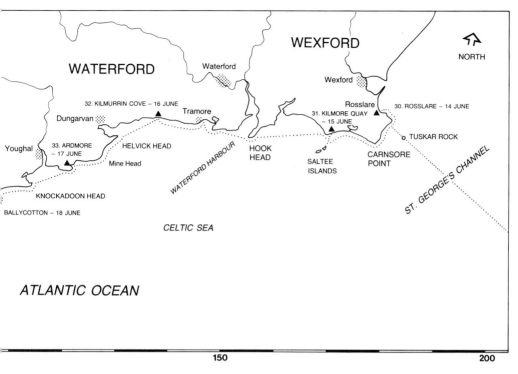

WEXFORD

NORTH

WATERFORD

Waterford

Wexford

32. KILMURRIN COVE – 16 JUNE

Tramore

Dungarvan

Rosslare
31. KILMORE QUAY
– 15 JUNE

30. ROSSLARE – 14 JUNE

TUSKAR ROCK

Youghal

33. ARDMORE
– 17 JUNE

HELVICK HEAD

Mine Head

WATERFORD HARBOUR

HOOK
HEAD

SALTEE
ISLANDS

CARNSORE
POINT

ST. GEORGE'S CHANNEL

KNOCKADOON HEAD

BALLYCOTTON – 18 JUNE

CELTIC SEA

ATLANTIC OCEAN

150

200

safety demanded we head directly for the nearest coast at Helvick Head, requiring us
to paddle directly into the wind. It was hard, wet work as we crashed through a rising
sea to gain the shelter of the land.

When we beached at a little cove to the east of the Head, we changed into dry clothes
and walked a mile or so to a nearby pub. Our morale was inexplicably low and we felt
as if we had been cheated by the weather. At the time, this objectively insignificant
hitch seemed to us a major set-back, which gives an interesting insight into our state
of mind. It was almost as if we had been forced to take a break in some important race
of dreadful consequence, when with hindsight and a truer perspective, it seems more
likely that our morale reflected a combination of physical weariness and prolonged lack
of sleep. What our logs show on detailed analysis is that we had taken less than 20
hours' sleep in four nights but had paddled about 120 miles. The condition was no
doubt aggravated by being almost permanently hungry. A rushed breakfast, chocolate
pickings during the day and an enormous evening meal was simply the beginning of a
downward spiral of calorie deficiency. As a matter of interest, I had heard of slipping
morale developing through similar factors when the trio of paddlers from St. Hild's
and St. Bede's College, Durham, had made the first circumnavigation of Ireland in
1978. But now that it was happening to us I was insufficiently objective to connect the
effect with the cause.

It may seem ridiculous, but a pint of Guinness and a sandwich put a new lease of
life into us. We could even persuade ourselves that the wind had eased (when it hadn't)
so that we were prepared to push on again. We were soon cursing the wind when back

on the water however. The sun was shining, it was a beautiful coast of fine cliffs, there were nesting gulls and guillemots to add wildlife interest and under any set of normal circumstances we would have enjoyed it. But on this particular day it all became minor detail, dwarfed by our fight with the wind.

When we arrived at Ardmore – a beautiful little village dominated by a fine Celtic tower – our misery was complete when we could find nowhere near the harbour to set up camp. Back in our boats, we set off along the sandy beach and reluctantly settled for a long carry to a caravan park where we had to *pay* to put up a tent. Fortunately it was the first of only two occasions we had to do so in Ireland.

It was instinct rather than reason that sensed the tiredness factor in our morale, and this dictated a lie-in until 0700 the next morning, in spite of the beautiful weather. A F6 south-easterly blow was forecast for later in the day, but now it was completely calm. We had launched by 0930 and the contrast with the previous day could hardly have been greater. The sea was like a mirror, it was hot, we were paddling topless and our mood was buoyant as we left the fine sea cliffs of Ardmore and Ram Heads to cross the open bay which leads to Youghal. Just before Knockadoon Head we landed on the beautiful islet of Capel Island to relieve the calls of nature, but were soon off again to cross the seven miles of bay to Ballycotton. As we did so however, a south-westerly wind was steadily freshening and in view of the forecast we were prepared to call a halt at the lifeboat slip in Ballycotton harbour. A short day of around 15 miles would do us no harm and would give us a chance to get a big lunch inside us, as well as give us time to prepare an extra-large evening meal.

The south-easterly blow materialised during the night and kept us trapped at Ballycotton throughout the next morning. As the wind eased to a F4 in the early afternoon we happily braved the large sea that was running to press on westwards. Although the sky was grey and threatening rain, it was exceptionally warm. With the wind and sea behind us we kept well off shore and made very good time so that we were off Roches Point and the entrance of Cork Harbour in a little over two hours.

As we crossed the harbour approaches a tanker was circling, no doubt waiting clearance to enter from the harbour authority. In the large swell and poor light it was foolhardy to assume we had been seen. The circling manoeuvre also made it difficult for us to anticipate the tanker's course and as the third circle appeared to be closing on top of us, we took the precaution of priming a white flare ready for firing. Luckily, it proved to be an unnecessary precaution and we continued on our way to reach the great natural harbour at Kinsale at 2000, having covered about 24 miles.

As the weather closed in, we set up our tent in the car-park of a little pub called The Bulman at Summer Cove, much to the amusement of the locals. It was raining by this time, the pub was exceptionally friendly and we ended up drinking Guinness all evening, forgoing our evening meal in favour of the convivial atmosphere. It may not have been "character building" but it was certainly good for our morale and, as it turned out, it could not do us any harm for we were to lose the next two days in exceptionally bad weather.

It blew, visibility was poor and it rained so hard in the thunderstorms that our car-park was awash. We consoled ourselves in being chauffeured around Kinsale on an extended pub-crawl, courtesy of an expatriate Cockney called Don Lanyon. He was a grounded oil-rig worker who had taken upon himself the responsibility of ensuring we remembered our enforced rest. Here I can soberly record the success of his mission.

When we got away on Sunday 22nd June the wind had dropped off and we had an easy passage past the Old Head of Kinsale. It was 11 miles off this spectacular headland that the great liner *Lusitania* had been sunk in 1915, but it was noteworthy on this occasion only because the sun finally won its battle with the cloud as we paddled by and because we were treated to a "ringside seat" of the Round Ireland Yacht Race, the spinnakers of the yachts creating great splashes of bright colour on this sensational seascape as we set off across Courtmacsherry Bay for Seven Heads.

But our interlude of sunshine was to be a brief one and, by the time we passed Galley Head, the weather was deteriorating fast. In a rising south-easterly wind the leaden sky was lowering by the minute and visibility had become poor. We had hoped to make Castletownshend, but with 38 miles paddled we were happy to find a sheltered campsite in the ruined crofts of the Rabbit Islands, south-west of Glandore. No sooner were we camped than rain had set in again.

By morning the weather was clearing to give a fine day but a moderate swell was running in from the south. As we passed between Toe Head and the great reef known as The Stags we were wary to avoid the ugly-looking breaks, but with a favourable tide to speed us along these were soon behind us. On reaching Sherkin Island we turned north into the sound that leads to the sheltered harbour of Baltimore and the channels that would take us on to the west coast. Beaching in Baltimore harbour we took an early lunch out of the south-easterly breeze. It was most pleasant to be able to strip off and dry out in the warm sunshine, taking some satisfaction in at last arriving in the area of great bays and headlands that characterise south-western Ireland.

The ruined crofts of the Rabbit Islands.

By mid-afternoon, we were off again to make the natural harbour at Crookhaven by 1830, having at last seen the infamous Fastnet Rock as we crossed the wide expanse of Long Island Bay. As we sat in O'Sullivan's Bar that evening, it was difficult to imagine that this quiet backwater had been a major port for sailing ships, in its heyday at the time of the American Civil War. Its main significance for us, however, was that tomorrow, after so many months of anticipation, we would at last be on the British Isles' most westerly seaboard.

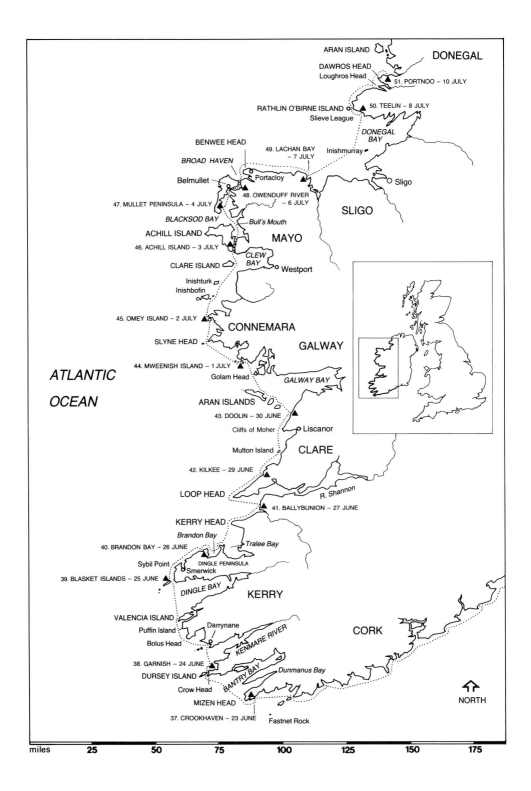

ARAN ISLAND

DONEGAL

DAWROS HEAD
Loughros Head

51. PORTNOO – 10 JULY

RATHLIN O'BIRNE ISLAND
Slieve League

50. TEELIN – 8 JULY

DONEGAL BAY

BENWEE HEAD

49. LACHAN BAY
– 7 JULY

Inishmurray

BROAD HAVEN

Portacloy

SLIGO

Belmullet

48. OWENDUFF RIVER
– 6 JULY

Sligo

47. MULLET PENINSULA – 4 JULY

SLIGO

BLACKSOD BAY

Bull's Mouth

ACHILL ISLAND

MAYO

46. ACHILL ISLAND – 3 JULY

CLEW BAY

CLARE ISLAND

Westport

Inishturk
Inishbofin

45. OMEY ISLAND – 2 JULY

CONNEMARA

SLYNE HEAD

GALWAY

44. MWEENISH ISLAND – 1 JULY

Golam Head

GALWAY BAY

ATLANTIC

OCEAN

ARAN ISLANDS

43. DOOLIN – 30 JUNE

Cliffs of Moher

Liscanor

Mutton Island

CLARE

42. KILKEE – 29 JUNE

LOOP HEAD

R. Shannon

41. BALLYBUNION – 27 JUNE

KERRY HEAD

Brandon Bay

Tralee Bay

40. BRANDON BAY – 26 JUNE

Sybil Point

DINGLE PENINSULA

39. BLASKET ISLANDS – 25 JUNE

Smerwick

DINGLE BAY

KERRY

VALENCIA ISLAND

Puffin Island

Darrynane

CORK

Bolus Head

KENMARE RIVER

38. GARNISH – 24 JUNE

DURSEY ISLAND

BANTRY BAY

Dunmanus Bay

Crow Head

MIZEN HEAD

NORTH

37. CROOKHAVEN – 23 JUNE

Fastnet Rock

miles   25   50   75   100   125   150   175

9

The Far West

Crookhaven – Portnoo: 24th June – 10th July

When planning the expedition, it had become increasingly clear that the west coast of Ireland has a very special character. In poetry and song it is synonymous with wild beauty, tinged with Celtic sadness and a reputation for spontaneous hospitality. In the cruising club guides and pilots it stands out for its sustained seriousness, requiring planning, seamanship and commitment from all seafarers who wish to experience its magic grandeur at first hand. We were not to be disappointed on any of these counts.

We were somewhat apprehensive when we set out from Crookhaven. The inshore and offshore shipping forecasts were so different, it was difficult to know what to expect of the weather. When we launched at 0800 it was pouring with rain from a dark sky and a fresh south-easterly wind was blowing. A moderate swell was working in from the Atlantic as we left the shelter of the inlet, to head west on a good tide that took us to the impressive sea cliffs of Mizen Head in under two hours.

As the rain stopped and the cloud began to break up, a 5–6m fin whale surfaced to blow 10 metres from my port bow, accompanying us for half an hour as we began an open crossing of about 18 miles to cross Dunmanus and Bantry Bays to reach Dursey Sound. The wind aided our progress for the first couple of hours, but as this dropped off, so the cloud thinned and it became oppressively hot. We continued to work hard, however, so that we entered the Sound between Dursey Island and Crow Head just as the tide began to turn against us.

Where the tidal narrows closed in, Mick and Richard fell into conversation with some fishermen who turned out to be off-duty keepers from The Bull Lighthouse. We were surprised to learn that they had been alerted to look out for us through the Irish Lights jungle network. They went on to recommend a beautiful sheltered campsite to the north-east of the peninsula at Garnish Strand, where we arrived about 1515 after a 30-mile day. Although attacked by swarms of midges, we experienced a warm welcome characteristic of this coast. The local postmaster, who lived in the only building around, volunteered his services to run me by car to the nearest store and also made his tools available to help fix a broken tiller bar on Mick's rudder.

Of all our paddling days in Ireland, Wednesday 25th June was to be the most special. The shipping forecast at 0555 predicted F3–4 southerly winds and fair weather. It could not have been better. By 0815, having discussed the weather prospects with the local salmon fishermen, we had set out on a dead run off the wind to make a 10-mile crossing of Kenmare River to the little settlement at Darrynane – a perfect natural

Repelling a midge attack at Garnish.

A lenticular cloud over Scariff Island.

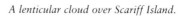

harbour with a silver sand beach, tucked beneath the foot of a steep mountainside. By the time we arrived for a bum-rest, the sun was shining from a clear sky, apart from lenticular clouds – like piles of plates – that capped the steep-sided and spectacular Scariff Island, just off the coast.

From Darrynane we had to paddle west to clear Bolus Head. As we passed Ballinskel-ligs Bay we could see on the distant western horizon what appeared to be pinkish clouds in the shape of fairy-tale castles. As we grew closer, however, we could see they were not clouds but the precipitous flanks of a group of islands – the Skelligs. It was an altogether remarkable piece of coastline with sensational sea cliffs and headlands.

Once clear of Bolus Head we could run off the wind again. With the tide and swell to assist us into the bargain, we were soon speeding along past the great rock buttresses of Puffin Island, where we encountered overfalls. As the tall cliffs of Valencia Island drew close, we had to make a decision as to whether we would have a short day and finish in the Port Magee Channel, or use the excellent conditions to cover the remaining 17 miles to the famous island of Great Blasket, on the western extremity of Dingle Bay.

It was an easy decision and we kept going, giving ourselves a superb paddle with a hazy view of the Kerry mountains to our right, the Dingle peninsula ahead and at the very tip, a great mass of orographic cloud which was marking the position of the whale-backed plateau of Great Blasket Island, which we could not actually see. There were numerous porpoises and shearwaters were skimming the wavetops as we grew closer to the island. We entered Blasket Sound (between the island and Dunquin on the mainland of Dingle) on the last of the fair tide. It was just 1830 when we hit the steep slip up the little quay of Great Blasket after a 43-mile paddle.

We camped out in the atmospheric ruins of the deserted cottages and completed a wonderful day by being invited to the hostel, one of the few buildings still intact. Plied with tea and cake, we sat in a cosmopolitan gathering before a tiny coal fire in a room lit by an oil-lamp, candles and the last of the twilight. After hearing of the island's history, and we had each contributed a song for entertainment, we wandered along the grass-grown roadways back to our tent, the shearwaters calling out all around us in the darkness. We were at our furthest point west.

When we awoke the next morning, there was no rush to be away, for the tide runs hard in Blasket Sound and would not be favourable to us until the afternoon. It was calm and cloudy, although the sun was slowly but surely dispersing the cloud and it was very warm. We used the morning to wander around the ruined settlement, savouring the atmosphere and taking photographs. There was much to appeal to the imagination: the ruins themselves were the result of forcible evictions by the Irish government in the 1950s, whilst the local waters are the graveyard of numerous ships, including some from the remnants of the Spanish Armada.

By this time the sun had broken through and there was a stir of excitement, for the ferry arrived from Dunquin, reporting the presence of a school of killer whales in the Sound. During the previous evening we had met two Irish sea paddlers who asked if they could join us as far as Smerwick. We were only too pleased to have their company. Just as we were about to leave, the summer residents at the hostel arrived with freshly made scones to give us a good send-off.

It was still calm when we paddled away from the tiny breakwater towards the nearby island of Beginish, in spite of a forecast of fresh north-easterly winds. Between the island and the mainland we were engrossed in conversation with our Irish colleagues when the distinctive fins and black and white flanks of killer whales sliced through the still water. There were at least three of them, and they circled us for several minutes while we sat still in the hope of getting some photographs. They had a strange knack of appearing in the wrong place at the wrong time and we felt quite disappointed when they finally left us.

Shortly afterwards, the north-easterly wind sprang up and immediately set up a short, sharp chop, blowing as it was against the tide. As we approached the mainland of the Dingle peninsula at Sybil Point, we were beginning what turned out to be a very hard six-hour slog into the wind. However, the coastal scenery was excellent with steep and pointed slabs dropping several hundred feet into the sea. Our new Irish friends left us at Smerwick and we carried on along the foot of Brandon Mountain. The weather was becoming increasingly stormy with fierce thermals and downdraughts, no doubt accelerated by the way Brandon Mountain drops from over 2,000 feet straight into the sea. The gusts were well over gale force in strength, flattening us onto our decks and snatching at the paddles. At one point, where we crossed a cove biting deep into the mountainside and funnelling the wind, there was a very real chance that we would be capsized. It was therefore a relief to turn Brandon Point and arrive at the little harbour at 1945.

We camped in the overgrown garden of a pub overlooking the quay, just as a torrential shower hit the village. Later that evening we sat cooking in the tent doorway, watching a magnificent thunderstorm working around the Kerry Hills to the west. The storm raged all night, with heavy rain and a gusty wind.

The downpour had cleared the air sufficiently to give a hot sunny morning with mist patches over the calm waters of Brandon Bay and the enclosing mountains gave a dramatic backdrop to the fishermen using traditional curraghs (constructed like large coracles, with tarred canvas over a light frame) as they fished for salmon, their one concession to the twentieth century being the use of "inboard-outboard" motors. We stopped to stretch our legs on Rough Point, opposite the Magharee Islands, and then set off into a fast-thickening haze towards Kerry Head – the southern point of the river Shannon Estuary. We were in fact ferry-gliding the tide running out from Tralee Bay in very poor visibility and were navigating by compass, but the tidal information for the west coast of Ireland is minimal and I hoped our estimate of the situation was realistic. After paddling blindly in this manner for about six miles, the dark cliffs of Kerry Head loomed out of the mist.

We now paddled as close as possible to the rocky shoreline, in order to keep out of the tide which was ebbing from the Shannon, knowing that at about 1500 the tide should begin flooding in our favour and enable us to move off shore. This was not to be, however, for as the tide turned, so the sea fog closed in and we had to keep near the shore to pick up landmarks. We were making for the major seaside town of Ballybunion (where we had arranged to be met by some relatives of one of Richard's neighbours) and we were beginning to feel despondent as the weather appeared to play

Rock formations in the Shannon Estuary.

tricks on us at every turn. Then, quite dramatically, the sea cliffs gave way to a coast of sand dunes, the visibility began to improve and we knew we were nearly there. By 1715 we had landed and were being swamped by the generosity and hospitality of the Sheehy family of Listowel, who were to be our hosts for the next two nights.

Although we were complete strangers, we were treated as long-lost brothers. Storage had been arranged for our boats, tea and scones were made available to us by a local beach café and then we were whisked away to an endless round of entertainment, feasting and drinking that was to last the next 36 hours. We also had the luxury of sleeping in *real* beds!

We left Ballybunion with reprovisioned boats and our own batteries recharged, just before midday on Sunday 29th June. The forecast was not very promising and within an hour we were paddling in fog across the Shannon's mouth towards distant Loop Head. The fine sea cliffs of this exposed headland were not done justice by the foggy conditions; indeed, they seemed to stretch on interminably. Once round the head we had to battle the tide all the way to the seaside resort of Kilkee, where after over 30 miles of paddling we were anxious to get off. It was altogether a dismal day, its drabness emphasised by the parting from our newly made friends in Listowel. It seemed a fitting end to the day when it began to pour with rain, but the last straw was when a fire siren went off in the middle of the night and the local fishermen decided to hold a reunion outside our tent at about 4 a.m.!

Approaching the Cliffs of Moher.

It was raining so hard the next morning it would have been foolish to break camp and it was nearly midday before we dared to get away. By this time the sky was brightening from the south and the wind was light and variable. We set off northwards with the Clare coastline stretching on as far as the eye could see – sheer rocky cliffs with no break in their defences. We took a quick lunch on Mutton Island and in a little over two hours we were clear of Liscanor Bay and approaching the world-famous Cliffs of Moher. This is a coast which can only be described as awe-inspiring, and we had anticipated its passage for many months. It has an imposing atmosphere which suitably complements its powerful visual image. Topped by isolated medieval towers, the cliffs rise many hundreds of feet in a truly vertical sweep to dwarf sheer-sided, needle-like sea stacks of up to 300 feet. We were lucky. At this point the sun dispersed the cloud to provide the appropriate level of dramatic lighting.

That evening we camped at Doolin, after an awful boat-carry over large boulders to a proper campsite. We watched a fine sunset over the island of Inisheer and had just enough time to walk a mile or so to the little pub – by reputation the finest pub for folk music in the whole of Ireland. We had made another 28 miles' progress and were in the best possible position to visit the Aran Islands.

It was the 1st July; a new month and mid-summer already behind us, along with ten weeks of our expedition. To stay sane, however, we always had to think in terms of realistic and achievable objectives. Today we wanted to visit the Aran Islands, famous for their classic sweaters and Gaelic-speaking community.

After repeating our awkward carry – 40 minutes for about 300 metres – we got launched at 0920 with a fresh south-easterly wind to speed us on our way. In less than an hour we had surfed the five miles to Inisheer. It was something of a disappointment. On this overcast and dreary day, there seemed little point in visiting the undoubtedly more picturesque and swell-battered southern cliff-line. The grey stony islands with little relief, symmetrical stone walls and fairly high-density population were not at their best. Paddling past Inishmaan we reached the pier on Inishmore in a little over three hours from leaving Doolin. By this time the wind had strengthened considerably and it had started to rain.

After buying some supplies we brewed up in the lee of the lifeboat station and debated whether we should stay or press on. The wind was now blowing F5 but it was still south-easterly and so would aid us on our run back to the mainland, cutting off the corner of Galway Bay. I was particularly anxious not to get stuck on the Arans when the forecast westerlies came away. It was a ten-mile crossing to Golam Head on the island of Gorumna, but a local fishing skipper assured me the sea state would not get too difficult. This clinched the decision, and it turned out to be a good one. It took only 1¾ hours to cover the distance as we surfed along on flying spray, sou'westers pulled down to keep off the worst of the rain. For all the fisherman's assurances, however, the seas were quite demanding, particularly now the wind had picked up to a F6 and was blowing the crests off.

This paddle put us on a technically demanding piece of coast that is a veritable maze of islets, rocks and shoals, where the Atlantic rollers break with a disconcerting regularity. We had to navigate on a very tight rein to avoid being in the wrong place at the wrong time when the bigger swells rolled through. It was mentally as well as physically demanding and we could never afford to relax.

Having passed the ruined tower on Golam Head we set off towards the relative shelter of Mweenish Bay. Even on this grim evening the stark beauty of the coast could not be ignored. Crescents of silver sand beaches are broken by low, rocky headlands before rising to low hillocks of machair, at this time of year a mass of wild flowers. Just beyond the coastal bays loomed the purple masses of the high mountains of Connemara – The Twelve Pins. In some places we could see sand dunes in the process of engulfing ruined crofting settlements. That evening we camped in the machair of Mweenish Island. A squall and heavy shower marked the passage of a front as we cooked our meal. A little later, the farmer on whose land we had camped paid us a visit. Short, with twinkling eyes, he sported a virtually toothless grin in his brown face. He was also a friendly old fellow and during the course of our conversation a chance remark led us to the conclusion that this was not the first time we had met. Twenty years before, whilst the A2M arterial road was being constructed through Kent, he and I had worked in the same road construction gang – I as a labourer during my university vacation and he as a kerb layer. Discussing the merits of various pubs in the Medway towns, perhaps we were not so far from home that evening as we at first thought.

If our paddle to the Blaskets was our best day's paddling in Ireland, our passage of Slyne Head on 2nd July was the most memorable. The forecast was for south-westerly F4–5 but freshening, putting pressure on us to get round the head before a westerly air stream became established.

Setting off in a squally shower, as soon as we were clear of the shelter of the bay we were in a heavy groundswell from south-south-west which was causing a ferocious break all along the shoreline. Our course to Slyne Head was approximately north-west, so it was a quartering sea. We had to pick our way very carefully through the maze of shoals to avoid the breaks and the nervous tension kept our reflexes sharp.

By the time we cleared Mason Island, the sun was shining, although towering plumes of convective cloud remained over the mountains, keeping them in dark shade and providing a dramatic backdrop to our sun-bathed endeavours. We island-hopped through a chain of picturesque islands – St. Macdara's with its lonely Celtic chapel, finally Croagh-nakeela – and then there was 12 miles of open ocean to Slyne Head itself. It was not featureless ocean, however, for wherever there were rocks or shoals the swells of about 5–6m were creating horrendous breaks. We dared not relax.

Steaks for dinner at Omey Island.

It was a great relief when at about 1500 we slipped through one of the inner channels of the tiny island chain that is Slyne Head. We could now run off the wind and swell, with the tide to assist us as we paddled north. There were still a number of dangerous breaks to avoid but we eventually made the shelter of the narrow channel protected from the Atlantic swells by the low islets of Inishturk and Omey Island. We camped on Omey, overlooking the channel at the point where it dries out to form a great expanse of silver cockle sands connecting to the mainland at low tide.

This time we camped in the back garden of a croft that had become a holiday cottage. The rich tall grass was once again a mass of wild flowers, but the most vivid memory of the camp has to be our unusual host. Staying at the cottage for his holiday was a bushy-bearded, fuzz-haired and overweight Breton. Living in Dublin, he stayed at home to run the house and look after the baby, whilst his Irish wife went out to work. Having met his wife whilst leading a solitary life as a fisherman on an island he shared with 100 cows on the Donegal coast, he was interested in all things nautical, asked a stream of questions in very good English about our adventures and continually reminded us to watch out for the nor'-westers on the Donegal coast!

The next day we left Omey on a fair tide and with a fresh south-south-westerly breeze to surf us north at an average speed of 6 m.p.h. The sky was grey and the cloud occasionally dropped to sea level to give drizzle and force us to navigate by compass. Having picked up the eastern tip of Inishbofin, we tucked inside the tiny island of Devillaun to kill the groundswell and flew on north-eastwards to the beautiful island of Inishturk and then Clare Island. Such was the scenic attraction of this mountainous island with its beautiful little harbour at its south-eastern corner that we were sorely tempted to cut our day short. However, the weather was now getting decidedly worse. The wind was a good F5 from the south-west and there was a fierce cross-sea running in the channel between Clare Island and the entrance to Achill Sound. By the time we reached this sound (which separates the rugged Achillbeg Island and then the mountain-ous island of Achill from the sand-dune coast of the mainland) Clare Island was lost to our sight in the heavy rain. The tide was running out against us, river-like, at about 4 knots and we made progress only by dodging from eddy to eddy.

A ruined fort and barracks overlook the tidal narrows at the southern end of the channel and we looked in vain around it for a suitable campsite. It proved to be far too boggy, however, and we eventually set up our tent in the teeming rain on a patch of grass next to a lay-by, a couple of miles up the Sound.

We had to wait for the flood tide to progress through Achill Sound and this meant a late start the next morning. We had looked forward to paddling in these sheltered waters, dominated by mountains on both sides, but the experience for me was marred by the bruised condition of my backside. It had given me nagging pain for several days, but on this occasion, with no technical problems or rough conditions to distract me, the pain became an obsession akin to a raging toothache. I guessed that the stretched muscles over my pelvic bones had become tenderised like steaks, after so many hundreds of hours' paddling, but awareness of the cause was little consolation when I could think of no cure other than to give up the trip.

Having completely restocked our provisions at the settlement of Achill Sound, we crossed the tidal "hump" and fought our way out of the north end of the channel. The northern entrance is aptly named the Bull's Mouth, where the Irish Cruising Club pilot estimates the flooding tide to run at 8 knots on spring tides. We had to cross about half a mile of white water and standing waves at about 6 knots to make an eddy on the Achill shore in order to break out of the Sound.

Now this major obstacle was behind us we concentrated our attention on the worsening weather. The wind was a F4–5 from the south-west but forecast to veer to the north-west and strengthen. Ominous black clouds were building up fast over Slievemore and squally showers regularly reduced the visibility to a few hundred metres. We stopped to put on our buoyancy aids and sou'westers before setting out on the six-mile crossing of Blacksod Bay, where we would be exposed to the full force of the wind and Atlantic swells until we reached Blacksod Point. I knew we would be cutting it fine to complete the crossing before the frontal squall came through to give us a head wind, so we struck out very strongly as the sky became inky black.

We reached the squat, square, granite tower of Blacksod Lighthouse in just over 1½ hours, arriving in the lee of the jetty as the squall struck with heavy rain and a wind gusting to gale force. We smiled knowingly and took satisfaction in "outwitting" the weather gods on this occasion. Then, having run our boats onto the beach, we made a bee-line for the keeper's cottage, hoping he would have been alerted to our enterprise, which would put us in an advantageous position to scrounge a shelter out of the dreadful weather.

Our concern was not necessary. Vincent Sweeney had taken over the keeping duties at Blacksod in 1980 from his father, who had been keeper since 1933. Vincent had been watching our crossing through his field glasses and no sooner had we introduced ourselves than we were given an outbuilding for accommodation and were whisked inside his cottage for coffee and biscuits. With a poor forecast on the morrow, we were to be the guests of the Sweeney family for the next two nights.

Our stay became something of an educational visit, although perhaps the lessons needed to be taken with a pinch of sea salt. The first lesson we learned was that local stone had been used to build the British Houses of Parliament. Secondly we learned that it was a weather report despatched by Vincent's father which had prompted Churchill and Eisenhower to unleash the D-Day landings in June 1944, and last, but not least, we increased the depth of our knowledge on the recession in the Irish fishing industry, for Vincent ran a sea-angling charter business and had once worked for the Irish Ministry of Agriculture and Fisheries.

But we did not spend all our time at Blacksod on improving our minds. We took the opportunity to rinse the salt out of our clothes, repaired a leaking keel-line on Richard's boat, serviced Mick's rudder and ate a constant stream of snacks. The highlight of the day was when we demolished a 6-lb piece of boiling bacon, along with 3 lbs of potatoes and other sundries in a single sitting!

We did not get away from the lighthouse until late the following day. Thanks to Vincent Sweeney's knowledge of the coast, he was able to confirm information that I had suspected but had been unable to verify – namely that towards high tide a small craft could travel up the *inside* of the Mullet Peninsula and reach the bay of Broad Haven by cutting through the old channel at Belmullet. In effect, it meant that the Mullet Peninsula is really an island, and could therefore afford us a further section of sheltered paddling on our journey north.

With Belmullet behind us and with evening approaching we had decided that the weather (it was blowing a strong north-westerly) would not allow us to get round Benwee Head, so we were looking for a place to camp whilst still in the shelter of Broad Haven. As we approached the jetty at Ballyglass, a yacht flying Danish colours came into view. When we paddled over to see if they had an updated weather forecast, we were surprised to be hailed by none other than the met. forecaster we had seen at R.A.F. Brawdy before our Irish Sea crossing.

That night we camped on rabbit-cropped sweet turf adjacent to the peaty brook known as the Owenduff River. The spot was particularly attractive because the sward was a carpet of tiny yellow flowers and we found enough driftwood to have a cooking fire. It was a windy evening and cold for July, although the squally showers were interspersed by short sunny spells that bathed the scene in the clear golden light of a late summer evening.

As the expedition progressed, so our instincts appeared to attune themselves to our needs in the natural world. This was particularly true in respect of my *feel* for the weather. We never missed an opportunity to take a forecast; I have been a keen amateur forecaster since my days working with the British Antarctic Survey in the 1960s, but we could now make our own judgements on the timing of developments with an

Our attractive camp by the Owenduff River.

uncanny degree of accuracy. This instinct had allowed us to cross Blacksod Bay and it was about to come into play again.

Although the forecast had made it doubtful if we could get away from Owenduff River, I woke sharp at 0500 the next morning sensing we could move. Sure enough, the wind had dropped away, and by forgoing breakfast we were paddling by 0630.

We spent the next three hours to make 11 miles in a very difficult sea. A big north-westerly swell was rolling in and reflecting back from the spectacular sea cliffs to create a confused and tiring wave pattern. By the time we could see the craggy rocks known as the Stags of Broad Haven, our life was made more difficult by the tide turning against us, steepening up the swells even further, so we were relieved to enter the long, narrow and rocky cove that led to the sandy beach of Portacloy.

The weather appeared to be deteriorating fast, so in view of the forecast we had taken at Owenduff River, we set up our tent by a group of upturned curraghs where the road met the bay. Having breakfasted, we dozed in the tent until midday, waiting for a local inshore forecast. It was not what we expected; we packed camp once more and set off on the next flood tide to make further eastward progress into Donegal Bay. It was a very committing day. The swell was thundering into the great sea cliffs of this north-facing coast and it was 10 miles to the next possible landing-place at Belderg and with this behind us, a further 14 miles to the next – the little quay at Lachan Bay, where the coast took a sharp turn to the south.

We were very tired after such a long day and it started to rain heavily almost as soon as we arrived at the slip. There was nowhere to camp properly, so we had little choice but to bivvy in the car-park among a party of French scuba divers. Confined to a leaking fly-sheet bivvy we watched the salmon-boats arrive at the jetty to unload enormous catches of salmon. We did not know it at the time, but we had reached the half-way stage in our journey, both in terms of distance and time.

It was a great boost to our morale when, after so many days of dull weather, we woke to bright sunshine. A fresh breeze enabled us to get our equipment dried out and we decided to undertake a six-mile walk to visit the nearest shop. The little lane petered out onto the great, flat, silver sand beach of Lachan Bay's "inner strand", passing a number of prosperous-looking bungalows. These bore testimony to the benefits brought to the crofting communites by E.E.C. subsidies and the Irish government's own programme to discourage further depopulation of the Gaelic-speaking area. There was a great deal of fishing activity just off the coast.

With our boats restocked and a reasonable forecast, we set off at 1350, heading north-east for the low island of Inishmurray, about 25 miles into Donegal Bay. It was a pleasant surprise when both the sea and the wind were less than we were expecting, and in the warm sunshine we could actually enjoy the paddle. We were making good progress towards the plateau peaks of the Sligo mountains, for somewhere at their foot lay Inishmurray. However, on the port bow of our course loomed the great bulk of Slieve League on the north-western extremity of Donegal Bay, continually "beckoning" us to where we needed to be, only it was a great distance away.

Four hours into our paddle we held a hurried conference and I put to Mick and Richard a simple proposal. The weather seemed settled, Inishmurray was two hours off but Teelin (in Donegal and at the foot of Slieve League) was only about twice that distance. We would go for it. A boiled sweet and a mouthful of water later, we changed our heading and set off for the north shore of Donegal Bay.

It was a superb summer evening. In the clear light the detail of our landfall teased and fooled us into underestimating its distance. I had not measured the new course with any degree of accuracy since our maps had been cut up and stuck back-to-back in smaller units, so the two-thousand-foot sweep of slabby rock that comprises the sea cliffs of Slieve League eventually took over five hours to reach rather than the four I had forecast. Meanwhile there had been a magnificent sunset and it was nearly dark when we slipped into the sheltered natural harbour at 2320. Another hour and a half had passed before we had set up our tent and prepared a meal. Our 38 miles without a stop had taken a heavy physical toll but we took great satisfaction in having crossed Donegal Bay. As we crawled into our sleeping-bags we noticed that the northern sky had still not grown completely dark – irrefutable testimony to our northerly progress.

After such a beautiful night it came as a cruel shock to be woken by the sound of heavy rain beating onto the fly-sheet. Our paddling clothes had been strung out to dry on a nearby fence so we cursed our casual optimism before rolling over to go back to sleep!

But really it made no difference. We spent the whole day tent-bound in a heavy downpour while the mist swirled around the inlet. We consoled ourselves by cooking an extra meal, but Mick's one comment said it all, "It's jacking-it-in weather". The best part of the day was reserved for the late evening when we visited The Rusty Mackerel pub. The locals were friendly and one ancient character called Micky (a sprightly 80-year-old) kept us amused in conversation for most of the time. The pub walls were decorated with a variety of old posters and advertising material going back many decades. I remember one that amused us in particular: Ronald Reagan, youthful and fresh-faced, was smiling down at us to push the social benefits of his favourite, mild cigarette!

The next morning was just as wet and misty as the previous day, but the wind had dropped off. Our sodden clothing still hung on the fence and it was with great reluctance that we accepted the inevitable and began to change and pack up camp. By the time everything was stowed in the boats we had about four hours of favourable tide left to break out of Donegal Bay and put ourselves on a northward-trending coast again. In mist and heavy drizzle we paddled westwards along the foot of Slieve League to reach the sound of Rathlin O'Birne. From time to time we would encounter tiny fishing craft working their salmon nets. On the oily swells, everything that could float was being utilised and in the foggy conditions the poachers were no doubt having a fine old time. It seemed remarkable to us that the salmon could survive at all in such aggravated overfishing.

Passing between the lighthouse on Rathlin O'Birne and Glen Columbkille we were making good time, but when the tide turned against us about 1500 it was as if we were dragging sea anchors. We moved in close to the shore but were still fighting about 2 knots of a spring ebb. With the turn in tide, as so often happens, came a change in the weather, this time for the worse. The wind freshened from the west to give a lumpy sea and the cloud dropped to sea level. Progress along the steep cliffs of Slieve Tooey was extremely slow. It did not help to know that there was no reliable landing ahead for another 12 miles.

At last, having reached Loughros Bay, we escaped from the worst of the tide, and set off on compass headings to headland-hop to Dawros Head. In the lee of the tiny island of Inishbarnog we came ashore to rest our bums and eat some chocolate. It was already 1800; we were soaked through and cold, but there was no water on the island so we were reluctant to camp. One more drive saw us past Dunmore Head and we eventually rounded the island of Inishkeel to the quiet waters of the anchorage known as Church Pool. By now it was 1945 and it came as a disappointment to find that the fine-looking silver sand beach, overlooked by the ruins of an ancient chapel, stank like an open sewer. On the far side of Church Pool, across a narrow sound, was a large village called Naran, but it was a coast of sand dunes and with so much of our gear wet we could not face the prospects of a gritty camp there. The air was blue as we paddled back the way we had come, heading for the tiny quay at Portnoo, which we had seen on passing but was not marked on either our chart or our O.S. map.

In spite of the unseasonable weather and the time of day, the quay was exceptionally active with children and holiday-makers who took an immediate interest in our arrival. There were no obvious places to camp and I eventually asked permission to set up our tent on a small patch of grass attached to a holiday cottage. Wet and caked with salt we must have looked a sorry sight, for we were immediately invited inside to have unrestricted use of the cottage, including the luxury of a shower and beds to sleep on. The Cooper family from Drumgary, Enniskillen, promptly went out for the evening, leaving us to cook our meal in their kitchen. Our luck had taken a turn for the better, but more to the point, the morrow would see us round Bloody Foreland and onto the north coast.

10

Very Wet and Watery Wanderings

Portnoo – Arisaig: 11th – 21st July

The character of the canoeing was about to change. Whilst on the west coast of Ireland, apart from a few local and notable tidal anomalies (such as the one we had experienced in the Bull's Mouth of Achill Sound) the tides had in general terms not been very big. In particular, tidal streams – the rates at which the tide flows *along* the coast – had been mostly weak and had rarely created technical canoeing problems such as tide races or overfalls. At least, this was our experience, for there is a disconcerting lack of information available about tidal streams on Ireland's west coast when one consults Admiralty Charts or books on pilotage.

In contrast, the north coast of Ireland and the islands of south-west Scotland create constrictions on the tidal flow as it floods from the Atlantic to fill the northern part of the Irish Sea and along the south-western seaboard of Scotland. This "funnelling" effect accelerates the tides so that overfalls form over shoals, and tide races are to be found off the tips of headlands and in narrow channels between islands. Such phenomena manifest themselves as white-water conditions similar to river rapids and if the wind happens to blow with any strength against the tide, it creates very rough seas. Since these coasts are exposed to the Atlantic winds and swells, it makes the canoeing potentially very serious. It certainly requires tight planning if the tides are to be used to give maximum benefit (as opposed to being a major hindrance) and if the roughest water conditions are to be avoided.

We therefore approached the coast with mixed feelings. We were excited at the prospect of doing something different and because we were getting close to the British mainland once more, but we were also apprehensive about the scale and number of the possible difficulties, any one of which would cause us serious problems and delays.

We had left Teelin in soaking clothes and with wet tentage. It was raining within minutes of our arrival at Portnoo and it was still drizzling when we got up the next morning; our gear would have to stay wet!

During the morning we restocked our provisions from the local store and finally bade farewell to our hosts about midday, just as the sun burned off the cloud. There was very little wind so we had an easy paddle on calm seas towards Aran Island. With most of the cloud now gone, we had fine views of the Donegal mountains, but the most memorable visual image of the day was when our course intercepted that of a traditional

Off the Donegal coast we encountered the 'Connaught', the oldest Galway Hooker.

working sail-boat known as a Galway Hooker. This specimen – the *Connaught* – had been built in 1842 and was the oldest known vessel of her type. We had heard a lot about such boats during our stay in Ireland, for one of them had crossed the Atlantic to Boston earlier in the summer.

Bright sunshine saw us through the picturesque islets that are scattered along the channel between Aran Island and the settlement of Burtonport and we were pleased at the extent to which the tide was assisting us. Because the islands were protecting us from the swell, we enjoyed the novelty of a relaxing paddle until, at about 1700, we

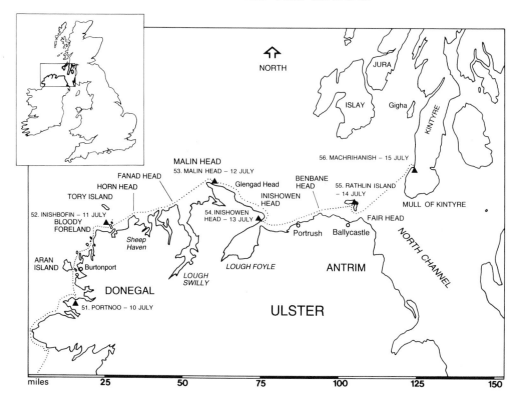

stopped for a snack on a silver sand beach set amid pink granite boulders on Gola Island. By now the cloud was racing in from the south-west and thickening fast, but we were still able to enjoy a fine panorama of Inishfree Bay with the dark hills beyond. These fell away to the north-east in the purple bulk of hillside which runs down to the sea as Bloody Foreland, which we now had to round to put ourselves on the north coast proper.

This exposed headland enjoys a notorious reputation for its rough seas, for it catches winds from all directions except the south-east and tides run hard. On this evening of gentle winds, however, we experienced no difficulties, the only event of note being when a fishing-boat stopped in our path to wish us luck with our journey. They had guessed our identity and purpose having read of us in one of the Irish national newspapers – fame at last! But we had no idea how we had come to gain such press coverage.

By now the visibility had deteriorated considerably, so that we could barely discern Tory Island to the north, but our morale had been lifted by the fishermen and also because we were at last paddling east. When we reached the low, treeless islands neighbouring Inishbofin, there were already touches of drizzle in the air and we paddled down between the main islands hoping to find a suitable camping place before conditions got any damper. Eventually we chose to land on the southern tip of Inishbofin, where the settlement overlooks the exceptionally high sand dunes of the mainland coast and the tide race that guards the crossing.

Two small boys had been running along the low cliff-top to observe our progress, but as we hit the stony beach, they mysteriously disappeared. As we stepped ashore, a silent crowd of onlookers appeared on the cliff, studying our every move without uttering a word. They simply stared. We looked at each other and felt strangely uncomfortable. Our audience was mostly middle-aged; they were dressed in old working clothes and each person looked alarmingly like the others, even the dogs were alike. In the grey light of that miserable evening it was as if we were looking at a sepia photograph taken half a century ago.

To break the silence and the spell (it was far too like an opening scene from a cheap horror movie) I put on what I hoped was a relaxed and friendly air, ascended the cliff and asked where we might camp. The replies came in such a thick brogue it was difficult to understand, the situation being aggravated by what seemed to be a general lack of sound teeth. There were no smiles to back up the offer to put our tents up where we pleased, so we still felt uncomfortable as we searched the patches of grass fronting the village for a spot that was not covered in goose droppings.

The settlement itself was very run down. Some of the cottages were no longer lived in, although the general lack of maintenance extended to those that were. We were still feeling uneasy when an older man approached and watched us erect the tent, then hang our wet gear over the wall guarding the village hall. Perhaps he was amused by the strange ritual that prompted us to put wet gear out in the rain (which would at least wash the salt out of it) but he eventually gave a little smile and told us we could put a line up *inside* the hall if we wished. In fact, we could cook in there too if we liked. We needed no urging to accept the offer and ended up sleeping in the musty and junk-strewn hall.

The next morning we were able to laugh at our sinister misgivings of the previous evening. In the sunshine that occasionally penetrated the early fog, the villagers seemed happy to speak to us and the fishermen gave us as many fresh crab-claws as we could carry.

We were to have relatively calm but wet and foggy conditions all along this north coast. Therefore our main problem focused on the large tidal eddies (running contrary to the main tide) for unspecified and unpredictable distances of up to a couple of miles off the coast which we attempted to use but not always with success. Thus, the day we left Inishbofin we made good time to the great rock buttress of Horn Head, paddled across the entrance to Sheep Haven in a fog bank but were able to relax in pleasant sunshine as we took a lunch-stop and cooked our crab-claws at the little harbour of Ballyhooris-key. As the tide flooded up from Tory Sound we sped past the lighthouse on Fanad Head, crossed the mouth of Lough Swilly and moved well off shore to pass Dunaff Head – in the hope of avoiding inshore eddies off Malin Head.

As this low, craggy head with its square tower came into clear view, our 3 knots of tidal assistance suddenly became half that rate flowing *against* us. By this stage we had paddled over 36 miles so our last hour to win the harbour at Slievebane became a frustrating and wearying battle. It was 2200 when we landed, about 100m west of the quay, in a complex of rock-guarded beaches giving access to a good campsite. It was a still evening of atmospheric light that streamed in under the cloudbanks from the north-west to tint them in innumerable shades of grey, mauve and purple. But our main attention was not on the beauty of the scene; we were obsessed by our desire to cook and eat before darkness overtook us. It was nearly midnight when we crawled into our sleeping-bags.

The early hours of Sunday 13th July were warm and sticky and I eventually found it more comfortable to run the risk of midge bites and sleep on top of my sleeping-bag. The weather forecast taken the previous night had spoken of rain in the morning and, since we would not be able to use the tide until the afternoon, I lay in until 0700 and did not call the other two until 0800. While they were getting up I walked along the beach to see what chance there was of buying any supplies in the village. The only shop was the village pub and that would not open until the late morning.

Once back in camp we cooked our porridge and began eating just as the first spots of rain arrived on a gentle southerly wind. This would be yet another day when we failed to get dried out. Breakfast over, our first job was to call at the nearest habitation and get our water bottles filled, then we wandered off to see if the pub had opened, to buy some food.

Slievebane occupies a very scenic site and is potentially a picturesque village. However, the atmosphere was spoiled by the rubbish and litter which lay wherever we looked. Even the beach was spoiled by piles of scrap metal and the dilapidated caravans which occupied the land between the sea and the houses. The highlight of our stay here came at lunchtime. Any locals observing us would have witnessed a re-enactment of a primeval scene. Squatting on our haunches on the pebble beach, oblivious to the rain which we had come to accept as part of our existence, Richard and I sat cracking open the cooked crab-claws with a couple of large stones. Pleased at our good fortune in being given such delicacies and knowing that Mick never eats sea food, we greedily demolished the tender white meat of eight large claws squashed between hunks of bread.

We then sat in the tent, waiting for the weather to clear as forecast. Instead, the rain grew heavier. With all our paddling gear soaked it really made no difference, so we decided to pack and leave at 1500 regardless of any weather improvement. Meanwhile, visibility had closed in to give intermittent sea fog, sometimes obscuring the jagged rocks of the Garvan Islands which lay only a few hundred metres off shore from where we were camped.

When we left the beach a north-westerly breeze had sprung up. Around the Garvans the tide was swirling in all directions. The tidal eddy which in theory was to take us along the foot of the high cliffs of this coast was as frequently flowing against us and we settled down to a frustrating paddle. In good weather the spectacular coast would have been a pleasure to paddle, but today it proved tedious. Sometimes the sea would be mirror-calm and we could look up at high rock buttresses, a little later the breeze would freshen to give a fierce, choppy cross-sea and we could see nothing as the fog banks swirled around us. So the journey continued, with us hugging the cliff-line until south of Glengad Head, being buffeted by the wind as we crossed the more open coast of Culdaff Bay and then back to the cliffs again.

It was now early evening. It had become absolutely still and we were paddling in fog again. As we closed with Inishowen Head our position was confirmed by the eerie sound of the horn of the lighthouse on Dunagree Point, where the entrance to Lough Foyle cuts back on itself towards the south-west and Londonderry. Just to the south of the light a sluggish creek joins the sea by a tiny quay. We arrived here at 2120 and we could make no further progress without crossing to Ulster. It had been a short day of only 21 miles but we had by now had our fill of being wet through.

We quickly pitched our tent in waist-high wet grass and draped our sodden paddling gear over our boats. If it rained hard in the night it would wash out some of the salt.

The cliffs of Horn Head, County Donegal.

By 2200 we were inside the tent and preparing our meal. Looking from one salt-encrusted face to the other, at the miserable weather and back to our wet "hovel", we simultaneously burst into laughter.

"What a poxy way to spend a fortieth birthday!" I exclaimed.

"You haven't even wet your whistle," said Mick.

"When was the last time you didn't have a drink on your birthday?" asked Richard.

"Can't even remember," I replied forlornly, "probably some time before you were born."

"Poor old sod," said Mick before he and Richard collapsed on their sleeping-bags laughing.

Had there been a pub within walking distance we would still have been unable to get a drink after 10 p.m. on a Sunday evening. We had one good shot of whisky left in the bottle that had been thrust upon us on the day we left, but we had promised ourselves not to finish it until we got to Scotland. Amazed at my own will-power, I lazed in the tent, content to let Richard get on with the cooking. Such was my 40th birthday party.

When the alarm went at 0445 I was thankful to hear it was not raining. On looking out, it was another dull and miserable morning but at least the fog had dispersed. The tides today could be running up to 6 knots in Rathlin Sound (where there are only four hours of west-east flow in any tidal sequence) so our timing to enable us to get to Rathlin Island was absolutely critical. We responded to the urgency by breakfasting, breaking camp and launching in under 1½ hours. We then set off towards Portrush on the far side of Lough Foyle at a brisk pace. To the south, across a calm sea dotted with fishing craft working their salmon drifts, lay Magilligan Point at the eastern entrance to the Lough Foyle narrows. A low coastline of sand dunes stretched eastwards from here to Portstewart, backed by the hills of Ulster. On this particular morning, many of those hills had a cap of mist.

Fighting the tide that was flooding into the great sea loch (for on this coast the tide rises or floods from the unexpected direction of east to west) it took us three hours to cover the ten miles to Portrush. We were about 20 minutes behind our tight schedule at this point, where we picked up a powerful and predicted tidal eddy that would take us from the Skerries Channel and across the bay of Bushmills to the Giant's Causeway and the great cliffs of basalt columns that make up Benbane Head. We had won back our lost 20 minutes by the time we had crossed the bay and still had time to look at the famous causeway, its stepped hexagonal pillars like some elongated and disorganised trail of giant pencils stood on end. Arriving off the tall cliffs of Benbane Head at 1140, we were just in time to pick up the main tidal ebb that would carry us through Rathlin Sound.

The chart of this notorious area of water looks like a pilotage nightmare, showing one mass of eddies and overfalls. I had read up everything I could lay my hands on before committing us to the course of action advised by the *Irish Cruising Club Guide*. In winds of any strength, small craft would be at considerable risk, but the prolonged period of slack air streams that had produced the wet and foggy conditions now worked to our advantage. Where we would normally have expected to find broken white water, today were great oily boils that slid one into another. In under 1¾ hours we were off Bull Point on the western extremity of Rathlin and at 1415, having put about 30 miles behind us, we came into the anchorage of the main settlement at Church Bay.

Our arrival coincided with that of the Irish Lights Commission service ship, so when we beached our boats alongside the main quay we assumed that the large crowd of smiling faces had turned out to welcome a launch from the Irish Lights vessel. However, we soon found out that it was us whom everyone wanted to see. We were immediately surrounded by eager hands that carried our kayaks and escorted us to the campsite behind the single terrace of cottages that fronts the quay. We had no idea how they had been alerted to our arrival, but this did not stop us making the most of being celebrities. The local postmaster was also skipper of the ferry from Rathlin to Ballycastle on the Antrim coast; acting as a spokesman for the other islanders, he made us as welcome as possible and placed himself at our disposal should we need anything.

Basalt cliffs of Benbane Head and the Giant's Causeway, County Antrim.

Just before we had reached Church Bay, the sun had made a brave attempt to break through the cloud canopy, enabling us to make our first priority washing the salt out of our clothes while there was some chance that they would dry. With the whole afternoon and evening in front of us we had time to cook an extra-large meal and also catch up on some sleep, for we had been on early starts and late finishes for a long time. It was early evening when we woke and it had started to rain again. This had wet our clothes yet again, but it did not dampen our spirits, for we were in position to make our jump across the North Channel to Scotland.

To make the best of this special occasion, we went straight off to Mcuag's Pub and it turned out to be a memorable evening. To use the local parlance, "it was a good crack". A guitarist and banjo player from Belfast had set themselves up in one corner of the bar and had established a party atmosphere. From time to time they were hushed into an awed and appreciative silence by the incredible performances of an ageing fiddler who revealed to us later that he was a professional musician and violin-maker from Aberdeen. The Guinness and Bushmills single malt flowed into the early hours, as the lads ensured that I made up for missing out on my birthday.

Like most occasions of this type, the festivities in Mcuag's seemed a good idea at the time and were no doubt good for our morale, but the direct consequence was that we overslept the next morning. It was 0745 when I woke up. More alarming than the time, I did not yet have a clear head! By the time I had pulled myself together, I was in time to catch the inshore shipping forecast and this put us under immediate pressure. Outside the tent it was foggy, raining gently, and there was no wind. The forecast was for the light south-westerly wind to increase to a F6 later, before veering to give a full gale from the north-west. If we wanted to avoid being stuck on Rathlin for several days we had to make our crossing to Scotland before the gale arrived.

The hectic packing in the rain meant that my head was clear to make a final check on the navigational calculations to provide compass headings for each hour of our crossing of the North Channel to the Kintyre Peninsula, where we intended to land at Machrihanish – the first civilisation to the north of the Mull of Kintyre's rugged wilderness. Although this is only a trip of 23 miles from embarkation to landing, and only 16 miles between the two nearest points of land, it is for all that fairly serious. These narrows create enormously powerful tidal streams which we had to *cross* more than use. It was a condensed version of our St. George's Channel crossing but with a more difficult finish. We had to leave Rue Point on the southernmost tip of Rathlin near slack water. As the tidal stream running *into* the Irish Sea picked up in strength it would give us a partial lift towards the Scottish coast, but as we got near to Earadale Point on the Mull of Kintyre, the tide would reach its maximum strength and be running with a more southerly set of 4 knots or more, making it difficult to make the last few miles to Machrihanish. In a wind of any strength, this would create a very dangerous sea state. Hence my concern to beat the arrival of the wind. The alternative was hardly acceptable, for it would require us to drop off the tide to the southern tip of the Mull of Kintyre, giving us less of a fight but costing us another day's paddle to win back the lost ground.

In spite of our late start, we arrived at Rue Point at 1030, only ten minutes later than a best possible time. The sea was calm and the fog banks thickened and thinned to give visibility of anything between a kilometre and a mile. Hoping that the timings given in the weather forecast were reasonably accurate, we set off eastwards, leaving the Irish coast for the last time.

The plan was to ferry-glide the tide so that we stayed on a rhumb-line connecting Rue Point with Machrihanish. All was going well when, after two hours, the fog dispersed to give us a clear view of the hills on the Mull and back to Fair Head (on the Irish mainland). It was reassuring to see we were in our previously calculated positions. Meanwhile, although the air was still calm, a heavy groundswell was working in from the south. It was another example of the sea preceding the wind and we knew we were on borrowed time. As the swell had picked up into great, oily rollers, this had created problems for Richard. In the fog, with no visible horizon, the motion had made him queasy, and at the very moment the fog lifted, he had paddled over to me to express his disquiet and discomfort.

Leaning on my bow for support, he had been violently seasick. It was neither a good place nor a good time to be feeling ill.

"You'll be O.K. now we can see where we're going instead of looking down at the compass all the time!" I assured him.

Richard's pained and drained face did not show any great confidence in my assessment of the situation. Mick, in his usual phlegmatic manner, shrugged his shoulders but winked at me when Richard was no longer looking.

"Too much booze, that's your trouble," Mick said with a laugh. "Serves you bloody right!"

Richard, of course, did not see the funny side of Mick's joke and, while I did laugh, I was sincerely hoping that it was seasickness and that it would disappear now we had an horizon to relate to. If this were not the case, we were all going to be in trouble.

For the next hour we made steady progress towards the steep cliffs and hillsides that fall into the sea at Earadale Point. With about two miles to go before reaching the Point I began to feel ill at ease. The south-east-going tide was running very hard and *against* the swell, which was being kicked up to about 3 metres and was so steep-faced that we began to fear it would break. Quickly taken transits (a technique to judge one's speed and direction of movement by observing the apparent movement of one close and one distant fixed object) showed we were making no progress whatsoever towards our landfall at Machrihanish. Two options were worth considering: one was to stick it out and "mark time" until the tide slackened, which we could not risk because of the coming blow; the other was to abandon our rhumb-line and ferry-glide towards the cliffs, hoping to find slacker water near the shore. We *had* to try the latter.

The next two hours were hair-raising. Having run the gauntlet of what was in fact a giant tide race, near the coast we had to ensure we were not caught in the large shore-break. At one stage I was tempted to try a landing in an open cove, just to the south of Earadale Point, but on observing an extra large set of rollers collapse across the entire width of the little bay, we were immediately dissuaded from that course of action. There was nothing for it but to string out in single file (there was no point in all getting wiped out together) and force a passage of the Point. It was nerve-racking and required a carefully timed sprint for what seemed to be several minutes to make the necessary progress and avoid the frightening area of broken water. I was dry-mouthed with sweat dripping into my eyes by the time I cleared the Point, which turned out to be the worst of the hazards. The rest of the paddle was simply less frightening and we were mentally as well as physically drained as we turned the last set of reefs into Machrihanish Bay, where a good surf was building up.

By now it was 1610. Scattered rocks provided some shelter to the western end of Machrihanish and we were able to slip between them into the shelter of a little bay holding the ruins of a lifeboat station. We were dehydrated and the sudden release of tension made us suddenly aware of just how exhausted we were. We had but one thought, "Get out of the boats!" Normally we would have scouted for a campsite that was out of the way, but now we were no longer prepared to paddle one more stroke than necessary. Not far from the old lifeboat station stood a very large and prosperous-looking cottage which was set in a large lawn, one end of which had not been cut. There was also a seaweed-covered beach giving access to the lawn. It seemed too good to be true when the owner (Mrs Lyle-Barr) gave us permission to camp at the bottom of her garden.

Our sense of lethargy was absolute as we pitched camp in slow-motion. We had expected to experience intense elation on getting back to the British mainland with over 1,500 miles behind us, but it did not happen. Later on, it was easy to see that our traverse of the Irish coast (just 32 days for the 799 miles since leaving Whitesands) had taken a heavy toll on our nervous as well as our physical energy. We were puffy-eyed from prolonged lack of sleep. The lines round our eyes were picked out beautifully by their lack of sun and wind burn after so much squinting into the light reflected off the water. I had lost a stone in weight. Our looks had been aged by about five years that could be extended to ten years when we were caked in our daily ration of salt-crust!

Indeed, our appearance compared to when we had left home had altered a great deal

At Machrihanish in Kintyre after our crossing from Ireland.

more than we were aware. After more than three months away and continuous living out of doors we had tanned to a nut-brown around the face, neck and hands. Richard normally has very short, dark hair which had grown to a great curly mop, turned auburn by the sun. Mick's brown hair had been bleached fair and his face now sported a full, blond beard. My dark hair had some light ends and quite a few extra grey bits, while my moustache had been left untrimmed and become blond and walrus-like. I must confess that I had been too vain to let my beard grow when it demonstrated a determined inclination to sprout white!

That first evening at Machrihanish we were too lacking in objectivity (and possibly too tired) to understand why we were not feeling any elation. Mick summed up how we felt at the time when he casually remarked, "I'm tired and I'm pissed off living in wet, salty clothes."

In a similar manner we had not noticed the physical changes that had occurred in our appearance. It would take people who knew us from home to point these out.

What we in fact needed was a proper rest. Knowing we could not sustain our high-pressure momentum indefinitely, one had been planned into the trip, but it had been earmarked for when we would meet our friends, and that would not be until we got to Arisaig, about 130 miles north of us. Before leaving home I had estimated we would be there in the last week of July. It was now the 15th, so we phoned to say we would be at Arisaig on the 22nd of the month, just seven days away. It was a very optimistic estimate, particularly when the next weather forecast ruled out any possibility of paddling for the next few days. A south-westerly 5 was blowing within minutes of our landing and it was now forecast to become a full gale before veering to give a north-westerly gale later the next day.

Our two days trapped at Machrihanish did something to rest us physically but we could not afford to be idle. The first job was to get cleaned up and this task began early the next morning when we took a bath in a nearby stream. We then took all the clothes we were not wearing to the local pub (The Beachcomber Bar) where the daughter of the licensee had offered to put them through the pub's washing machine. She also gave me a lift into Campbeltown so that I could buy a completely new stock of food. It meant that when we left Machrihanish on 18th July our gear was in its best condition since leaving the Shannon.

The phone call home obliged us to reproduce our Irish-style work rate if we were to honour our commitment to reach Arisaig on time. At first it seemed almost impossible, but we would have two factors working in our favour. One was that the direct line northwards would keep us on the inner and therefore protected side of the mass of islands; the other was that the islands would be constricting and therefore accelerating the tidal streams to give us a faster speed over the ground. Thus, when the wind began to abate during the late evening on Thursday the 17th, it gave us sufficient time for the seas to subside and allow us away early the next day. We were up for 0600 to begin packing, but because Mrs Barr insisted we should have some extra breakfast before leaving, we did not launch until gone 0830.

It was a very cold day for July. A few spots of rain were falling from a cloudy sky, but the visibility was exceptionally good, so we could see the low island of Gigha, for which we now headed, even though it was 15 miles away. Passing Cara Island, we kept to the sheltered eastern side of Gigha, landing for a bum-rest and a bite to eat in the main crofting settlement of Ardminish Bay. We could not afford to waste the tide, so by 1320 we were off northwards again, paddling into the narrowing Sound of Jura, the scene now dominated by the hills of Islay and Jura while the islands themselves protected us from the Atlantic swells.

We continued to make good progress, even when the tide turned against us and the wind made an unexpected shift to the north-north-west. The Paps of Jura slowly receded astern and we moved close to the Kintyre shore to stay out of the worst of the tide. As afternoon passed into evening, the clouds thickened with the promise of yet more rain but our efforts were eased when, at about 2000, the wind dropped away. We would happily have stopped to camp, but with strong south-westerly winds forecast we could find no suitably sheltered campsite among the rocky inlets. The map suggested there would be numerous camping possibilities in the maze of channels and islands south of Carsaig, but they all proved too boggy and it was 2100 before we wearily stepped ashore in Carsaig Bay, having put a creditable 45 miles behind us.

The race was now on to establish camp and eat before the onset of darkness on this unpleasant, murky evening. Drizzle was already falling and after battling the wind all day, Sod's law ensured that there was a complete calm – a perfect combination heralding an assault of midges. One must expect to be plagued by these exasperating insects during a Highland summer. We had, therefore, included in our kit a "beany hat" with a fine-mesh net sewn around the brim, so that the enclosing cylinder of gauze could be tucked into clothing at the neck, rather like a narrow-brimmed bee-keeper's hat. Such a hat works well enough – but it is hardly a convenient form of headgear when trying to eat a meal! Notwithstanding these many discomforts, the campsite did produce for us an unexpected bonus. The occupants of another tent pitched nearby began questioning us about our equipment and on hearing about our journey felt it appropriate to press upon us a bottle of wine and a plateful of fresh strawberries. Once again it was nearly midnight before we had finished our meal and could turn in to get some rest.

There was still no change in the weather when we got up at 0615 the next morning. It was still drizzling, the Sound of Jura was perfectly calm, while the island itself was just visible below the low, featureless blanket of stratus cloud. It seemed sensible to dress in our wet paddling clothes and pack at full speed to be away for 0800. By 0915 we were paddling into Crinan Harbour, having put six miles behind us, along with the mist-shrouded slopes of the Knapdale Forest. We had no choice but to come into Crinan, for we needed to visit a chandler's. Somehow I had misplaced the maps and charts that would get us to Arisaig and I had been unable to find anything suitable in Campbeltown. A middle-aged lady was attending the chandler's shop as we walked in, still dressed in our wet paddling gear. As puddles formed around our feet, I began to realise that we were not quite her usual type of customer. Her face displayed a look that was a mixture of disgust and horror as I borrowed her scissors, knelt on the floor and cut the new chart up into manageable sections that I could tape into a plastic wallet.

This delay was a nuisance. We were determined to reach the Sound of Mull by the end of the day, so we now had to work extra hard to ensure we did not lose the tide. Once clear of the Crinan anchorage we were in an area that experiences some of the most powerful tidal streams in Britain. Just south of Dorus Mor we sped through the islets of Eilean na Cille on a tide race that spilled into a confusing mess of tide – standing waves, overfalls and boils – which carried us at high speed past Reisa Mhic Phaidean. To the west of us, in spite of the low cloud ceiling and heavy showers, we could see the gap between northern Jura and the island of Scarba. This was the Gulf of Corrievreckan, possibly the most spectacular tidal phenomenon in Britain. Here the tide flooding up the inside of Jura can be up to four feet higher than that in the open sea, only half a mile to the west, causing it to spill westwards through the gap in a huge tide race that can be turned back on itself in strong south-westerly winds to form a giant whirlpool known as "The Hag" and reputedly the second largest whirlpool in the world. Having experienced its adrenalin-producing qualities on a previous visit, today we were deliberately avoiding it!

A fresh wind from just west of south had sprung up just after we left Crinan, which was ideal for giving us yet further assistance as we negotiated the confined Sounds of Shuna and Seil. When the island of Luing began to fall astern, we paddled into what appeared to be the blind end of a Norwegian fjord, so narrow does the channel become between the island of Seil and the mainland.

By 1345 we had reached the sweeping, single arch of the Clachan Bridge (sometimes called "the Bridge over the Atlantic") and the sound had the appearance of a small river. The 18 miles from Crinan had taken 3½ hours but we only had about two hours of tide left to reach the Sound of Mull.

Clearing Seil, we came into the open water of the Firth of Lorn, finding ourselves fully exposed to the wind and squalls that were moving up from the south-west, setting up a moderate sea with a very short wavelength. Between the heavy showers

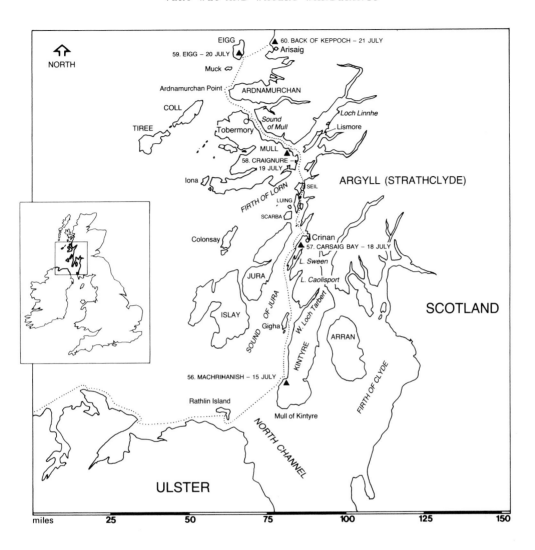

accompanying the squalls, our navigation was kept simple by taking a direct route to keep the distinctive entrance to Loch Spelve on our port bow, but as each squall hit, visibility was reduced to a few hundred metres and we judged our course by the wave pattern with only occasional glances at the compass. As Duart Point (on the Mull shore of the entrance to the Sound of Mull) came nearer, we could enjoy long surf rides that brought us just below the magnificent castle and through the tidal narrows by 1545. We had just beaten the tide.

One more hour of paddling saw us across Duart Bay and into the shelter of the small bay at Craignure. It was the old familiar story of being soaked, cold and ravenously hungry. Our reward was that we had 35 miles less to paddle, the luxury of a properly equipped campsite with easy access from the beach and the prospect of a long *dry* evening in the local pub.

Next morning, the wind had shifted to become a fresh north-westerly. It was the worst possible wind direction for a passage of the Sound of Mull. Knowing we had a long day ahead of us, we set off at 1015, before the tide had turned in our favour. Buffeted by the heavy showers, we made painfully difficult progress along the Mull shore and crossed to the mainland side where the Sound changes direction, thus cutting the corner and getting the best from the tide by Eileanan Glasa and Fiunary Rocks. At last we had turned off the wind a little, making progress easier and enabling us to cross to the Mull shore yet again, where we cut inside Calve Island to enter the harbour of Tobermory, overlooked by its picture-book rows of brightly painted buildings.

We were now a long way behind schedule because of the head wind. If we were to be sure of making Arisaig the next day we had to be prepared to paddle into the late evening, so while we had the chance, we bought a proper meal before setting off again at 1630. The immediate problem was to get round the swell-battered promontory of Ardnamurchan Point – the most westerly point of the British mainland and an area of rocky wilderness which guards the northern entrance to the Sound of Mull. In the fresh wind that had now backed to south of west, a heavy swell was running into the rocky headland and reflecting back to produce clapping seas. We had anticipated a grim time here, so it came as a pleasant surprise when the cloud broke sufficiently between the showers to allow low-angled crepuscular rays of sunlight to filter through. This created a dramatic seascape dominated by the tall tower of the lighthouse, standing out starkly against the backdrop of dark rainclouds. From here we could run directly off the wind and swell towards the Isle of Eigg, about 10 miles away.

Although it had been an arduous day we were able to enjoy the next couple of hours. It felt good to be in familiar waters and, as I caught occasional glimpses of Muck and Rhum between showers, it brought back a flood of happy paddling memories. The real interest, however, was generated by our becoming involved in a strange race.

A yacht had rounded Ardnamurchan shortly after us and it was soon evident that its course was the same as our own. Flying "goose-winged" before the wind, it could make very little progress in overtaking us because we were frequently surfing on the sizeable swells. Our amusement was provided by trying to hold her off from overtaking us for as long as possible. We had started with a lead of about a mile and it took about 1½ hours for the yacht to draw level. In a shouted conversation the skipper expressed his surprise at encountering us at all on such a wild evening, but he was even more impressed by the speed at which we had been travelling. It also earned us a reward, for, having established that we were all heading for the anchorage at Galmisdale on the south-eastern corner of Eigg, we were invited to join them on board for a drink when we arrived.

It was 2130 when we at last came inside the island of Eilean Chathastail to enter the shelter of the natural harbour. The yacht was still not anchored, having had to manoeuvre more cautiously than we had in the confined channel approaching the anchorage. We had covered another 23 miles since leaving Tobermory. Now that we had arrived we were soon beginning to chill and so we wasted no time in disembarking at the slip and erecting our tent opposite the estate office. It was a site where we would normally have sought permission to camp, but the lateness of the hour and the unthinkable possibility of a refusal prompted us to abandon such niceties. The invitation we had been given did nothing to improve our sense of propriety.

Forgoing our evening meal, we changed into dry clothes, returned to the slip and hailed the yacht to get ferried aboard. The tiny tender had barely sufficient free-board once we were all seated to begin the row back. I remember thinking that we were probably more at risk then than at any time during the day's paddle. But the row back to the shore was to be even more dangerous. It took place three hours later; it was a dark night because of the cloud and we had seen off our hosts' bottle of whisky on empty stomachs. We may have had the gall to drink them dry, but had not been so rude as to reveal our hunger. It meant that when we got back to our tent we found ourselves cooking a large pot of porridge at 0130!

By 0630 we were up again for the last leg of our paddle to Arisaig, now only about 10 miles off. It was another cold morning with heavy showers but at least we knew that it would be the last time for a few days that we would have to dress in wet clothes and pack in the rain. Our only anxiety was caused by the late shipping forecast which had predicted that our south-westerly wind was soon to become a F7 westerly.

Shortly before 0900 we paddled over to our friendly yachtsmen to bid them farewell. None of them were up, however, so we immediately set course for the Back of Keppoch – a peninsula protected by a complex of islets and rocks to the north of Arisaig village, where I knew of a campsite that would make us welcome. We were already in good spirits when the sun broke through the cloud to add to our cheer. It treated us to a fine view of the distinctive and precipitous miniature mountain known as the Sgurr of Eigg – a veritable cockscomb of columnar pitchstone porphyry which dominates the island and is one of the great landmarks of the Inner Hebrides. Between showers, we were also able to enjoy fine views of Rhum – Eigg's even more spectacular neighbour.

Our paddle was relatively fast and without incident. Thankfully, the swell of the previous evening had dropped off, enabling us to negotiate the complex reefs off the Back of Keppoch without problems. At 1125 we ran our boats onto the narrow cove of silver sand that faces west from "The Croft" campsite. It was Monday 21st July and we had covered the 131 miles from Machrihanish in under 3½ days. Having kept our tryst with a day to spare we could enjoy the novel prospect of a prolonged and proper rest.

11

Reflections, Reunions and Rest
Arisaig – Inverguseran

It was our arrival at the Back of Keppoch that produced the euphoria we had been expecting at Machrihanish. Our mental attitude was completely different from that which we had experienced on that dull evening when we had first stepped ashore in Scotland, for now we were finishing an easy day, we were less tired and we had focused our minds on the positive.

By dead-reckoning, we had paddled 1,647 miles since leaving home. This was considerably less than I had originally allowed for and was a testimony to the extent to which we had taken on both more and longer open crossings. More to the point, it meant that we had about 1,000 miles of paddling left in front of us and while under normal circumstances this would sound a daunting prospect, after what we had already done it did not sound too bad – particularly if we said it fast!

We were also inside what one might call our "best-projected schedule". Given that we had done so badly in May, this was quite surprising. Had we enjoyed very good weather in those early weeks, it was theoretically possible that we could have reached Whitesands ten days before our actual arrival, thus enabling us to tackle the St. George's Channel crossing on the cycle of neap tides around the beginning instead of the middle of June. This scenario also presumed that we would have the right weather for the crossing itself.

Had this happened, however, and had we taken the six weeks we had allowed to get round Ireland, plus a week to get up to Arisaig (instead of 3½ days), then we would still have expected to arrive at Arisaig in the last week of July.

The lesson to be learned from us now being ahead of that schedule is both edifying and unusual. All my previous experience, backed by what I had been told by other long-distance sea paddlers like Geoff Hunter, had suggested that a good overall average distance for a day's paddle is about 20 miles. When we had met up with Geoff at Whitesands our overall average after 50 days from home was a miserable 14+ miles. This was due to the exceptionally poor weather we had suffered and at the time we had cursed our luck. But on analysing how we came to arrive at Arisaig when we did, that same period of wretched weather may have in fact been doing us a great favour.

We had only been able to paddle for 28 days of our first 50 away from home; even then we had felt forced to push our luck by taking on very marginal conditions. We had also taken on bigger distances than we had wanted in order to compensate for the lost time. The average length of our actual paddling days had therefore been about

The view from the Arisaig camp, towards Eigg and Rhum.

Partying on the beach at Arisaig.

25 miles. When we left Wales we knew we had to take advantage of any reasonable weather. The result had been that we had made an overall average of over 24 miles per day since seeing Geoff, achieved by pushing up our average day's paddle to exactly 30 miles. Having maintained that level of work rate for just over five weeks, we had good reason to feel pleased.

It is not hard to imagine less technical reasons for our morale reaching a high at this time. We were confident that the worst was behind us. Being back on the mainland meant we would be able to replace broken equipment more easily if the need should arise. Most of all, we were looking forward to seeing faces from home.

When we arrived in the cove at the Back of Keppoch we were confronted with the prospect of a long carry, for it was low water and we were approaching spring tides. However, from a grassy hillock overlooking the beach, a lone figure had been watching every move of our arrival. He now walked over to introduce himself as Tony Campbell, an art lecturer from near Dundee. We gladly accepted his offer to help carry our boats up to the main site and were even more pleased when his wife Alison emerged from their tent to present us with coffee and biscuits.

The weather also responded to the occasion. The showers had died away and from time to time we were treated to periods of sunshine. In a short while the camp fence was festooned with the fluttering pennants of our drying gear. The other campers looked on in astonishment at the mounds of equipment that were being pulled from the depths of our boats. Having used the site as a base for previous visits to the Small Isles, it was reassuring to know that the MacMillan family who owned the site would tolerate our peculiar ways which, for a short time at least, would turn our corner of the field into a good imitation of a gypsy encampment.

The Campbells had their own newly purchased sea kayaks with them and took great interest in every item of equipment we were carrying. We answered the many questions as best we could and in return received regular supplies of hot drinks. By late afternoon we had managed to get most of our gear dry, had cleaned ourselves up and dug out clean clothes for the occasion. It was then time to take up the Campbells' offer of a lift into Arisaig so that we could buy some supplies. We needed little persuading to retire to the hotel afterwards for a few beers, and it was here that the girls from home found us a couple of hours later.

Richard's Mandy had driven up with Sue. They were going to spend a few days with us before the rest of our club friends descended on us the next weekend. We had not seen Mandy since Clovelly; Sue had visited us in Pembrokeshire while we were stuck at Dale. In our original planning she was to have joined us here to paddle around Scotland, but the ankle injury that had stopped our D.–W. training had also cost her the fitness she would need for the next leg of our journey. There was so much news and so many stories to exchange that the evening passed all too quickly.

The rain returned in the late evening and stayed with us throughout the next day. It was also very cold, but the weather no longer seemed so important now that we had company from home.

Wednesday 23rd July was the day of the Arisaig Highland Games. During the morning we walked into the village to see a Highland Wildlife Art Exhibition before going to visit the games. The weather improved during the late morning and we spent a very pleasant afternoon. Sprawled beneath a tree in the sun, pints in hand, we watched impressive feats of strength in the "heavy" games and dancers whirling in competition to the skirl of the pipes. That evening, back at the campsite, we had a barbecue on the beach before visiting the pub and a wild ceilidh in the village hall. Just after midnight, we left the dance to walk back to the camp along the famous "Road to the Isles". A full moon was shining in a cloudless sky, so pale that only the brightest stars showed. The northern horizon was still bright from the Arctic sun. There was not a breath of wind.

Sue and Mandy's visit passed all too quickly and on Friday morning the girls packed the little black "Mini" to travel south for the rest of their holiday. The wretched weather matched our mood, so we decided to concentrate our misery and get all our washing out of the way. Everything we were not wearing went through the washing machine of a nearby campsite that boasted a proper laundry. It also made us determined not to spend another inactive and purposeless day, so we resolved to spend Saturday riding the West Highland Railway into Fort William.

This we duly did and it proved to be an experience that we would recommend to anyone. There can be few railway lines anywhere on earth that run through such a concentration of contrasting and wonderful scenery. Between Mallaig and Arisaig the line passes Morar, where the white sand coves and turquoise waters look out to the spectacular seascape of the Small Isles and Skye. Climbing to cut inland, the line leaves Arisaig to run through luxuriantly wooded glens of natural forest before emerging into the austere beauty of classic Highland scenery – rock, heather, cascading burns and steep, bare mountainside.

Late that Saturday evening Bev arrived, bringing with her yet more heavy rain. She was followed by Ian Bourn and the rest of our club visitors during Sunday morning and our corner of the campsite was taken over as a village of expedition tents sprang up, set within a laager of sea kayaks. We were swamped by deliveries of food parcels and, as the sun came out, we settled down to enjoy the luxury of being thoroughly spoiled. A barbecue on a grand scale was prepared around us as the day became an extended feast of eating and drinking.

The party atmosphere was sustained through to the following Monday. For three of us it was our hundredth day away from home and the others needed no persuasion to share in the occasion. We drove into Mallaig to stock our boats for the journey north. This inevitably included a visit to the pub and on the return journey to the campsite the mood was right for a mass bathe in the falls of Loch Morar. The rest of the afternoon was spent in preparing our gear for our departure on Tuesday, before yet another barbecue. As the evening wore on, we sat on the beach around a bonfire of fish boxes. Beyond the dark silhouettes of Rhum and Skye the sun set in a calm sea, reflecting the vivid hues of a copper, pink and orange sky.

It was a very different team that set off from the Back of Keppoch to the one that arrived on 21st July, for Bev would be paddling with us until we got to the east coast, and five other friends were going to paddle north in our company to our next camp.

Our flotilla of nine kayaks crashing through choppy waters in the Sound of Sleat. Photo: Ian Bourn.

Because Wild Water had replaced our worn-out cags and spray-decks we looked different. But the main change was in our attitude to what we were doing.

Properly rested, we had considered the paddle still ahead of us with a cold objectivity. The uncompromising approach that had seen us around Ireland was probably inappropriate and as yet impossible to repeat. Our intention was therefore to treat the remainder of the Scottish west and north coasts as a "holiday" – we would resort to our more usual form of sea paddling, allowing ourselves time to look at points of special interest, camping at the end of each day with sufficient time to get properly established and with the intention of cooking on open fires. Having Beverley with us would force us to adopt a more leisurely pace and abandon our ruthless obsession with covering big mileages. In the long run, we thought this would allow us to face the less interesting east coast with a positive mental attitude when we were hungry for miles and this would see us all the way home.

A large gathering of well-wishers turned out to see us off. Our stay at The Croft had aroused the interest of many campers and the MacMillans would accept no payment for our very intrusive stay on their property. It was about 0945 when we eventually paddled out of the shelter of the numerous rocks to hit a fresh northerly head wind. This was whipping up the Sound of Sleat into an annoyingly short, choppy sea that ensured we were soon soaked through. With fully loaded boats we were having to work very hard to keep up with our relatively lightly laden companions who had mistakenly expected our fitness-level would allow us to pull away from them. The weight of our boats ensured that we had to crash through the waves that they easily bobbed over.

A hard pull saw us past Mallaig and Loch Nevis. We stopped for lunch just south of An Fhaochag, where a tricky landing in the rocks gave us access to a steep beach piled high with fish-box driftwood. Out of the wind, we built a huge fire to warm us up and to get dry. By the time we left we were having to fight the tide, but at least the wind had backed from being straight onto our bow and Bev was treated to a close encounter with an inquisitive otter.

After passing the picturesque hamlet at Airor we decided we had best cut our losses for the day. Accepting that the head wind was a cruel fact of life that was not likely to go away, we began looking for a suitable campsite.

We were now traversing the coast of the rugged wilderness known as the Knoydart peninsula. Where the river draining Glen Guiserein meets the Sound of Sleat it flows between stony banks of pebbles which give access to level pastures stepped in well-defined terraces. It was here, amid ruins overlooked by the isolated sheep station of Inverguseran, that we set up our encampment. There was plentiful driftwood to fuel our fire for our last evening spent with friends from home. As darkness settled, we were joined at our fire by the tenant of the sheep station. He kept us enthralled by the explanations of his unusual life in this very isolated spot. His account of problems caused by foxes and golden eagles were a refreshing reminder that at least some parts of our island still offer a truly rural existence to a man prepared to face a hard and lonely life.

12

Highlands and Islands Holiday

Inverguseran – Helmsdale: 30th July – 17th August

We said farewell to Ian and the lads at about 0830. We had both enjoyed and benefited from their company, but now I made a point of not looking back as under grey skies our four kayaks were being carried north-east on the tide flooding into the narrowing Sound of Sleat. The entrance to the great sea loch of Hourn (with its views of gloomy peaks) was soon astern, and with an entourage of friendly seals, we ran through the scattering of rocky islets known as the Sandaig Islands. To the west of us the Isle of Skye was slowly crowding in on us. Reaching Glenelg, the mainland shore sweeps in an arc to the west and so forms the narrow channel which gives the shortest of the ferry crossings to Skye. This is Kyle Rhea – the tidal narrows which are overlooked by high ground on both sides and connect the Sound with Loch Alsh, about two miles to the north-east.

Our passage of Kyle Rhea was without incident. A neap tide and absence of wind combined to produce nothing more than oily boils, swirls and a few small waves in mid-channel. It was certainly not what we were expecting. The Admiralty publication, *West Coast of Scotland Pilot*, reports regular spring tides of 6–7 knots and recounts how, during a period of melting snow in the Spring of 1943, H.M. Surveying Ship *Scott* could make no headway against the north-flowing stream when steaming at 12 knots!

Crossing Loch Alsh in a perfect calm, just after midday we arrived at Kyle of Lochalsh and landed at a run-down Ministry of Defence slip amid unsightly piles of scrap and rubbish. The rain set in shortly afterwards and we took an extended lunch break to buy some fresh meat (while it was still available) and eat a sausage-and-chips lunch in what we all agreed was an exceptionally grotty café.

When we set off north again to cross Loch Carron and reach the Crowlin Islands, low cloud hid the mountains from view and heavy rain danced in high-spouting splashes from the calm surface of the water. The rain slowly eased and on the eastern shore of the main island we stopped by a burn to fill our water bottles, during which time a fresh north-easterly breeze blew up. This being Bev's first day with us she was beginning to feel it. To ease her efforts we set off towards the more sheltered water of the mainland shore and shortly afterwards we saw a lone white kayak which we decided to intercept. The occupant introduced himself as Graham Almack and told us he was attempting a solo circumnavigation of the British mainland, having set out from the Solway Firth 18 days earlier. We would have been happy to share our company and food for the evening but he seemed reluctant to socialise, and quickly made his way ashore to remove himself from us. We did not see Graham again, although we were to follow his progress with great interest.

Before reaching Applecross we came to Ard Bhan – a small promontory which presented us with a shell-sand beach backed by a bank of sweet turf. It would offer protection from the strong northerly winds which had been forecast, so we stopped to camp in spite of the early hour. No sooner had we established ourselves and cooked a hurried meal in the lee of a wall than the rain set in for the evening.

We woke next morning to a wild day. Rain was driving in sheets before a strong north-easterly wind which whipped a grey sea into ranks of white horses. Between the squalls we caught glimpses of the symmetrical, volcano-like cones of Skye's Red Cuillin, visible across the Inner Sound along with the island of Raasay. But it did not matter. Being "on holiday" meant we need feel no guilt in not trying to press on.

Instead, when the showers became less frequent, we explored the narrow neck of land on which we had camped and its adjoining shoreline, causing Mick and Richard to stumble across another otter. Later, we went for a long walk into the local crofting settlement of Camusterrach and scrounged a lift into Applecross. This proved most fortuitous, for it led to a meeting in the Post Office with the Warden of Applecross House (a residential centre for the Drake Fellowship*) and we spent an enjoyable evening as his guest.

The next day we were able to press on again. By late morning the sun was shining and we could paddle without cags into a gentle northerly breeze. These conditions gave us exceptional views into the hills of Applecross and out to Raasay and Rona. When we stopped for lunch just south of the entrance to outer Loch Torridon, the panorama had improved even further, for beyond the north-eastern headlands of Skye were the distant hills of the Outer Hebrides.

As always, when stopping in such idyllic surroundings the temptation to cut short the paddling day and camp was very strong. A poor shipping forecast forced us to be more objective, however, and it was confirmed shortly afterwards when the sky was rapidly invaded by high cloud streaming up from the south. When the sun's strength became dissipated behind a veil of milky cloud, the beach lost much of its colour and attraction and we steeled ourselves to move on across the mouth of Loch Torridon with its fine views of the mountains of Liathach and Beinn Alligin. A chill north-easterly wind freshened quickly during our crossing, so by the time we had reached Red Point on the far side, we were finding the going increasingly difficult.

The paddle along the southern shore of Loch Gairloch became one of plodding drudgery into the full force of the wind and a short sea that ensured we were soon soaked. Conditions were particularly arduous for Bev. She was considerably disadvantaged in having to respond to the general pressure to keep up with our level of paddling fitness, as well as having to paddle her Anas Acuta which was a slower boat and not fitted with a rudder. We were all pleased to tuck in behind Eilean Horrisdale to the sheltered anchorage and village of Badachro to make camp. If get stuck we must (and this was a strong likelihood in view of the forecast), it was one of

---

* The Drake Fellowship is now called the Fairbridge Drake Society; it is a registered charity which provides residential outdoor opportunities for disadvantaged young people from the inner cities.

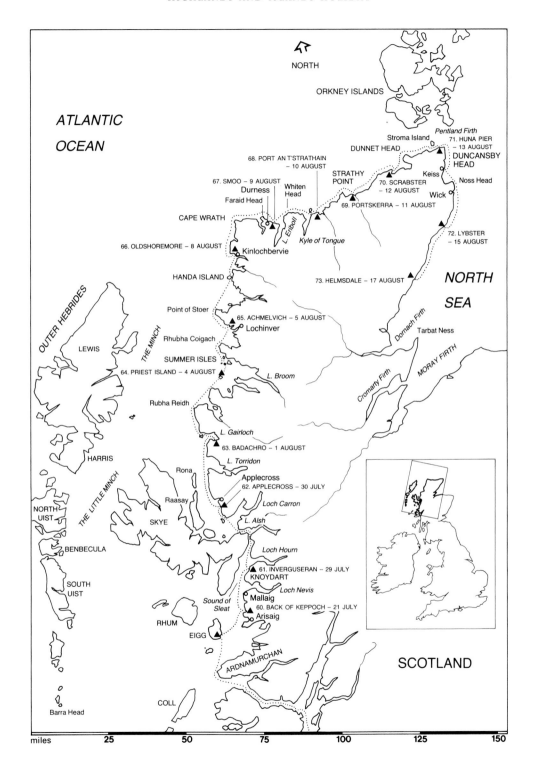

the better places on the north-west coast to be. Having sampled the pleasures of the Badachro Inn on a previous visit, I must confess its attractions had figured highly in my assessment of the options open to us!

During the night the wind came in blasting gusts between ominous calms. Lying in my sleeping-bag, I could hear it rushing and roaring along the loch shore like an express train. It would hit the tent with a great shudder that shook everything, then rush on into the distance, the night and the next silence. Whilst the weather kept us at Badachro on Saturday 2nd August, it was the consequences of Richard's over-indulgence during our incarceration that prolonged our stay through the Sunday. He lay in the tent in silent despair, having gone beyond the stage where he could put a brave face on his self-inflicted suffering and ignoring the occasional tirade of cruel jibes that we threw in for good measure. Meanwhile Bev, Mick and I soaked up the sun, walked into Port Henderson and took to our boats to fish for mackerel. The evening was a particularly fine one and, in keeping with the holiday spirit, we spoiled ourselves with a barbecued beef joint.

When we paddled north from Badachro we cut inside Longa Island and found ourselves on a section of coast boasting numerous caves, stacks and arches. We were about to traverse the great headland of Rubha Reidh where the coast takes a distinctive trend to the east. It was unrealistic to attempt its passage without a favourable tide so we stopped to kill time and eat a late lunch until the tide had turned in our favour. Later in the afternoon we turned the head below the lighthouse to cut across the mouth of Loch Ewe towards Greenstone Point in what can only be described as superb conditions.

The wind had disappeared completely to produce an oily, northerly swell; late afternoon sun bathed us in its warmth and light, picking out the coastal detail and accentuating the contrast with the dark, sombre skies to landward, the calm conditions enabling us to see the large number of porpoises that were swimming around us. Most of them would almost certainly have remained hidden from us if there had been any sea running.

Once clear of Greenstone Point we headed directly for the Summer Isles, arriving at Priest Island (31 miles on from Badachro) in the late evening. It was a wild place of craggy cliffs and boulder beaches that made landing awkward on the west-facing shore. A deep gash in the low cliffs offered the only weakness in its defences and this provided a corridor of access followed by a steep gradient. It gave an awkward boat-carry to a level hinterland of small boulders, partly grown over by wispy grasses and overlooking a lochan dammed back by an ancient storm-beach. The island is uninhabited, but a ruined wall bore testimony to its past occupation and now made a suitable hearth for our cooking fire.

The awkward landing made an even more difficult launching point on Tuesday. We eventually set off under overcast skies in mid-morning, although the cloud ended in a distinct line only a few miles to the west of us, bathing the Western Isles in bright sunshine. Hopefully, we would be getting the same conditions later.

Priest Island behind us, we paddled into the heart of the Summer Isles. They are low-lying, very rugged and almost devoid of easy landing spots. After passing between Tanera Mor and Tanera Beg we found a beach on Isle Ristol where we could stretch

[ABOVE] Approaching Priest Island, the most westerly of the Summer Isles, the largely uninhabited group near the entrance to Loch Broom. [BELOW] In the rugged heart of the Summer Isles.

our legs before paddling up the narrow channel that leads into the natural harbour of Old Dornie. Shortly afterwards we landed at Reiff Sands and ate our lunch.

About mid-afternoon we forced ourselves to leave, just as the cloud edge at last cleared us. This was a real bonus, for the next few miles of coast ranked as being the most spectacular we had paddled in the entire expedition. Turning the cliffs on the headland of Rubha Coigach the views across Enard Bay to the mountains of Sutherland and the Inverpolly Forest were magnificent. Mesa-like, the mountains rise in classic shapes from the surrounding wilderness of scoured gneiss. The scene was dominated by the pillar and ridge of Suilven, with the quartzite screes of Canisp glistening just beyond. Further south rose the darker masses of Cul Mor, Cul Beag, Stac Pollaidh and finally Ben Mor Coigach.

As we crossed the bay towards Assynt and Loch Inver the sea was virtually calm. It enabled us to paddle without thinking, concentrating the senses on absorbing the surroundings. Having attempted to take in the magnitude of the whole, attention to detail was no less rewarding. The scene was in a constant state of transition, for as the sun moved on its westward arc and we paddled on to change our view point, so the purples, mauves and browns made subtle shifts of hue. We indulged ourselves in a photographic extravaganza.

We had already decided during our lunch break that we would stop early; the forecast was for an easterly gale and we would be better off if we camped on a west-facing coast before turning the Point of Stoer. Accordingly we turned into Achmelvich Bay where a white beach faced north to offer the option of using a commercial campsite. It was certainly a wonderful spot but spoiled by over-development and too many other campers for our taste. We opted to paddle a little further over clear, green waters to a west-facing crescent of sand. This led to a small terrace of turf beside a steep burn and offered a perfect site with an outlook to the Minch and Lewis.

We did not try to move the next morning because of the dreadful forecast, but as the day wore on, we continued to remain in sunshine and the south-easterly breeze became fresh, but no stronger. This was a lost opportunity in paddling terms but once again it was a beautiful spot in which to waste time. In fact, the gales saved themselves for the next day, although thankfully there was little rain and the steep hillside protected us from the worst of the wind.

Friday 8th August gave us yet another fine paddle. On a clear morning with only a light north-westerly breeze we were away by 0815 to use the spring tide flooding round the Point of Stoer. To avoid the tide race, we stayed close beneath the lighthouse and stayed well in to look at the sensational 200-foot sea stack known as the Old Man of Stoer (a name aptly taken from the Norse "Staurr", meaning Stake) but avoiding the breakers that seethed along its foot in spite of the good conditions.

From the stack we headed north-east across the open bay to the nature reserve at Handa Island, about nine miles off. Here we stopped on the beach on the south-eastern corner and whilst eating lunch admired the aerobatic dog-fights of both arctic and great skuas as they forced their victims to disgorge their hard-won food. The paddle through the Sound of Handa gave canoeing of a completely different character, for we now found ourselves hemmed in and had to weave our way through a maze of skerries opposite Port of Tarbet.

Passing the Old Man of Stoer.

About 1715 that evening we paddled up Loch Clash into the fishing port of Kinloch-bervie, with the intention of picking up fresh supplies. The store had closed 15 minutes earlier but the local postmaster took pity on us and gave me a lift to the shop in the next village, just as that closed too! We resigned ourselves to having a frustrating ending to an otherwise good day, but all was not quite lost. As we were about to walk back to our boats a mobile shop pulled up next to us and we were able to purchase enough fresh food to see us through the next week. We had been similarly fortunate in Badachro, so any would-be travellers in the north-west would do well to take account of such shopping facilities.

Having bought the food we needed we had a more immediate problem to solve: there was nowhere to camp. At 1830 we set off again and found an ideal site at Oldshoremore, where King Hakon began his invasion of Scotland in 1263. Ringed by green and rocky hills it has a tiny natural harbour among the rocks with an old slip. Trapped in a triangle of land between the peaty river and the beach is an area of rabbit-infested sweet turf where we could set up camp. The burn had some large pools offering us a chance to bathe, there was an ample supply of old fish boxes to provide a cooking fire and we kept the sun until late in the evening. It was a splendid situation in which to spend our last night's camp on Britain's western seaboard.

Cape Wrath! An evocative name if ever there was one. It conjures up images of stormy seas, and no wonder: one glance at the map will show that it is fully exposed to the North Atlantic storm track and catches all winds in a northern arc between south-west and south-east. Yet the name has nothing to do with such phenomena. It is derived from the Norse, "*Hvarf*", meaning "turning-point", and is in fact a reminder that in the early Middle Ages it was on the regular longship routes, linking the Viking bases in the Orkneys with their settlements along the west coast.

Whether our ancestors saw it as an everyday hazard or not I do not know, but its passage in a small craft has to be treated with respect. It is a place of confused tides as well as winds, so sea conditions are likely to be unpredictable and settled weather is an advised ingredient for a safe passage by sea kayak.

In this sense we were extremely lucky. The morning of Saturday 9th August dawned clear and calm. Once the sun had cleared the hilltop, our main problem when trying to get away from Oldshoremore was avoiding being eaten by the midges. But the forecast was a deteriorating one and as soon as we launched (at about 0845) a sheet of cloud raced in from the west. Undeterred, we set off to make full use of the spring tide and made fast time through a little race between Eilean an Roin Mor and the mainland. Once clear of here we had no more shelter and were committed to rounding the Cape, now looking less than inviting under a dark and threatening squall.

At the southern end of the great sweep of sands known as Sandwood Bay we passed the impressive sea stack of Am Buachaille, but kept well off shore to get the most from the tide. From here, our intention was to keep out to sea, hoping in this way to avoid the worst of the turbulence that would be caused at the foot of the Cape, where the east-going flood tide would collide with a west-going eddy current that runs along the north-facing shore. Just over two hours after leaving we entered an area of confused

Negotiating the Atlantic swells off Cape Wrath.

but lazy swells about two miles north-west of the Cape. My theory was about to be put to the test as we set a course due east.

Wind was minimal. We ran through a long series of overfalls when north of the lighthouse that tops the high Torridonian cliffs, all the time expecting the going to get worse. But it never did. Travelling "over the ground" at well over 6 knots, we did not want to waste our good fortune and kept out in the tide until off Balnakeil Bay. The tide was now slackening so we headed straight for Faraid Head with its rocks and islets. We were beginning to feel the effects of dehydration – no doubt exaggerated by a degree of nervous tension – but the north-easterly swell we were now in denied us anywhere to land for a break. When we reached Durness a moderate surf was running. We pushed on a little further to the steep-sided and narrow inlet or "geo" at Smoo.

This very unusual coast requires further description. The cliffs in this part of Sutherland are comprised of deep beds of limestone. They form a headland at Durness which was known to the Vikings as "*Dyra Ness*", (meaning "Cape of Beasts" or "Wolf Cape") and the name is a grim reminder that Sutherland was plagued by wolves in these times. The "geo" at Smoo is a classic limestone gorge that has been invaded by the sea. At its landward end is a great open cave system where the Allt Smoo disgorges its peat-stained underground river. It was here that we hauled out our boats nearly six hours on from leaving Oldshoremore and, after eating some lunch, we set up camp a few metres from the cave entrance.

It was to take us another three days to traverse Sutherland's north coast and get to Scrabster, from where we would have to tackle the Pentland Firth. Each of these three days was similar in character. The weather tended to be fine and sunny but we could not help wondering what we had done to upset the god of wind. During each morning a most annoying easterly breeze built up to frustrate our progress; each day we had to stop early because either the tide or the groundswell denied us easily accessible landings; each day we were impressed by the fine scenery – completely different in character from the west.

Leaving Smoo on a superb summer morning, we cut across Loch Eriboll to the cliffs of Whiten Head, where we were slowed by a stiff easterly breeze. Pushing on, we put the Rabbit Islands and then Kyle of Tongue behind us. Around lunchtime we were exploring the caves and arches sculptured in the pudding-stone of Eilean nan Ron when the wind strengthened even more, encouraging us to seek shelter and a break in the sandy cove at Port an t'Strathain.

By the time we had finished eating there was very little favourable tide left. The prospect of battling tide and wind was hardly in keeping with our "holiday" pact. Besides, we did not want to reach the Pentland Firth before the neap tides due around the 13th/14th August. So we set up camp where we were and had just got established when we received a visit from the Gregory family who owned the holiday cottage overlooking the bay. They had their own general-purpose kayaks and were so enthusiastic about the natural wonders of neighbouring Ron that we agreed to set off early the next morning to pay a second visit. In the meantime we enjoyed a most pleasant camp. It was a sunny afternoon, the burn provided a bathing pool and when Bev took her boat out to fish, she returned with two mackerel to start our evening meal.

Our idyllic campsite in Port an t'Strathain.

The secret entrance to the inner sanctuary of Eilean nan Ron.

During the night the wind veered to the south-east, producing a calm sea between the cove and Ron when we set off for our "guided" visit to the island. Our imaginations had been fired by the Gregorys' description of a "secret" entrance to a hidden natural harbour that once served the abandoned settlement. It lived up to our expectations. We were taken through a cave that was navigable to small craft at half-tide or less and emerged in a tiny, open inner sanctuary, completely enclosed by steep walls of rock, but with path access to the ruins. We would never have suspected its existence had we not been taken there.

Leaving Ron, we set out for Neave Island and immediately found ourselves in a moderate north-westerly swell. Given that we had experienced over 24 hours of easterly winds this came as a surprise. I could only guess that it had been generated by some deep depression off Iceland or Greenland. Whatever the cause, it put a new complexion on the day's paddle, for our offshore wind was steepening the swell in the shallower water to produce an awkward shore-break. Getting ashore might now prove troublesome.

Before coping with this potential difficulty, we first had to tackle the immediate problem of getting past the low, rugged headland of Strathy Point. This juts out several miles into the tidal streams, producing a tide race and overfalls that we now had to run. The swells had been picking up all the time with the flooding tide and we were glad to find that the faster flow on the point took some of the steepness off them. We could now concentrate on getting ashore.

Melvich Bay offered us more than one possible option, the first being what the O.S. map showed as a natural harbour just east of Rubha Bhra. Having made this decision, we had only progressed a short distance when we were distracted by the appearance of some very large dorsal fins cutting through the wavetops just to seaward. We watched them for some time, speculating on their identification.

We had not reached Rubha Bhra when the tide turned and began to ebb against the run of the swell. It grew and steepened accordingly, creating an evil-looking break that surged over an offshore reef to our left and dissipated its remaining energy in a heaving mass of sloppy seas and gaping holes on the point itself – to our right. It was a situation that Mick, Richard and I had become accustomed to during our months in the west, so without consultation or any consideration for the fact that this was probably the worst sea Bev had been in, I set off into the "corridor" between the reef and the point.

Bev's notes on what followed bring the incident to life through fresh eyes.

. . . I was paddling with Mick. Bill and Richard were some way in front. I had been aware of the swell building up for some time. The others seemed to have a nonchalant – almost arrogant – attitude towards it that I found niggling because I found the swell unnerving.

. . . Suddenly I was aware of a large reef to our left on which the sea was breaking with disturbing force, causing turbulent water between it and the shore . . . Bill didn't appear to hesitate but went straight into the gap while Richard waited. By the time Mick and I arrived Bill was waving us on from 100m ahead and Richard set off. It was watching him that caused me a momentary loss of nerve. Feeling trapped and oblivious to all other considerations I simply wanted

"out"; but I was still in sufficient control to appreciate that the only "out" was the way ahead.

Since the swell was running away from me, Richard appeared to be going down an enormous slide. His boat and the distant figure of Bill gave it all a frightening scale. As the swell bore on, Richard disappeared from sight on the far side. It seemed an eternity before he reappeared. He was alarmingly tiny in comparison to the sea breaking on his left. I didn't say anything but Mick must have sensed my uneasiness.

"Would you like to go round the outside?" he asked. I declined and set off into the gap, feeling very vulnerable and warily glancing at the reef-break. When I forced myself to look back the swell was steep. I kept wondering if it was steep enough to break and bring down a bus-sized wall of water on top of me. But it just ran on and away.

At last I came level with a narrow gap in the rocks on the shore, providing an entrance to a sheltered lagoon. Bill and Richard were already weighing up where to get out. I said nothing but I could see and sense Bill had now realised it had been a frightening experience for me. When they helped me out of my boat I sat on a rock feeling completely drained of energy and emotion. I was almost nauseous and very close to tears . . .

This was a natural harbour with a proper slip. At the top was a large area of tall grass where we made our camp. It was comfortably hot in the sun as we walked to the main village of Portskerra to find a shop and supplement our lunch rations. The road gave us a good vantage point to look down on Melvich Bay. We were thankful we only had to speculate on the "epics" we might have encountered in trying to run the surf that was thundering into the beach at Bighouse, where the river enters the bay.

In the bay at Portskerra after the eventful paddle round Strathy Point.

During the early evening, as we approached low water, the swell died away and the local fishermen arrived at the slip to go out and fish for mackerel (which they would use to bait their lobster pots). They told us how they had watched our arrival and informed us that the shipping forecast for Icelandic waters would give us future warning of such swell conditions. We had learned that lesson the hard way!

The same fishermen returned in a little over an hour with an enormous haul. We were invited to help ourselves to any fish that we wanted, along with as many crabs as we might care to take from their main catch. It was another example of the many acts of spontaneous generosity that would gain in momentum as our nightly stops brought us into increasing contact with coastal settlements.

It was virtually calm and the sun was already climbing above the distant Ork-

Bev at Scrabster, showing the strain of our passage along the coast of North Scotland.

neys when we rose early the next morning. Breakfast over, I cooked the crabs we had been given whilst fighting off the massed squadrons of midges that emerged from the long grass as the air rapidly warmed. They were a great encouragement to get on the water quickly and by 1000 Portskerra was behind us and we were heading east for Scrabster, on Thurso Bay.

Long before we reached the hideous nuclear power plant at Dounreay we were punching into a fresh easterly head wind. We had seen nothing to match the power station's ugly appearance since leaving Milford Haven. Its impact amid so much natural and unspoiled beauty was quite profound. The Chernobyl disaster was still fresh in our minds as we attempted to come to terms with the wisdom that could justify Dounreay's visual intrusion on the environment. One did not need to be a chemist or ecologist to guess at its unseen impact. In the midst of our discussion along these lines, a great jet of steam blossomed in the station's main complex. The loudness of the blast made me physically jump and sent a shiver down my spine. I think we all paddled a little faster for the next few miles.

Like the day before, the north-westerly swell began to build as the tide picked up. It was more apparent off the rock ledges of Brims Ness where we crashed through some tidal turbulence. Then, after a long slog, at about 1400 we turned the craggy headland into Thurso Bay and entered a strangely quiet world as we left the wind-against-tide conditions behind us. Passing under the lighthouse tower, we entered the complex of harbour breakwaters at Scrabster, a busy ferry port serving the Northern Isles. We landed at a slip next to the Royal Mission for Deep Sea Fishermen and, having rinsed and hung out our paddling clothes, we went inside to treat ourselves to a "fry-up" lunch at a bargain price.

During the afternoon I went to see the Harbour Master. The visit was partly to sound out the possibility of accommodation (to no avail) but mainly to test my tidal planning for the Pentland Firth against his expert local knowledge. I was concerned about the sea state we might encounter as a result of the easterly air stream but the Harbour Master assured me that this would be preferable to running the Firth in north-westerly winds – which seemed the next most likely weather sequence. Accordingly we made our plans to leave the next morning.

Meanwhile, we went for a three-mile walk into Thurso to undertake a bulk-buy of food for the next leg of the journey. It was the first time we had been in a proper town since our short visit to Fort William. The economic impact of Dounreay was immediately apparent in this very prosperous little community. It was the best shopping centre we had been in since Plymouth and although the traffic was somewhat overwhelming, we welcomed the opportunity to purchase a number of delicatessen-type items which had been unavailable in the village stores we had usually shopped in.

Once back at Scrabster, we were faced with the problem of finding somewhere to stay and we were very pleased when the superintendent of the Fishermen's Mission offered us carpeted floor-space. Unashamed luxury! We had not slept with a roof over our heads since leaving Portnoo, over a month before.

What seafarer has not read or heard gripping sagas of the terrible sea conditions that are sometimes produced by the infamous Pentland Firth? Constricted by the complex of glacier-scoured islands that make up the Orkneys, the tides that flood and ebb round the British mainland's north-eastern cape to fill and empty the North Sea achieve exceptional rates of flow – around the Pentland Skerries about 10½ knots on spring tides. The results of such flow include awe-inspiring overfalls and notorious tide races such as the Merry Men of Mey. During storms these have an evil reputation and at their worst are reported to have been a serious proposition for the powerful warships of the British Grand Fleet that once used the island-locked waters of Scapa Flow as its main base. The problematic section of coast runs from Dunnet Head (the most northerly point of the British mainland) for about 15 miles eastwards to Duncansby Head, where the coastline makes a dramatic turn to the south.

The *Macmillan & Silk Cut Nautical Almanac* (Macmillan, London) sums up the serious nature of the passage in simple and direct terms:

> *Any yacht going through Pentland Firth, even in ideal conditions, must avoid Duncansby Race, Swilkie Race, and Merry Men of Mey. A safe passage depends on correct timing and positioning to avoid the worst races mentioned above, regular fixes to detect any dangerous set, and sufficient power to cope with the very strong tidal stream.*

When we set off from Scrabster in the late morning of 13th August, the fine weather of the previous three days had given way to scudding cloud and we had psyched ourselves up to expect almost anything. It was critical that I had made the right allowances for timing. One certain factor in our favour was that we were coming onto neap tides, although the weather forecast was far from ideal. It was blowing 18 knots from the south-east when I telephoned the Coastguard for a weather update and the wind was due to strengthen as the day progressed. Had it not been for the assurances given the previous day by the Harbour Master we would not have set out at all. But now we were committed.

In spite of the strong beam wind and choppy conditions in Thurso Bay, we made good time to arrive off the tall cliffs of Dunnet Head around noon. The tide was running hard and setting us off shore; at the last minute we had to paddle hard on a southerly heading to avoid being swept past, barely managing to make the lee of the point beneath the lighthouse. We needed some shelter to rest from the buffeting we were receiving from the wind, which was now gusting about gale force as it funnelled over and around the head. While resting we ate chocolate and watched the tidal turbulence in the races off shore, but we could ill afford to lose time, so were soon on the move again.

Between gusts, the wind was blowing F5–6 and we could not escape from it once we were on the eastern side of the head. It gnawed away at our strength and morale like a relentless animal and in desperation we decided to punch straight into it for a while to put us in the shelter of the north-facing shore. For Bev it was particularly hard going and it took us over 1½ hours of soul-destroying paddling to cover the short distance to the broken harbour at the cove of Ham, where we stopped to alleviate our misery. In the lee of the tumbled slabs that once made a breakwater we crouched to avoid the chilling winds, all the while brewing tea and making up bread rolls to fortify ourselves for the next leg.

With only two hours of fair tide left us, we set off once more at 1500. Our progress had already been slowed to the extent that I knew we had lost our chance of turning Duncansby Head. The important thing now was to make sure we used the tail end of the present flood tide to take us past St. John's Point where we would have to run the Merry Men of Mey.

This race extends right across the Firth to the island of Hoy, making it unavoidable. The best we could do was catch it when it was *least* violent. Arriving there in the last hour of the east-going tide, it was a great anticlimax. I had spent most of the day wondering what we would meet here so it came as a strange sort of disappointment not to be frightened. It was simply "another tide race". Bev was able to take a camera out as we bounced through. Her attempt to get some photographs was frustrated by the grey skies and poor light conditions rather than an intimidating sea state.

With the tide about to turn against us, we began to search for somewhere to camp. Beating into the wind we managed to land on a new slip at Gills Bay, but there was nowhere to set up a tent to bivouac and we reluctantly returned to our boats. The wind had made it a particularly tough day for all of us and Bev was having to dig into her inner resources to keep going when we launched for the last time.

About two miles further on we came to an old lifeboat station at Huna Pier, only a couple of miles short of John o'Groats. Once ashore we were determined to camp and had to set up on a narrow piece of rough ground, sandwiched between the low cliffs and the store shed of a builder's yard. These were very "seedy" surroundings in

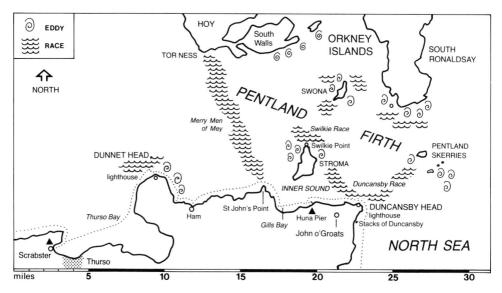

The tidal streams of the Pentland Firth.

comparison to what we had come to take for granted in the past few weeks, but we still had a very fine view of the Orkneys.

In real terms, the 20 miles we had made that day were among the potentially most technical of the expedition. However, we only began to appreciate the satisfaction of putting this behind us as the paddling aches began to ease, and we appeased our ravenous appetites with half a large billie of white crabmeat, followed by pork chops grilled on an open fire.

Thanks to a misleading weather forecast, we failed to move the next day. It was raining and blowing hard at dawn and the forecast I got from the Coastguard did not anticipate any real improvement until the late afternoon. We needed to get away around 1300 if we were to sneak round Duncansby Head just after low-water slack, before the tide picked up. But this would still mean a rough sea because of the high wind, so the day was written off.

The morning was spent confined to the tent, but about lunchtime the rain stopped and clear skies approached from the west. This prompted us to walk the coast to Duncansby Head, in order to observe for ourselves where the worst tidal conditions occurred. Before we got to the headland the wind dropped to nothing and gave us a sunny, calm afternoon to wander the cliff-tops and mentally note the areas of potential difficulty. We could see clearly into the heart of Scapa Flow and the Orkneys, and as the tide picked up in speed, some of the white water reached impressive proportions. Interesting and informative as this was, it was also frustrating. We were *looking* at an excellent opportunity to finish our paddle through the Pentland instead of *doing* it. But this was no place to ignore weather forecasts; it is almost always the timing of a forecast rather than the sequence that turns out to be wrong, so we had to be philosophical about it.

Our response was to walk back to the tents and treat ourselves to a barbecued feast that included steak, new potatoes in melted cheese and baked onions. As the tide slackened a serene calm settled over the Firth and we enjoyed another wonderful sunset. We planned to attempt to reach the North Sea the following dawn.

To use the last 2½ hours of the next favourable tide we were up in the dark at 0400. Just before launching I phoned the Coastguard and we were away shortly after 0530. A light easterly breeze was blowing and the cloud lowering by the minute. The first spots of rain fell soon after, but I could hardly believe our luck in finding the sea so calm – I doubt if a single wave broke over my deck as we paddled about a quarter of a mile off shore to pass John o'Groats. The only disappointment was the gloomy and dismal dawn that was too dark to allow photographs.

At 0630 we arrived at Duncansby Head. It was raining heavily and the wind had freshened and backed to the north-east. As the compass heading swung to the south it was a special moment for all of us. It was pointing towards a direct line home and it was easy to believe that the east coast was "downhill" all the way.

So it was that we passed the famous Stacks of Duncansby on a rising north-easterly swell. This assisted us off the cliffed coast onto our first lowland shoreline for many weeks. When the tide ran out on us we landed by the old harbour at Keiss, about 0930. Soaked through by the rain, we were quite chilled and because we were unable to find any shelter to cook breakfast, we walked up to the main village, hoping "something [would] turn up".

The Sinclair Bay Hotel was open. In spite of our dripping-wet paddling clothes we were made very welcome and stood steaming in front of the bar's coal fire. We then sat down to demolish a traditional breakfast. When, in the course of conversation, the hotelier heard what we had done, he refused to accept payment.

The weather improved dramatically while we were eating and we launched from the steep slip in the harbour at 1300. We crossed Sinclair's Bay with its sand dunes to reach the cliffs of Noss Head, just as the tide once more turned to flood in our favour. This flushed us past Wick, where the wind suddenly picked up to produce a strong westerly. To seek shelter, we tucked in to the foot of more fine cliffs with caves and stacks. Unfortunately, the coast was slowly trending towards the south-west so that the wind became an increasing problem as it came onto our bow. We slogged it out until 1830, when we turned some rocks which suddenly brought us to the little fishing harbour at Lybster, set back in a natural amphitheatre with high and steep enclosing walls. A level area of cut grass overlooked the harbour basin and provided an ideal site to put up the tents. Our first 30 miles of the east coast were behind us.

It rained for the rest of the evening but there was almost complete shelter from the wind. We slept well and woke to a sunny morning that was oppressively humid. The midges were having a field day in the still air, although looking east towards a distant oil platform in the Beatrice Oilfield, I could see there was plenty of wind over the North Sea. Being a Saturday, there was minimal activity on the quayside when I wandered down to telephone the Coastguard for a weather update. A "small-craft" warning was in operation; it meant another lost day and from lunchtime onwards we were period-ically hit by heavy, squally showers on a cold and blustery north-wester which continued into the late evening.

The spectacular cliffs south of Dunbeath, the haunt of seals.

The forecast I took on Sunday 17th August meant this was almost certainly going to be the last day of our "holiday". The winds were due to moderate in the afternoon, so if we could get away and reach Helmsdale, Bev would be in a position to make her way overland, back to Arisaig, to pick the car up.

Lybster harbour at low water proved to be a very awkward place to launch our boats and it was 1315 before we finally got away. The wind had eased to a fresh westerly and the previous day's more vigorous air stream had completely killed the north-easterly swell, allowing us to paddle a few metres from the rock-ends when we chose. The cliffs were riddled with caves on this section of coast and wildlife abounded. South of Dunbeath, where a white castle overlooked the bay, the coastline was quite exceptional. Some of the seal herds were over a hundred strong; thousands of shags hurtled through the air around us as we disturbed them. Just before the isolated rock tower of Pinnacle Stack we paddled through a natural arch of gigantic proportions. The vertical sides were probably approaching a hundred metres in height and it was an even greater distance to paddle through the chasm.

One seal made a particular impression on me as well as on my paddles. It was one of a large group that conformed to normal seal behaviour by panicking to launch themselves from an offshore rock when we were only a few metres off. However, this particular young specimen remained in a cleft of the rocks so that I could sit my boat across it and deny him his exit. The seal remained very calm and allowed me to touch its head, so Bev paddled over to take a photograph. I gently laid my blade on the back of the seal's head to give the picture scale. It was not the right thing to do. The seal went wild, grabbed the paddle blade in its jaws and began a tug-of-war with me as it fiercely jerked the paddle from side to side, nearly pulling me in. When I did manage to release the blade it had a set of teeth marks etched into the glass as a permanent reminder of my folly.

The Ord of Caithness proved to be an almost featureless headland from our close position and shortly afterwards the hills fell away to the Strath of Kildonan. The mouth of the river that drains this valley is the site of Helmsdale and the heavy rain of the previous day was creating a strong current as the river spewed out of the harbour entrance. Once inside we found an easy landing-point on a beach, but camping possibilities looked to be very limited. There was one small patch of grass outside the Old Customs House, which displayed a "Bed and Breakfast" sign. I knocked and asked if we could camp. The response from Mrs Mackay was better than we had dared hope for.

"Yes," we could camp.

"Wouldn't you be better off in a caravan?"

"What caravan? I'm sorry, I don't understand."

"That one," she said, pointing to an almost new tourer parked on the edge of the grass patch. After a quick tour of inspection we gladly accepted the offer. As we organised our gear for this special occasion we received several other visits.

"Could I get you anything?"

"Are you sure you have enough to eat?"

Our "Highlands and Islands holiday" might be over, but if we received this type of welcome wherever we landed on the east coast, we had nothing to fear for our morale as we mentally prepared ourselves to finish the expedition.

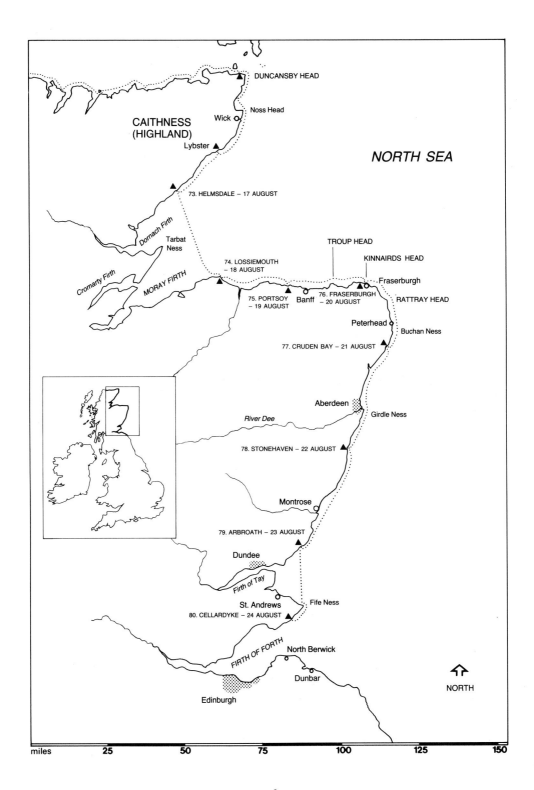

DUNCANSBY HEAD

CAITHNESS
(HIGHLAND)

Noss Head

Wick

Lybster

NORTH SEA

73. HELMSDALE – 17 AUGUST

Dornach Firth

Tarbat
Ness

TROUP HEAD

KINNAIRDS HEAD

74. LOSSIEMOUTH
– 18 AUGUST

Cromarty Firth

MORAY FIRTH

75. PORTSOY
– 19 AUGUST

Banff

Fraserburgh

76. FRASERBURGH
– 20 AUGUST

RATTRAY HEAD

Peterhead

Buchan Ness

77. CRUDEN BAY – 21 AUGUST

Aberdeen

River Dee

Girdle Ness

78. STONEHAVEN – 22 AUGUST

Montrose

79. ARBROATH – 23 AUGUST

Dundee

Firth of Tay

St. Andrews

Fife Ness

80. CELLARDYKE – 24 AUGUST

FIRTH OF FORTH

North Berwick

Dunbar

NORTH

Edinburgh

miles   25   50   75   100   125   150

13

Back in the Old Routine

Helmsdale – Cellardyke: 18th – 25th August

Beverley's departure from Helmsdale was a moment to which none of us were looking forward. We had enjoyed her company for its own sake and it had added special qualities to our passage of wildest Scotland. According to plan, we had taken more time over what we were doing; we had enjoyed it and, just as we had hoped, this had established the positive attitude of mind to "finish the job" as quickly and clinically as possible.

We were aware that we were about to revert to the long paddles we had got used to when canoeing round Ireland. Each day we would be paddling for as far and for as long as the weather and tides would allow. I had become preoccupied to the point of obsession with the idea that the faster we finished, the less likelihood there would be of getting caught by autumn gales. To our advantage, weather statistics supported the theory that we would be on a coast sheltered from a predominantly westerly air stream. To our disadvantage, the nights were beginning to draw in and it would become progressively more difficult to get our camping chores at the end of each day's paddle done in daylight.

Leaving her Anas and gear in the keeping of Mrs Mackay to be collected later, Bev caught the early morning train to Inverness and then hitched across to the west coast to collect her car at Back of Keppoch. Meanwhile, we had decided to make maximum use of a reasonable weather forecast to make a 30-mile crossing of the Moray Firth. By taking a direct line to Newtown we would save ourselves about a day's paddling.

Leaving at 0840 there were plenty of points of reference to plot our progress. As the great hills that plunge to the sea at the Ord of Caithness receded astern, we could just pick out the hills of Morayshire ahead of us – they appeared as tiny mauve islands on the southern horizon. Off to our right we could see an occasional flash of white as the sun broke through the cloud canopy and was reflected off the tower of the lighthouse on Tarbat Ness.

Every second hour we stopped for food and drink. We worked hard and progress was good, but the weather pattern did not develop exactly as forecast. As the wind slowly freshened, it backed from north-west to south of west. It was not enough to effectively slow us down, but it was enough to ensure we got wet. What we at first regarded as a "bloody nuisance" eventually prompted us to earthier and distinctly Anglo-Saxon expletives.

We were about eight miles from our landfall before we could pick out features with any degree of certainty. The lighthouse by Covesea Skerries and the radio masts at Burghead eventually fixed our position and showed that the plan I had made for the crossing had been too simplistic. This had been to head almost due south from Helmsdale, allowing the wind to balance the effect of the tide flooding into the Firth. In fact, the south-westerly wind had emerged as the clear winner in the battle between the elements and we were now about three miles east of where we had intended to be. To put this right would involve paddling into the wind. It seemed more expedient to choose a new landfall – Lossiemouth – that was downwind. In any case, this would give us that many miles we did not have to paddle the next day, or the next, or the next . . .

Having changed compass heading accordingly, it was 1630 and 32 miles on from Helmsdale when we ran ashore at Lossiemouth. From the sea, the area around the sailing club looked to be a potential camping place, but after searching the sand-blown environs we wrote this option off and took to our boats again. In the short time we were searching, the tide fell so quickly that we barely managed to recross the rocks that protect the beach to paddle round the main fishing harbour. It was the second stage of a frustrating attempt to find a place for the night.

Lossiemouth being a commercial port of some size, we were presented with an endless expanse of bricks and concrete amounting to a camper's nightmare. The one option we had not yet explored was a commercial site up river, behind the sand dunes to the east of the town, but by the time we considered this possibility, the tide was hacking out of the river so fast we could not get there anyway. Again we searched the dock area and eventually met a security watchman who suggested we sleep out under the roofed-in but open-sided fish market. A telephone call to the Harbour Master cleared this arrangement, so having changed into dry clothes, we phoned the Coastguard to

At Lossiemouth we were compelled to camp in the covered fish market.

tell them where we were and went off in search of the Mission for Deep Sea Fishermen, hopefully the source of a cheap meal. It was closed. Disappointed, we bought a snack in a chip-shop and returned to the fish market.

Now that the activity for the day was over, we put up a fly-sheet between the boats and cooked a meal of chili and rice that could be eaten later, for Bev was going to find us via the Coastguard and we did not anticipate her arrival until the late evening. As darkness descended, heavy rain set in and we were glad of the roof over the tent. There had been a constant coming and going of military air-traffic over the town throughout the evening, and even now, through the pouring rain and under a low cloud ceiling, Shackleton aircraft droned in from the sea, their headlights blazing through the murk.

Bev arrived in time for us to catch last orders in a local pub. When we returned to the fish market it was immediately apparent that our gear had been interfered with, although the only items missing from the mass of very expensive equipment were a cheap gas-lighter and a small hand-torch. This was the second time that we had suffered pilfering. On the previous occasion Richard's digital watch had been removed from the chart deck-lines as his boat sat on what we thought was a deserted beach on Omey Island in County Galway. Given that the security of our equipment had been at constant risk, we had in fact paid only lightly for our trusting and casual attitude.

When we set off the next morning, Bev was on her drive back to Kent. For her, three weeks of paddling had been enough and she was not intending to see us again before we reached the Tyne.

Whilst we had assumed that on the east coast we would be in a westerly air stream with minimal sea-state problems, in fact we found ourselves at the beginning of a prolonged period of onshore winds which on occasion set up a heavy groundswell. This forced us to plan all our landing spots with care and maintain an air of seriousness that we would have happily forgone. On the southern shore of the Moray Firth, many of the coastal villages have a man-made harbour dating from the expansion of the herring industry which followed the Napoleonic Wars. Unfortunately, some of the harbours have been allowed to fall into disrepair in recent years, so we could not always rely on them as a haven to effect a safe landing.

Immediately east of Lossie the coast is a low one of conifer-covered dunes extending many miles and fronted by a surf beach. It was a dull morning threatening rain when we set off on day 122 to do this section. A moderate surf was humping in with regular monotony, keeping us alert and wary. To begin with, we were also fighting the last of the tide so it seemed an eternity before we reached the area of overfalls and tidal swirls that marks the approaches to the Spey Estuary. We had just arrived off the river entrance when the weather brightened to coincide with the tide turning in our favour. We now made good speed to pass the settlements at Portgordon and Buckie.

Around mid-afternoon we came upon a complex of reefs where the swell was breaking fiercely. We paddled through these to come inside the harbour of Findochty, with its picturesque waterfront. Our arrival was watched with interest by a group of schoolboys. As the Primus was assembled to make tea and we made up bread rolls, the lads carefully scrutinised every item of equipment. Between the bombardment of questions of, "What's that for?" and "Why is it like this?" they bemoaned the fact that this was the last day of their summer holiday before returning to school. It was yet another reminder that here in the north, autumn was already upon us, so our stop was a short one.

East of Findochty, the coast is a series of promontories separated by small coves. This brought us to Portsoy, with its frontage of ancient warehouses. It was 1830. Having notched up our 2000th mile since leaving home, we felt we had done enough. Because of the heavy swell, approaching the harbour's narrow entrance was not straightforward – sandwiched as it is between a breakwater and rocks. Once inside, however, a concrete slip gave immediate access to a road and a steep, grassy bank, at the foot of which was a tent-size area of level lawn. This made as good a campsite as one could hope for inside a village and we had the added luxury of a bench seat to use while waiting for our evening meal to simmer on the Primus.

The following day began cold because of the fresh north-westerly wind. It had not been forecast, but we put it to good use by hanging out our wet clothing to dry, advertising our presence and attracting the attention of several fishermen who visited us for a chat and to wish us luck.

We launched at 1015 and once out of the harbour were immediately in a heavy northerly swell and lumpy sea. It was physically demanding and particularly difficult where the seas were clapping back, but the tide gave us a lot of assistance and before long the cloud dispersed to leave us in bright sunshine. One by one, we ticked off the major landmarks. First, after about an hour, came the harbour at Whitehills, then the larger towns of Banff and Macduff with an impressive array of church towers and spires.

As we approached the cliffs of Banffshire, the coastal scenery became quite impressive, as did the sea state. The swells increased in size east of Gardenstown and were reflecting back from the cliffs of More and Troup Heads to give us a rough passage. Then, quite suddenly, the seas eased, possibly because the tide was running so strongly in the same direction as the wind, enabling us to make around 6 knots. In this manner we were soon off the headland of Rosehearty, but once more we were aware of an evil-looking shore-break as we began to think in terms of finishing for the day.

When we had left Portsoy, our intention was to make Sandhaven, but as we stood off this harbour, watching the surf smash into and over the ruined breakwater, discretion prompted us to use the little tide that was left to make for Fraserburgh, only a couple of miles further on. It seemed a simple enough proposition but it did involve the risk that the tide would turn against us, the wind and the groundswell, which would steepen accordingly. With less than a mile to go, below the lighthouse on Kinnaird's Head, the tide *did* turn and the final run into the harbour entrance at Fraserburgh became traumatic.

The headland kept the wind off us but the tide was tanking out of the harbour into the long, heavy rollers that were steepened to breaking-point. Conditions would no doubt grow worse by the minute, so we paddled as fast as our fear of being forward-looped would allow. Anglers on the breakwater watched our progress with bemused interest. They probably thought we were crazy and at the time we would have been inclined to agree. I was dry-mouthed and pouring with nervous sweat by the time we cut right and came into the shelter of the harbour-light and breakwater.

Safe and no longer threatened with being smashed beneath a collapsing wall of water, our senses could switch from concentrating on survival to taking in the situation objectively. It was a warm afternoon. The sun was shining from a clear blue sky and the major town of Fraserburgh was certainly the busiest fishing port we had seen. Offshore fishing vessels were lined up at every quay, sometimes several boats deep. It was a hive of activity and industry. We had to seek a way through a complex of inner basins before finding a slip on the north-east corner where we could get out of our boats, but the prospects of discovering some out-of-the-way corner to camp or bivvy looked very remote.

Everyone we spoke to on the dock was friendly but pessimistic about camping possibilities. In particular, they thought our chances of spending a night in the harbour without having our gear stolen were non-existent. But we could not afford to accept this view, so leaving Mick and Richard to guard our vulnerable equipment, I set off to try to locate the Harbour Master.

About a hundred metres from the slip I passed a gateway to the Forbes boat-building yard. The name recalled memories of a boyhood friend, so feeling that I had nothing to lose, I wandered inside to ask for help and was quickly directed to the yard foreman, a thick-set and jovial man in middle age by the name of Jimmy Watt. Within the space of a few seconds I realised that we had once more fallen on our feet. Thanks to Jimmy, our accommodation problem was solved. Out of sight of the main harbour we had a strange campsite. It was a dirty corner surrounded by industrial junk, small boats awaiting repair, hull templates and piles of timber. The smells were a mixture of paint, diesel and stale fish. But it was private and we were only a few metres from a toilet block with a hot-water heater. We would be able to wash out our paddling clothes! What more could three weary and salt-caked paddlers ask? Some local fishermen stored their boxes of live crabs in the yard, and on stumbling upon us whilst unloading, they were quick to offer us as many as we chose to eat. The pessimism of our advisers had indeed proved ill-founded.

After a clear, chilly evening under a full moon, we woke early the next morning to the drumming of a heavy downpour on the fly-sheet. The shower fortunately proved to be short-lived, but it gave us a "dirty" start to the day, for the yard had become an industrial swamp of puddles and grey mud. We had to take great care to pack without getting everything soiled and we needed no encouragement to hurry and be off for 1000 just as the tide was beginning to flood south.

Leaving the entrance to Scotland's busiest fishing port behind us, we were relieved to discover that the heavy swell of the previous evening had dropped away on the intervening tides and we could make fast and easy progress across Fraserburgh Bay. We had learned from past mistakes not to take liberties with the swell, so we still gave the long reef and beacon at Inverallochy a wide berth. As we cleared the point to leave the Moray Firth behind us, the distant silhouette of the lighthouse at Rattray Head came into view. The coast itself offered little in terms of scenic interest – sand dunes fronting lowlands, but we took consolation in the good tide that carried us in under two hours for ten miles, past the lighthouse perched on its exposed rock ledge. From here, the rather dull coast ran south to distant Peterhead, where the size of the Russian timber ships at anchor tempted us to underestimate the great distance involved.

Passing the gaunt ruins of Slains Castle, south of Peterhead.

But the tide continued to run well and this was to provide Mick and Richard with some comic relief and amusement. I was paddling without my cag on and, to relieve the monotony of the journey, ventured into a tide race to the north of the port. I had underestimated the scale of the turbulence and got completely soaked by doing so, while the other two (wearing cags) avoided the worst of the bouncy water. They were not sympathetic.

Our fast progress continued past the lighthouse of Buchan Ness, where the coast improved in interest once again with rocks and cliffs. More encouraging still was a clearance of the cloud establishing itself from the north, so that shortly after passing the dramatic ruins of Slains Castle (reputed to be the inspiration for Bram Stoker's *Dracula*) we had bright sunshine to finish off one of our easiest days yet – just over five hours to make 24 miles.

Rounding the rocks on the northern extremity of Cruden Bay a vista of sand dunes opened up and, tucked into our right, the little harbour of Port Erroll. Being high water, it was an easy exit onto the slip and a straightforward carry before camping amid a complex of drying stake nets on good turf. It was still only mid-afternoon so we had plenty of time to rinse out our clothes in fresh water, assured of their drying in the warm sunshine. Then we walked along the little river into the main village to buy some supplies before eating a good lunch.

While resting at Arisaig we had been befriended by another camper at "The Croft". Eddie Davidson – a helicopter engineer based at Aberdeen – lived at Oldmeldrum, just a few miles from Cruden Bay. He too was a sea paddler and had insisted that we contact him when in the area, so I made a telephone call to let him know our whereabouts. His enthusiasm to help was a great morale booster. Within an hour he had driven over to pick us up and take us back to his bungalow for a shower and meal. Both he and his wife did all they could to make us feel spoiled for the evening. Later, Eddie dropped us back at our tent. It was another cold, still and clear night. Bright moonlight lit up the bay and the stake nets threw clear-cut shadows over our camp. Clean, with full bellies, we all agreed it had been a particularly good day.

Friday 22nd August proved to be another day of good progress when everything went well. It is always a bonus to get up to clear skies and the fair weather set the mood and tone for the day. By 0815 we were at the village shops to restock on supplies. Then, with full boats, we began a long carry over slippery kelp to the low-water mark in the outer harbour. Once afloat, a cool north-westerly wind helped blow us south and having cleared the Skares Rocks at the southern end of the Bay of Cruden, we began a tedious slog along the sand dunes of Balmedie Beach. Although the tide was running in our favour by this time, the distant tower-blocks at Aberdeen seemed to take an age to get any closer. Meanwhile, to seaward, we could look out to a number of oil platforms and the busy coming and going of helicopters.

At long last we put Aberdeen astern and having passed the lighthouse at Girdle Ness, we were once more paddling past sea cliffs which could absorb our attention and break the monotony of the journey. The buoys of the lobster pots and flag markers of the fishermen's dans monitored our good speed and assured us of our continued tidal assistance. We abandoned our original plan of stopping at Portlethen and decided to push on for Stonehaven to give us a 35-mile day by 1715. In fact, the tide turned to run against us just as we rode in on the swells of our last mile. As we entered the harbour, a Coastguard officer hailed us and announced he had observed our progress throughout the day from his Land-Rover, but he was unable to suggest a suitable place to spend the night in what was an austere but rather attractive harbour, with well-appointed buildings overlooking the main quay. There were certainly no obvious places to erect a tent, so I eventually contacted the caretaker of the Aberdeen and Stonehaven Yacht Club to see if they could help. This resulted in the club commodore arriving to offer us the freedom of their facilities. We commandeered a fish-barrow to move our kayaks into their dinghy shed, while we settled into their newly refurbished clubhouse, which had been converted from a traditional dockside warehouse. It gave us a proper kitchen, showers and a comfortable room to sleep in.

At Stonehaven we commandeered a fish barrow to move our kayaks to the yacht club.

It was soon made known to us that the club had an active sea-canoeing section. Some of the membership arrived to look at our equipment and this led to another very enjoyable evening in a local pub. George Farquhar led the proceedings. He had been a lifelong mountaineer and had recently taken to sea paddling. He is a little older than myself, and having a lot in common we struck up an instant accord. It led to George and his wife accompanying us back to the clubhouse to see off the remains of a bottle of Macallan and an agreement that George would paddle with us for the first part of the next day's journey.

Fortunately for all, no early start was needed on Saturday. We had to wait for the tide and so enjoyed a lie-in until 0730, making the best of our "luxury" accommodation by taking a shower, then walking into the main town to purchase the makings of a full, cooked breakfast, instead of just eating our usual bowl of porridge.

Later, we borrowed the fish-barrow once more to move our boats to the beach outside the harbour, where we launched at 1135, by which time George had joined us. Once again it was a sunny day and a fresh northerly wind was blowing to assist us.

The coast to the south of Stonehaven is of exceptional quality. Cliffs of conglomerate or "pudding-stone" resemble a fossilised plum pudding and so have been vulnerable to spectacular shapings by the erosive forces of the sea. Deep caves and arches abound. To lend atmosphere to the scene, at Dunnottar we paddled beneath the picture-book Scottish castle. George, acting as a good local guide, recalled for our benefit its associations with great moments in Scotland's history, and in particular the castle's part in saving the Scottish Crown regalia from being plundered by the occupying forces of Cromwell's army.

At the cove of Whistleberry we bade farewell to George. Shortly afterwards the cliffs were also left behind and we passed the settlement of Inverbervie and fishing village of Gourdon. It meant that we had left the Scottish Highland Zone, for here on Montrose Bay, with its mainly sand-dune coast, we were undoubtedly in the Central Lowlands.

[ABOVE] *The cliffs of Tramore in southern Ireland.*

[BELOW] *The ruins at Great Blasket, the most westerly point on our journey. The abandoned cottages are the result of forced evictions by the Irish Government in the 1950s.*

[ABOVE] *Our best day of paddling round Ireland – passing Puffin Island near Valencia on 25th June.*

[BELOW] *In misty conditions we kept close below the cliffs of Loop Head, County Clare.*

[ABOVE] *The slabby coastline of the Dingle Peninsula approaching Smerwick.*

[BELOW] *The beach of Gola Island, Inishfree Bay, County Donegal.*

The 900ft Cliffs of Moher, County Clare.

Portage across a beach with view across the Inner Sound to Skye.

Our sheltered camp at Badachro, Loch Gairloch.

On the crossing of Donegal Bay.

The magnificent view across Enard Bay to the mountains of Sutherland.

In Scarborough Harbour on 9th September. This is one of the many harbours that provide havens on the east coasts of Scotland and England.

Meanwhile, the swell had been picking up on the tide and was causing an intimidating break along the shore all the way to Scurdie Ness, where a lighthouse marks the entrance to the great natural harbour of the port of Montrose. We then had to cross Lunan Bay to reach the distinctive cliffs of red sandstone that culminate in Red Head. Knowing we would soon be running out of tide we considered trying to land at the ruined harbour of Auchmithie, but odd swells were crashing over the top so we kept going, against an ebbing tide, to reach Arbroath.

Just north of the fishing port, the coast kicks sharply westwards so, turning the point, we found ourselves out of the wind at long last and paddling into the blinding light of the setting sun. We arrived at 1830 but our scout of the harbour failed to find a slip. Returning to the western end of the outer harbour we ran ashore and settled on another unusual camping place. This time we set up the tent on top of a sewage installation! It was hardly ideal, but we were pressed for time and had to work fast to get established before darkness descended.

While we had been plagued all day by a wind we did not want, just as it could be useful in drying our gear, it dropped completely. But it left us a fine evening. To the east, against the darkening sky, blinked the loom of the Bell Rock Light. A large red moon rose over the harbour entrance to grow steadily smaller and more yellow as it ascended its traverse of the heavens and became mirrored in the calm waters.

In spite of our compromises on campsite and our sense of urgency, before we had time to eat we had been overtaken by nightfall. We finished cooking by candle-light.

The weather was still fine the next morning. We had time to kill to await the tide, so Mick and I went for a walk round the harbour before cooking breakfast in the sunshine. What had been an easy boat-carry the previous evening would now be an exceptionally long one, for the outer harbour had just about dried out. We finally launched at 1130 and paddled straight out to sea to begin an offshore crossing of St. Andrews Bay, on a direct line for Fife Ness – the northern extremity of the Firth of Forth. Paddling close to shore would have given us a greater distance on a relatively uninteresting coast of sand dunes where we would also have been fouled up in military firing ranges, so we would be better off in the open sea.

Although there was very little wind, a long, heavy swell was running from the north-east. It gave a little help to cross the last of the tide ebbing from the Tay Estuary, but after about an hour we adjusted our compass heading to point straight to Fife, still around 19 miles away and well below our visible horizon. Much of the time we were paddling in sunshine, although surrounded by towering cumuliform clouds producing dark precipitation trails. There were double rainbows too, but somehow we seemed to miss most of the showers.

All the time we were paddling, I was nagged by a concern for where the heavy swell had come from. We had been caught out too often by violent weather changes following hard on the heels of such unexplained sea conditions. It did not fit the forecast we had taken, but for the time being, it did not get any worse.

When, after several hours, we did arrive off the low headland of Fife Ness, we took no chances with the swells breaking on the extensive area of reefs that lie between a fixed beacon and a cardinal buoy. We felt more comfortable when we had put these behind us and entered the Firth of Forth, where a choice of action now faced us. We could either make a big push to cross the Firth to the Lothian shore, or find a campsite on the north side, perhaps in one of the numerous Fife fishing harbours. It was already 1645 and it was the prospect of another "candle-light dinner" that swayed us to choose the second option.

The first harbour where we could effect a landing was at Crail. This was a quaint and unspoiled village with an olde-worlde charm and fine views out to the Isle of May. But there was nowhere suitable to stop for the night. When we were caught in a heavy rain shower, our boats seemed the driest shelter at hand, so again we set off westward. We were still looking for a campsite when we came to Cellardyke, the most easterly of the complex of villages that merge to form Anstruther.

Cellardyke is a lovely old harbour with stone cottages crowding in on the ancient quay and breakwater. At the eastern end we could see a narrow patch of sandy turf jammed between bench seats. It was just big enough to take a tent, so having checked that the occupiers of the nearest cottage did not object, we began to establish our camp.

We had barely begun this task when the local Harbour Master arrived on the scene. Coull Deas proved to be one of the more memorable characters we met on our journey. In his sixties, Coull was quietly spoken but with an air of strength and authority about him. His rugged face – the product of a lifetime at sea as a fisherman – wore a wide, friendly smile. Whereas I had expected to be admonished for not seeking his permission to camp, he in fact had come to insist (in very strong terms) that the proper procedure to permit camping was first to come into his cottage so that he could administer tea and home-made cake in suitably generous portions. Having questioned us while we ate and drank, he was reluctant to let us escape to cook our supper. When we did get away, he was quickly on the scene to take our wet clothing away so that it would be properly dry for the next day.

It seemed to us that the life of Cellardyke focused on the harbour and we were repeatedly made welcome. First we were invited into another house to get a teletext weather forecast; then a local antiques dealer offered us a room for the night; finally, we were driven off to the home of Crispin Heath, who was in the process of building an outdoor centre at East Neuk, on the western side of Anstruther. Again we had to insist on being taken back to our boats, for we needed a very early start in the morning if we were to cross the Firth of Forth before more unsettled weather arrived.

I doubt if we will ever forget Monday 25th August. We were up at 0515 to find it cold and clear. The night sky was just beginning to pale overhead, while to the east, the first flushes of pink and orange tinged the horizon, throwing the outline of the Isle of May into stark silhouette. We worked fast because we wanted to get away, and had just eaten our porridge when Coull arrived. He had simply assumed we would accompany him back to his cottage to eat the proper breakfast his wife had prepared for us. We could hardly refuse, so it was 0715 before we had donned the dry clothes that had been returned to us and were ready to be off. Then, just as we were about to launch, a reporter from the local press arrived (more of Coull's work) and we lost another 15 minutes. By the end of the day these wasted moments had come dangerously close to bringing the expedition to a premature and disastrous conclusion.

14

Running South

Cellardyke – Whitby: 25th August – 8th September

While taking our second breakfast I had used the opportunity to phone the Coastguard and been given a weather forecast which warned of strong north-easterly winds developing in the afternoon. To play safe, we decided we would make for Dunbar rather than Eyemouth, so I checked the sailing directions, compared them with Coull's local knowledge, then memorised the map of the harbour from the Almanac. There was good reason for these precautions, however, for I knew the actual harbour entrance would be hidden from seaward by a complex of dangerous rocks which we would have to avoid by locating leading marks over an old swimming-pool. Duly armed with this information and having said goodbye to Coull and Elsie, we headed south into the Firth.

So far, so good. It was a lovely autumn morning. There was a fresh north-easterly breeze and a moderate swell, but overhead were clear skies and we were bathed in sunshine. The atmosphere was crystal clear, affording excellent visibility and extensive views across to the Bass Rock and the distinctive hummock of Berwick Law.

After over two hours of paddling we had made good progress. It was still sunny and clear but the wind had strengthened considerably and was blowing about F6 – pushing us further west than we had expected, given that the tide was ebbing from the Firth. Hundreds of gannets from the Bass Rock colony were soaring around us. But I was uneasy. Something was not right. Where were all the fishing-boats?

It became very hard work when we tried to win back the lost ground by turning more to eastward. We were straining every muscle and sinew to make any meaningful headway as the wind continued to pick up in strength. The sea state was rapidly deteriorating. Odd wave crests were getting blown off. Rudders had to be kicked hard over to balance the kayaks on the wind. It was the worst possible moment for my rudder cable to break and I now had a continuous fight to prevent the boat from heading up into the wind. We had been warned by Coull that the tides on the south side of the Firth can be unpredictable. On the pot buoys it was now clear it was running against us. But very slowly, we gained ground to put us off the rocky shoreline of Dunbar.

The wind was blowing almost directly onto this shore and, once close in, the sea state was formidable. Breakers foamed over the reefs and clapped back off the cliffs and breakwater. But where was the harbour entrance? To be more precise, where was the swimming-pool to give us our leading marks to find the entrance amongst those evil-looking rocks and breaking seas?

In freshening winds we crossed the Firth of Forth, passing Bass Rock, on the way to Dunbar.

Raging seas pounding the Dunbar harbour walls the morning after we made our hazardous entry.

We made two traversing runs along the frontage of the harbour area, standing sufficiently off to avoid the breaking water. We could not see anything that remotely resembled a swimming-pool. Conditions were deteriorating quite swiftly. Was it perhaps time to cut our losses, turning to run with the tide and wind into the inner part of the Firth, to North Berwick or beyond? These were desperate moments.

It was at this time that, out to sea, we noticed a lone fishing-boat – at least, we could see it when not hidden in the wave troughs. We had to shout to converse as we held a council. We would have to anticipate the fishing-boat's course and attempt to intercept it to seek guidance on where we might get in. It was really up to Richard and Mick, for I could not keep up with them without a working rudder in this sort of sea and wind.

Richard did well to get to the vessel. He had already finished his conversation with the fishermen and the boat had steamed off towards Dunbar before I arrived on the scene. There was no swimming-pool to give us leading marks. We had to trust our judgement to clear the obvious rocks and breaks to the west of the breakwater and head straight for the low cliffs. The fishermen assured Richard that we *would* eventually see the entrance, on our left, at the last minute before hitting the cliffs. It would be difficult – an act of faith – but we had no choice. The fishermen would have liked to have waited and shown us the way but they dared not risk running out of water to make the harbour on the falling tide.

We came through the reefs in a very nasty sea, it seemed with breaks all around us. Running along a natural rock wall we could now see the staffs of the leading marks that apparently led to a blank cliff-face. With only a few metres left and absolutely committed, the entrance suddenly appeared on our left and we pulled with full power to head into it. In a few moments we were safe inside the Victoria Harbour.

"Jesus Christ! What a relief!"

The approach to Dunbar harbour.

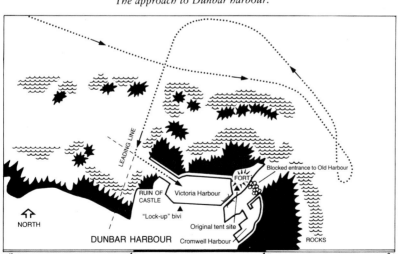

Amidst all the emotions of accepting that we had lived to paddle another day was a feeling of mental exhaustion, mixed with anger and frustration that one piece of faulty information could put so much at risk. I knew it did not help to feel this way. It was irrational, a waste of energy and purely subjective. But that is how it was.

A little later we were told that the swimming-pool had been washed away in a winter storm. We had also survived (by too fine a margin) the first onslaught of what was later called "Hurricane Charlie".

Our first night in Dunbar was an exceptionally wild one. We had set up our tent on a small area of quay that divided the new Victoria Harbour from the old inner basin, built in the time of Cromwell. The position was barely tenable, for the bigger seas were breaking against the main breakwater to send regular volleys of spray and foam over us. The fierce gusts of the howling gale were making the whole tent shake, causing the main panels to flap and crack with resounding slaps. Heavy rain went almost unnoticed in the general misery.

The morning brought a slight improvement in the conditions but we had to accept the need to move camp. Some fishermen suggested we move to a more sheltered site within the ruins of the old fort and we were just about to execute this plan when Billy Gillespie (a local builder) sought us out.

"Are you the lads with the tent and canoes?" he asked me, as I returned from surveying the fort. "What sort of night did you have?"

I told him.

"Would you like to move into some fishermen's lock-up huts? They're new, clean and have electric lights," Billy added. "I can send my son over with the lorry to help move your gear."

It was a godsend. A local yachtsman had already taken our salt-stiffened paddling clothes to get them washed for us. Life was beginning to look better by the minute. By lunchtime we were comfortably established in the garage-style accommodation and had disappeared into a neighbouring pub.

It was as we sat in comfort, watching the television news in the bar, that we began to appreciate we were not alone in being caught out by the freak weather. Northern England had suffered a much more severe battering. It was also clear from the forecast that the weather would preclude paddling for several days. We began to plan for a tedious and no doubt frustrating stay.

When camped at Badachro on Gairloch, we had met Rod and Eleanor Pengelly, proprietors of the outdoor gear wholesale business trading under the name Adventure Equipment Ltd. They had invited us to contact them when in their home area of Edinburgh, so we phoned them and were invited out for a meal the next evening. That would stop us getting too bored on Wednesday, but we still had the remainder of Tuesday to fill in. The prospect of an evening spent in the lock-up was distinctly unsavoury. An evening in the pub would be expensive. Grasping at straws, we responded to a poster we had seen earlier in the day and went off to the local theatre which overlooked the harbour, where we expected to hear a "folk concert" given by "The Tartan Lads".

We should have realised we had misunderstood the nature of the entertainment on offer when we looked around our fellow members of the audience. It looked suspiciously like a convention for the local Senior Citizens. "The Tartan Lads", when they appeared, were only marginally younger. Their cold but slick delivery of corny jokes and renditions of Harry Lauder songs accompanied by an accordion seemed to delight the majority of the audience, while our greatest but possibly more cynical amusement resulted from the way the kilted entertainers repeatedly asked for strings of requests, which they proceeded to disregard as they got on with their rehearsed act. The serving of tea and biscuits during the interval was our cue to cut our losses and retreat to the pub, feeling both younger and wiser!

Just before midnight, as we settled into our sleeping-bags in the lock-up, there came a tap on the door. Mick got up to answer it. As the door began to open it was suddenly pushed wide by the squirming shoulders of a brown and white, floppy-eared dog. It was so unexpected I had to look twice before I recognised my own springer spaniel, shortly to be followed by Bev. She had realised that we would be fed up if gale-bound for too long and so had driven for over eight hours to find us, so that at least we would be stuck with a car to run us around.

Bev's arrival meant there were plenty of tasty food parcels from home to keep us amused in the morning, while in the afternoon we could now drive into Edinburgh. We wandered around the main shopping centre feeling overwhelmed by the traffic before meeting the Pengelly family in the Grassmarket, in the old part of the city. They looked after us extremely well and after dining us, Rod Pengelly took us on a high-speed tour of the city, ending up "on the fringe" of the Edinburgh Festival to enjoy a first-class cabaret in the "Beck's Beer Tent". We spent the night in the Pengelly flat and, feeling slightly the worse for wear, drove back to Dunbar in the late morning of Thursday.

That lunchtime I telephoned the home of Rod and Suzie Mitchell, old friends who lived at Cullercoats, Whitley Bay, and who were expecting to put us up when we reached the Tyne. The phone was answered by Suzie who told me that Rod, like us, was storm-bound in their 26-foot sailing cruiser, just an hour's drive down the coast at Seahouses, but with no crew available to help him sail *Stella Peacock* back to her berth at the Royal Northumberland Yacht Club in Blyth. We immediately set off to find him.

Quite predictably, Rod was "catching last orders" in The Ship at Seahouses. We spent the rest of the afternoon talking of our adventures while we cooked a meal in *Stella Peacock*'s galley. A short lull in the wind had been forecast for that evening, so it was eventually agreed that Rod and I would sail through the night to get his boat home, while Bev, Mick and Richard returned to Dunbar. Rod knows this coast as well as anyone, having been responsible for revising its sailing directions, so I had complete faith in his judgement that the trip would "go".

After a fair afternoon it was a dismal and grey evening with rain in the air, but the wind was dropping. We packed hurriedly and at dusk, as the tide began flooding south, we cast off. Several people had gathered to see us into the long groundswell off the harbour entrance. As soon as we were in open water, Rod cut the engine and we began a reach towards the low outline of the Inner Farne to clear the reefs, and after a single jibe, began a fast run before the north-westerly wind that took us the length of the

Northumberland coast. It was a most enjoyable passage and a fast one for the old clinker-built cruiser, putting us into Blyth about half past midnight. After a quick nightcap we turned into our bunks and slept soundly until 0730 the next morning.

It was still raining when Suzie picked us up from the House Yacht at 0900. We dropped off Rod's sailing gear at his house and then Rod drove me back to Dunbar. *En route* we called in at the harbours of Berwick-upon-Tweed, Eyemouth, and St. Abbs so that I could gain a clear mental picture of the landing-places we might use on the journey south. The sea was less rough than of late but the strong northerly wind was not due to disappear until later in the weekend. That Friday evening, when Rod had returned home, our reunited band sat watching the weather forecast on the television of the local pub. Another near-gale was forecast for Saturday, meaning yet another lost day. Richard had been unusually quiet all evening. He suddenly turned and said he had a favour to ask. We wondered what was coming.

"My cousin is getting married in North Wales tomorrow. All the family will be there. Can I borrow the car?"

"Just make sure you're back for an early start on Sunday morning," I replied.

Bev tossed him her car keys.

"I'll leave now then," he said and was gone in the night.

When I opened the lock-up early next morning there was a car parked across the door. Inside were Coull and Elsie Deas. They had been worried about us since our departure from Cellardyke and had diverted from their journey to Hartlepool to find us. Breakfast that morning was accordingly supplemented by Elsie's sandwiches and Coull's own rollmop herrings. This remained the highlight of our day until Billy Gillespie invited us home for a shower that evening. In spite of all the hospitality, however, we were becoming very impatient to be on our way. But for the first time we did have a promising forecast for the next day. As we walked back to our strange home that evening, it was reassuring to see the sky clearing and notice the wind was dying.

Some time in the early hours of Sunday morning, Richard returned from the wedding. We were all up again for 0630 and relieved to find we had a fine morning and only a light north-westerly wind to continue our journey at last. Just before eight o'clock Billy Gillespie arrived with a fork-lift truck to help move our boats to the slip. It was a final and very welcome gesture that saved us a lot of hard work.

Even though the wind had abated, the groundswell was slopping around the harbour entrance, making the timing of our exit critical. Once clear, we were able to enjoy the sunshine and remove our cags for a long haul. Tidal assistance was very little, so the pull past Tor Ness and Fast Castle Head to reach the rock headland of St. Abb's took four hours. The swells breaking in the entrance to the little harbour there were still quite disturbing and worse still when we paddled past the rocky shore of Eyemouth. Stopping to see Bev was out of the question. Besides, the sun was now obscured by a thickening veil of cloud and a fresh westerly wind had sprung up to make it feel quite chilly. We also knew that the offshore wind would be steepening the swell when we had to land, so we were quite happy to put this off for as long as possible.

The northern approaches to Berwick-upon-Tweed are dominated by the extensive breakwater and attached light tower which protect the north side of the Tweed Estuary.

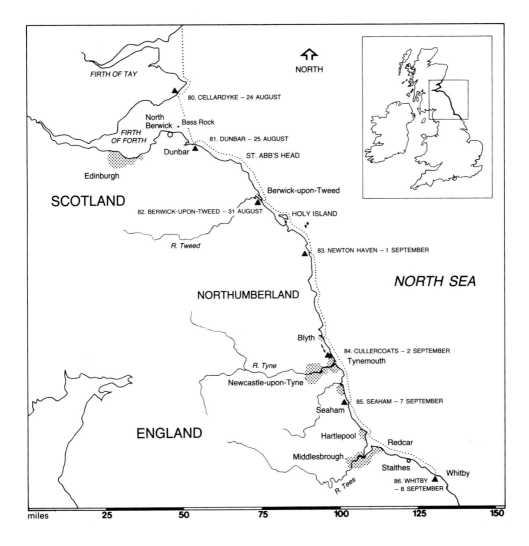

FIRTH OF TAY

NORTH

80. CELLARDYKE – 24 AUGUST

North
Berwick · Bass Rock

FIRTH
OF FORTH

81. DUNBAR – 25 AUGUST

Dunbar

ST. ABB'S HEAD

Edinburgh

SCOTLAND

Berwick-upon-Tweed

82. BERWICK-UPON-TWEED – 31 AUGUST

HOLY ISLAND

R. Tweed

83. NEWTON HAVEN – 1 SEPTEMBER

NORTH SEA

NORTHUMBERLAND

Blyth

84. CULLERCOATS – 2 SEPTEMBER

R. Tyne

Tynemouth

Newcastle-upon-Tyne

85. SEAHAM – 7 SEPTEMBER

Seaham

ENGLAND

Hartlepool

Redcar

Middlesbrough

Staithes

Whitby

R. Tees

86. WHITBY
– 8 SEPTEMBER

miles   25   50   75   100   125   150

A big surf was running into the bay that fronts the magnificent Elizabethan defence works and bastions that once protected this ancient fortress, while the wind blew the breaking tops back out to sea in great sheets of spray. We approached with great caution and with some measure of apprehension, for it was past the time of high water and the tide running out of the river would be steepening the rollers in the deeper water off the entrance. As a precaution, we strung out to make our run in, but in the eventuality we did not experience any problems more serious than an increased work-load to fight the ebbing tide. Beaching our boats on the southern side of the river at the point of Spittal (Tweedmouth), we found Bev waiting to see us in and share our first moments back on English soil since leaving Devon at the beginning of June.

Just inland from the point was a car-park and obvious camping place, sheltered from the west wind by a tall factory wall. We had all developed a keen eye for spotting

COMMITMENT AND OPEN CROSSINGS

potential aids to improving our creature comforts and on this occasion, being a Sunday, there was considerable sailing activity going on inside the natural, stony bar that protects the inner part of the Tweed's mouth. Sailing boats usually mean sailing clubs and comfortable changing facilities. So we walked along the shore to the Berwick Sailing Club, where we scrounged the use of their showers and a hot drink before hurrying back to the kayaks to take the 1750 shipping forecast. It warned of a south-westerly gale "soon" (meaning in six to twelve hours), for the slow-moving depression that had once been "Hurricane Charlie" and given us the prolonged northerly winds was now unexpectedly moving west again, bringing to mind a conversation with Coull.

He had told me that "a north wind has nine lives". This statement certainly fitted with our experience and the weather lore passed on to us by fishermen all the way down Scotland's east coast. They were adamant that whilst our Meteorological Office are generally reliable in their forecasts concerning weather systems generating west winds, when northerlies and easterlies are involved, then the forecasts are much less accurate in terms of timing and wind strength.

Having set up camp and eaten, we had two reasons to celebrate when we walked to the pub that evening. It was Richard's birthday and we still had the whole of September in front of us to traverse England's eastern seaboard.

I fell in love with the Northumberland coast many years ago, but its attractions on the occasion of this visit were not the scenic ones that had previously inspired me. Splendid as this coast is, I viewed it simply as a stepping-stone to a haven of comfort and hospitality that would become available to us when we reached the vicinity of Cullercoats and the Mitchell household. We were all looking forward to arriving there so that we could relax in home-from-home surroundings, in a way that had not been possible since leaving Plymouth. Now, with luck and some effort, it was only a couple of paddling days away.

Monday 1st September, gave us a clear bright morning after a night of gales and frontal rain. The wind had eased to being a strong westerly and on looking out to sea we were immediately aware that the northerly swell had been killed at last, making it possible to paddle close to the shore for a change. Shortly before eleven o'clock we left Berwick. After a limited section of low cliffs, a great open bay of sandy beaches and dunes makes a sweep towards Lindisfarne, otherwise known as Holy Island. Because the wind was virtually behind us, we could travel very fast along this section and were soon at the pyramidal beacon of Emanuel Head (the northern point of Holy Island). By turning the head we came into the lee of low, stony cliffs and once out of the wind we stopped paddling to eat some chocolate. Off again almost immediately, we reached Castle Point from where we had our best view of the little castle perched on its plug of jutting rock, but we then had to make a wind-buffeted crossing to the great castle of Bamburgh. This leg was fully exposed to the wind, for the low-lying coast offers no protection whatsoever. Without proper materials, my temporary rudder repairs carried out at Dunbar were unequal to the task, so once again I found myself struggling in a fight with the cross-winds while the other two kayaks with functioning rudders coped with ease.

There was no respite until we came to the shore below the imposing walls and towers

Bamburgh Castle, the fine sentinel above the dunes of the Northumberland coastline.

of the magnificent medieval fortress. Standing on an isolated rock above the dunes, Bamburgh Castle dominates both the eye and the coast for many miles. Fine as this prospect was, we would have preferred to have been paddling out to sea, where we could have run down through the Farne Islands, but in the strong westerlies it was not the right day for such a route. Instead, we continued to hug the shore until we could pull into the harbour at Seahouses, where we were met by Bev with a supply of rolls and drink.

As soon as we stopped paddling we were aware of how wet and wind-chilled we had become, so we were keen to keep going and use the last of the favourable tide to reach the natural harbour of Newton Haven, its arc of white sand protected by a scattering of reefs and supporting a small community that focuses on an open-sided square of single-storey cottages.

This scenic section of coast is National Trust property and Bev was unable to convince the warden that he might bend the rules in our "special" case and allow us to camp. An hour after arrival (and feeling very cold) we were still searching for some possible site when a local teacher took pity on us. She decided that her neighbours – the owners of an unoccupied cottage that served as a windsurfing centre – would almost certainly have helped us out if they had been in residence. She therefore arranged for us to camp in the sheltered orchard of the centre's back garden which made a very acceptable site.

During the evening I telephoned Rod Mitchell and warned him that, weather permitting, we would be with him the next day. This in fact proved to be another sunny morning but the west wind was still blowing strong and a "small-craft warning" was in operation. Paddling in a F6 would be strenuous but we had every intention of getting to the Mitchells that evening. Being realistic, we knew it would be difficult to reach Cullercoats on one tide but getting 30 miles to Blyth was a reasonable objective and it was the target that we set our minds on.

As we carried our kayaks across the sands to the low-water mark at 0930, there was barely a ripple on the surface of the inner haven but, looking out beyond the reefs, we could see the dark lines of wind ripples scurrying across the water and away from us. Once afloat and outside the rocks, we found that the wind "ripples" were being kicked up enough to produce white horses less than half a mile off the beach. Our route throughout the day was therefore constrained by our attempts to stay as close to the shore as possible, without taking too indirect a line.

The landmarks were slowly ticked off in our southerly progress. First came the rocky headland and fine ruins of Dunstanburgh Castle, closely followed by the tiny harbour and lifeboat stations of Craster. Once past the rock platforms of Boulmer, we could get no shelter at all to cross the wide expanse of Alnmouth Bay. The coast cut away from us westward as we rounded the northern point and paddling directly into the wind to retain close contact with the coast was not feasible. To make progress, we resorted to an extended and very physical ferry-glide off the wind, forcing us to paddle on a heading 45° adrift from the course we were actually moving along to reach the broken breakwater in the harbour entrance at Amble.

Just south of here, opposite the lighthouse on Coquet Island, we had arranged to meet Bev for some lunch. We spotted the distinctive markings of the spaniel "Boy" as he ran along the ridge of the sand dunes before seeing Bev, so pulled into the beach over polished rock slabs. We were about to search the foot of the steep sandy bank for a place out of the wind to eat our lunch when the problem was solved for us. Holiday chalets sat on top of the escarpment and we were invited inside one of the buildings for hot drinks and the chance to eat in comfort.

It was about 1400 before we forced ourselves to abandon our comfortable surroundings to cross the uninspiring expanse of Druridge Bay. The effort of crossing Alnmouth Bay was fresh in our minds, so it was decided to abandon the tidal assistance to be gained by taking a direct line and instead we paddled as close to the beach as possible. The dunes dragged interminably on as far as Cresswell. In the few, brief miles that followed, the scene significantly changed for the worse. In sharp contrast to the wild and rural landscapes which had been the norm for many months (with only minor exceptions), we found ourselves on an industrial coast. Rounding the low rocks of Snab Point to pass Lynemouth, our view was one of open-cast mining and a power station complex. The sea clouded, changed colour and we could smell the pollution. It was a grim reminder that not all aspects of getting closer to home would be for the better.

Newbiggin Point is a distinctive feature of this landscape because of its imposing church. Passing it, we could look across the open bay to the Pier-Head Light of Blyth. Meanwhile, the wind had dropped considerably in the last two hours, so we paddled a straight course towards the storage tanks visible to the north of the harbour at Blyth and came in about 1750.

Rod and Bev were waiting on the south-western pier arm to see us in and ten minutes later we had beached on the sands outside the south harbour. A photographer from *The Journal* – a Tyneside local paper – was also there, so having satisfied our commitment to sponsors by giving a brief interview to back a press statement, we left our boats in the Rushforth Shed of the Royal Northumberland Yacht Club and were driven off to Cullercoats and the delights of home cooking.

Our strenuous push to Blyth proved to be a particularly worthwhile effort because the next morning it was blowing a full gale from the north-west. One look at a map will show any reader not familiar with the area the long north-westerly fetch and explain why this sets up a big sea on the Northumbrian coastline, so while the weather did its worst, we remained warm, dry, well fed and comfortably accommodated in the Mitchell home.

Later in the day we received Canoe Club visitors from Kent when Micky Bowles and Duncan Cox arrived and were put up by Rod's twin brother. This swelled the size of the party that took place in the evening and went on into the early hours.

> *Keep your feet still Geordie Hinnie*
> *Let's be happy through the neet,*
> *For yer may not be sa happy*
> *Through the day.*
> *Give us that bit cumfort*
> *Keep yer feet still Geordie lad . . .*

Rod's "squeeze box" gasped and fell silent. The player ceased his march around the sitting room, skilfully avoiding the scattered beer cans, bottles and glasses.

"Come on you miserable sons of Onan! Sing you buggers! Let's start again."

Rod was seriously ill and had been to the hospital for further tests that day, but tonight, for us, he was his old self and performing his host-duties as only he could. The melodion began playing once more and Rod's strong bass voice rang out clear, perfectly matched by the voice of his twin brother Quent.

> *Wor Geordie and Bob Johnson*
> *Were lyin' in one bed . . .*

This time there was a greater volume of raucous howling from the inebriated rabble that took up the chorus. This brought a twinkle to Rod's eye and encouraged him to lead straight into another unaccompanied Gilbert & Sullivan song. The fact that it was two o'clock in the morning could not be allowed to spoil the fun, although to be fair, Richard was already sound asleep in the armchair and when Rod abandoned his "box" to play a reel on the whistle, others began to waver in their determination to keep awake.

Of such stuff is Geordie hospitality made – particularly in the Mitchell household. It almost certainly did a great deal of temporary harm to our weary bodies, but it also encouraged a pleasant euphoria. Our morale fed and thrived on it.

The result was that none of us were very keen to paddle our boats from Blyth down to Cullercoats the next afternoon. Although the wind had gone back to being a strong westerly, the gale had left us with a groundswell which encouraged us to keep well clear of the rock ledges below the disused lighthouse on St. Mary's Island. South of the resort area of Whitley Bay, we turned the rocky promontory which protects the little harbour of Cullercoats and landed on the sands below the lifeboat station. From here we could carry our boats up on to the promenade and eventually to Rod's house.

We intended to stay with Rod and Suzie until Sunday 7th September. The two clear days that we had until then were earmarked for rest, relaxation and making our final preparations for the run home. Most of the time would be used in amusing ourselves socially but some work had to be done. Richard overhauled the boats, making some minor fibre-glass repairs and completely replacing the rudder cable that had caused so many frustrations since Dunbar. We restocked on basic supplies and covered the maps and charts that we needed for the last section of the journey, for in our frantic rush to get jobs done before our departure in April, this particular task had remained incomplete.

We left Cullercoats as planned on the Sunday afternoon. The weather was generally fine but a fresh to strong westerly was still blowing as we waved goodbye to the Mitchells and their children. Bev had already driven home, as had our two clubmates. All three of us were keen to get going again. Unless we were very unlucky with the weather, we felt confident that we could get home before the end of the month.

Our paddle from Cullercoats took us along the sands of Tynemouth and so past the huge breakwaters that protect the entrance to the Tyne. The cliffs of South Shields and Lizard Point were behind us when we arrived off the rifle ranges at Whitburn. This being a Sunday, we had not expected to find them in use but the red flag was flying. Perhaps the Territorial Army were at practice. We could see the look-out and felt sure he must have seen us, but shots continued to crack through the air. Since the butts were parallel to the cliff-top and it was obvious that some spent rounds would be coming directly over the sea there was an obvious danger. It was annoying rather than alarming that the proper, common-sense procedures were not being followed to let us pass through the range.

The weekend anglers were out in force on the Sunderland breakwater as we began picking up speed on the rising tide. The wind had eased and become more north-westerly so we reached the industrial harbour of Seaham quickly and decided to make this our stop for the night. Fourteen miles was a very short day but it was already 1700 and to press on to Hartlepool would take us into the darkness.

As we looked for the easiest landing-point we were hailed by a lone figure on the breakwater arm. We had already spotted him watching us and he now identified himself as the son of Ernie Guy, whom we had attempted but failed to contact by telephone when staying with Rod. In truth, it was a very tenuous contact that we had half-expected to come to nothing, for it had come about as a result of our canoe coaching activities at home through one of Ernie's distant relatives whom we hardly knew. With such a flimsy connection, we could hardly have expected that Ernie had been plotting the progress of the expedition for many weeks, first through his contacts in Kent and more recently through the Tyne Coastguard. It was therefore a most unexpected and pleasant surprise to land and find that our stay in Seaham was already arranged.

Soup, bread, chocolate and coffee were immediately thrust upon us. This job had been assigned to Ernie's son, while he negotiated with the Harbour Master's office to bring a touring caravan into the dock area to accommodate us. Everything we might need had been taken care of. Once the caravan was set up we changed in comfort and were driven off for a pub meal. Later, when we had returned to the caravan, Ernie showed us where to find all we needed to cook breakfast in the morning. Such concern for our comfort was difficult to come to terms with.

The pulsing bleep of the alarm clock sounded unusually loud within the echoing confines of the caravan. It was just 0450 and when I looked outside to check the weather it was still dark. Having had such a short day on the Sunday, our intention was to put in a long paddle. Hence the very early start, which would enable us to reach Hartlepool for a second breakfast, before the tide (which was soon to be ebbing against us) could gather its full strength.

During the night a northerly swell had developed. It was working into the harbour of Seaham and swirling in great rushes across the concrete slip where we had to launch. It made getting afloat awkward but by 0635 we were on our way south and the day had dawned fair to give us a straightforward paddle along the industrialised coast of Durham. The winding gear of silent collieries scowled down at us from the low cliff-tops and just before 0930 we were able to beach on the western side of the breakwater arm that juts south-east towards the Yorkshire coast at Hartlepool.

Here we found ourselves in complete shelter from the wind and the railings around a promenade paddling-pool area were promptly utilised as drying racks for our wet items. Within minutes we were befriended by an elderly lady who introduced herself as Mrs McNaughten and invited us into her home for tea and bacon sandwiches. Before long she had contacted both the local press and Radio Cleveland, so we felt like real celebrities by the time lunch had arrived and it was with some measure of reluctance that we started to organise our getaway.

Several people watched us as we struggled to carry our boats over the wide expanse of mud and rocks to the low-water mark. Fortunately they were too far away to hear the continuous tirade of cursing that our half-hour of boat carrying prompted and it was 1300 before we waved farewell. Once clear of the breakwater we were in a long, heavy swell, which was rolling the large ships at anchor in the bay. There was considerable shipping traffic entering and leaving the Tees. We knew we would not be seen easily in the swell, so no time was wasted in crossing the well-buoyed channel that marks the Tees approaches.

Throughout the afternoon, the sky remained clear and the visibility excellent. Across the wide bay, the industrial beaches of the Tees gave way to the cliffs of North Yorkshire which stretched to the south-eastern horizon. As we headed for Staithes (where we intended to stop for the night) the northerly wind was slowly picking up in strength. The swell, however, had grown out of all proportion to the wind strength that we were actually experiencing. As the swell continued to grow on the flooding tide, the sea state became intimidating. The bigger waves were 4–5 m – a size we had come to accept on our long haul up the Atlantic coast – but these North Sea swells were more frightening, being both steeper and much closer together. The north-west to south-east orientation of the coast meant the shore was taking the full force of the sea, so we stayed out to make life easier. Even then there were times when we thought the swell might break.

It did nothing to improve my state of mind when we noticed that the fishing-boats had all disappeared. It could only mean one thing . . .

The haven of Staithes occupies a flooded, gorge-like inlet protected by a single breakwater. It is one of the few harbours that breach the natural defences of this cliffed shoreline and by 1700 we could see our destination. The seas were breaking right over the breakwater. For something like 500m off shore, the sea was one mass of breakers and white water. The harbour was unapproachable. It was time for a change of plan and I called over to Richard and Mick, whose diary takes up the story.

> Bill called us together – a sure sign something was wrong – but I didn't need to be told. My stomach was already churning over. It didn't help that after "switching off" at Rod's house we were expecting an easy run home. Thinking of all the comforts we had left behind us in the shelter of Hartlepool, I now had to face up to surviving again. An argument was going on in my head. Perhaps Bill was getting too eager to get home and pushing our luck a bit too far. The other side of my nature argued that I trusted his judgement. But it didn't stop my swearing at him under my breath. It was decision time. Staithes was wiped out in a white heaving mess. The tide and wind wouldn't let us turn back. The next harbour was Whitby but Bill didn't seem very happy about that option either.

Mick was quite right in detecting my reluctance to commit us to Whitby. My reading of the local sailing directions had made it only too clear that the entrance to Whitby would probably be very serious in these conditions. Reefs extend over half a mile off shore with only a very narrow channel between them. The tide would be setting across the approach line. It was still two hours' paddling away and there would be precious little daylight to spare. If we could not get in there we would have a five-hour paddle to reach Scarborough. Given the conditions and that we would be both tired and cold, this prospect was quite appalling. These thoughts I shared with my companions. I did not go on and tell them that we might be forced to use the radio to summon a lifeboat to show us the way in. My pride made it difficult for me to face this possibility. I was certainly not prepared to tempt the others into forcing the decision on me by teasing them with the possibility. The main thing was to keep a clear head and weigh the options carefully. For the time being we had to keep a grip on our fear and press on for Whitby, where time would no doubt force decisive action upon us, one way or the other.

In the event, my mind never stopped churning over these possibilities for the next few hours. Motivated by instincts of survival, senses alert and sharp through fear, we paddled on with surprisingly good speed. There were many anxious moments, but one wave in particular I felt sure had my name on it. I was paddling on the shoreward side of Richard when the wave bore down on us and absorbed my total attention as it seemed so much bigger than the others. Richard appeared to loom house-high above my head. I could see by the look on his face as he looked down at me that he too thought the worst of my chances. "Shit! Don't let it break!" is all I remember thinking. Had this crude prayer not been answered I would have been in very serious trouble. As it was, the wave ran on unbroken for some way before it toppled, leaving me shaken but unharmed, shouting out a list of obscenities at the elements in my relief. The mocking, tearing wind simply threw them back in my face with the next deluge of spray, unheard even by Richard, just a few metres away.

Eventually, in the evening sunshine, the beacons of Whitby harbour came into view. With a good tide running under us they came up very quickly, along with the cardinal buoy that pinpoints the entrance to the channel. As yet, we could not see the gap in the breaking white-caps that we hoped to find in the main channel. Then, as the entrance marks lined up, sensual awareness created a slow-motion impression of the next few, critical minutes. Without speaking we fell into a well-spaced line ahead. I began the approach, acutely aware of the waves breaking on both sides of me. Mick's journal:

> We inched towards the harbour, back paddling to avoid getting picked up by a wave and surfed in . . . saying my prayers again, it seemed to take an age. We all knew what it would mean if one of us went in . . . Burning in my mind was but one idea – get both feet firmly on land.

The harbour entrance was itself a hazard because of the confusion of wave pattern as the seas were reflected back to form clapotis. It would be a moment of truth but it could not be avoided. Suddenly, before me, the confusion seemed to ease. It was an opportunity not to be missed. Now it was a full-powered sprint, reckless to the risk of getting surfed or looped. I was vaguely conscious of anglers peering down at us from the western pier extension, then we were in. I could risk pulling up my neoprene cuff to look at my watch. Just 1900. The danger was past. Mind and senses tuned in on new discomforts. The wind was very chill. We all agreed we were cold (we had not noticed before). The unanimous agreement was that we were knackered (we hadn't noticed that either). I felt nervously and emotionally drained. The immediate reaction was to make profound curses and belittle the whole incident. Like the "epics" before, it would now be just one more story, occasionally told in some pub.

15

Nearly Home

Whitby – Happisburgh: 9th – 18th September

The implications of the Whitby episode are all too clear and reinforce some lessons from the early stages of the expedition. Any section of coast can be deadly serious if tackled in the wrong conditions; weather forecasts cannot be regarded as an absolutely reliable guide to the sea state; sea paddlers may sometimes be required to draw on resources that go beyond technical know-how and physical skills.

Our entry to Whitby harbour was not the end of our troubles for the day. We were unable to find a good place to camp or shelter, but in the light of what had happened, we were happy enough to find a small apron of derelict land perched between the harbour below and a waterside pub above called The Duke of York, where we changed into dry clothes and beat a hasty retreat to the bar. For fear of being moved on, we dared not erect the tent between the boats until after closing time and we were up again to pack by 0540 the following morning, before it was light.

The sky promised a day of fine weather and both the wind and sea had eased. Fishing-boats carrying angling parties were on the move. Launching at 0730, we headed out of the harbour into a northerly swell and had been thoroughly soaked by the time we reached the pier ends. The seas were still big enough to break on the rock ledges on either side of the channel, so we did not turn to run south-east until well off shore. We could then afford to relax a little and enjoy the fine cliff scenery, shown at its best in the early morning sun.

The coast was steadily trending southwards. With both the wind and tide to assist us, we arrived off Robin Hood's Bay in under an hour and by the time the tide turned about 10 o'clock we could already see the silhouette of Scarborough Castle, standing high on its rocky promontory. Our response was to move closer to the shore to escape the full effects of the ebb tide – a course we would have been reluctant to adopt had the wind not dropped away by this time. It was exactly midday when we entered Scarborough harbour, having covered about 17 miles, but there was no question of paddling further in spite of the early hour, for we had a long-standing offer of accommodation in the town.

Milton Bowers, the headmaster who had first backed my request for leave of absence, was now Head of the Graham School in Scarborough. We were to be his guests for the rest of the day, so my first task on getting ashore was to alert him of our arrival. This plan was initially frustrated when we could find no accessible slip on the falling tide, so we eventually left the harbour to beach in the South Bay and gained permission to leave our kayaks in the lifeboat station. Meanwhile, Milton had arrived and we were

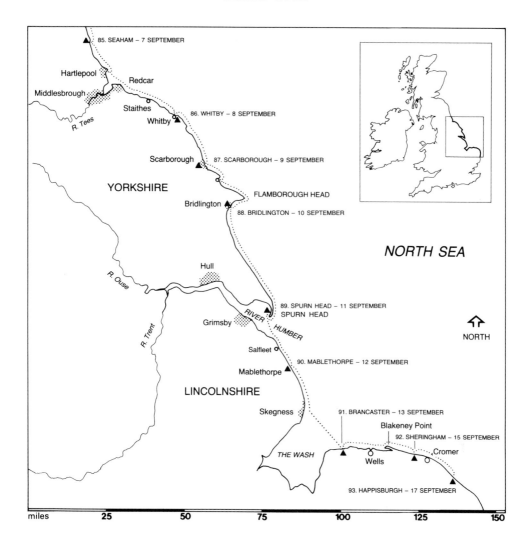

Inside the map:

85. SEAHAM – 7 SEPTEMBER

Hartlepool
Redcar
Middlesbrough
Staithes
Whitby
R. Tees

86. WHITBY – 8 SEPTEMBER

Scarborough   87. SCARBOROUGH – 9 SEPTEMBER

YORKSHIRE

FLAMBOROUGH HEAD
Bridlington
88. BRIDLINGTON – 10 SEPTEMBER

NORTH SEA

Hull
R. Ouse

89. SPURN HEAD – 11 SEPTEMBER
SPURN HEAD
RIVER HUMBER
Grimsby
R. Trent

NORTH

Salfleet
90. MABLETHORPE – 12 SEPTEMBER
Mablethorpe

LINCOLNSHIRE

Skegness
91. BRANCASTER – 13 SEPTEMBER
Blakeney Point
92. SHERINGHAM – 15 SEPTEMBER
Cromer
THE WASH
Wells

93. HAPPISBURGH – 17 SEPTEMBER

miles   25   50   75   100   125   150

driven to his home where his wife Greta had prepared a lunch for us. Later, when school had finished for the day, we were taken for an interview with the local press and then spent a very enjoyable evening as we were treated to a meal in a local carvery.

The weather appeared to be quite settled, so we were anxious to be away early on Wednesday morning to get the most from the tide. This led us to meet the lifeboat mechanic at 0700 to retrieve our boats and we were on our way once more by 0730. Although the sun was shining in a clear sky, the northerly breeze and swell had returned during the night, putting some degree of pressure on us since the day's paddle would take us round Flamborough Head – our last major headland involving complicated tidal eddies.

Paddling south from Scarborough we were making the most of the clear water and sea cliffs, for after Flamborough we would not be meeting such conditions again. It was already apparent that the swell was picking up, so we kept a wary eye on the shore-break. As we approached Filey, with over nine miles to the chalk headland of Flamborough still to cover, I began doubting our ability to turn the head before the tide turned against us and steepened the seas even further. Direct access to the sheltered bay of Filey is denied by a great reef which stretches south from the bay's northern point and is known as Filey Brigg. Being close to high water, the seas were breaking the length of the Brigg in a most sensational manner. In the bright sunshine it was quite picturesque but hardly encouraging. Great white explosions of spray and spume were rocketing skyward as the rollers collapsed on the reef. After the experiences off Staithes and Whitby we needed little encouragement to be more cautious, so once clear of the southern tip of the Brigg we reluctantly turned shoreward and back on ourselves to land by the sailing club, where the sands are protected by the point and the reef itself. To have pushed on would involve a commitment to turn Flamborough at all costs, for there were no other landing-places that would be easy after Filey.

There would now be a long wait for the next tide so we walked along Filey beach to the local Coastguard look-out. The auxiliary on duty was both friendly and sympathetic to our needs, offering us accommodation at her fish-and-chip shop if we were unable to get away. More practically, she telephoned the Coastguard on duty at Flamborough to give us an on-the-spot report of conditions. In view of the forecast, he urged us to move off in mid-afternoon, reinforcing the advice already given us by the mechanic of the Filey lifeboat, who happened to call in at the look-out about this time.

The result of these conversations was that we moved off just before 1400, heading south-east towards the distant chalk cliffs. There was far less wind than when we had landed, so progress was relatively easy in spite of the foul tide. We eventually picked up the east-flowing tidal eddy which assisted us towards the tip of the headland, making sure we followed the advice given about "keeping the lighthouse glass open". This meant using a crude form of transit to ensure we paddled a fixed distance from the shore, ensuring we would get caught in neither the tidal turbulence off shore nor the shore-break in the shallows off the head. What we in fact did was line up the bottom edge of the light itself with the edge of the cliff-top. Good advice it proved too, for in spite of the settled conditions that now prevailed, long lines of breakers were rolling across the rock platforms that extend from the southern side of the head.

By 1700 we had cleared the technical problems and were heading west towards distant Bridlington, its position clearly identified by the church spire. Here, on the south side of Flamborough, we were in a different world. Sheltered from the northerly breeze, the sea's surface was glassy calm, the air oppressive and hot with the sunlight glaring back off the water.

When we came to enter the busy harbour there was a bustle of activity on the fishing quays and many more yachts on moorings than I expected to find. But we could see nowhere to slip the boats that would give access to a likely stopover. The beaches south of the harbour proved no more promising, so we ended up back inside and disembarking on the mud. We could find nowhere to stay or pitch the tent and I eventually went to look for the local lifeboat station. The administrator for the R.N.L.I. was quite happy for us to sleep in their headquarters, but it was so far from both the harbour and the

Keeping well out from the cliffs, favourable tides helped us past Flamborough Head.

beach (they launch their lifeboat with a tractor) that the long carry of our heavy kayaks was impracticable. There was no alternative but to sleep rough. With this in mind, we moved our boats beneath an alcove within the harbour complex, whose roof was the promenade above. This fruitless search for more comfortable accommodation had wasted nearly two hours and it was almost dark before we had changed into dry clothes. Anticipating a long paddle the next day, we turned in early.

South of Bridlington, the Humberside coast is outstanding in its lack of paddling interest all the way to Spurn Head and the entrance to the river Humber. For something like 40 miles, the low shoreline is devoid of natural relief and runs almost ruler-straight from one groyne to the next, occasionally passing small seaside villages. It was a section I had been anticipating with distaste ever since we had covered the O.S. map showing it. There was no choice but to "switch off" and paddle it as quickly and clinically as possible.

Fortunately, the weather forecast was a good one and would at least provide the opportunity to clear the entire section in one paddle. Accordingly we were up in the dark at 0530 and, after a magnificent sunrise over the harbour, we were away on a calm sea for 0730.

Low boulder-clay cliffs fronted by sand or shingle stretched to the limit of visibility. Thankfully, this was only moderate, so the real extent of our monotonous undertaking was conveniently hidden from us in the haze. So, one by one, the villages and caravan sites shown on the O.S. map were ticked off. At around 1000, when off Hornsea, a north-easterly breeze came away, providing a little help when the tide turned against us at midday. The dullness of the scenery was accentuated by the sultry weather conditions. A tantalising blue sky stayed just behind us all day, while ahead the sky was veiled in a thick, stormy haze, affording only brief glimpses of watery sunshine. So anxious were we to put this all behind us that we did not bother to take a lunch break. At 1500, with the ebb tide in full flow against us, we were off Withernsea.

Interest returned briefly off the R.A.F. bombing ranges at Cowden. Tornados were swooping in overhead and their bombs sending up great plumes of water. We eventually agreed that they were too close for comfort and we were thankful to have our ICM 12 radio on deck to call up the range officer and gain an official clearance to paddle on. It was an incident which highlights an important use of marine wave-band radios that sea canoeists often overlook.

After this episode the miles dragged laboriously by until we at last came to the neck of the great spit which terminates in Spurn Head. This bank of sand and shingle extends several miles into the Humber Estuary, its human inhabitants – the Humber Pilots, the Coastguards and the full-time crew of the Spurn lifeboat – under the threat of finding themselves in residence on an island after every North Sea storm, so tenuous is the attachment of the spit to the mainland. The full force of the tidal flow in and out of the Humber sets off Spurn Head, creating considerable turbulence, so having paddled past the black and white hoops of the disused lighthouse, we approached the last few hundred metres gingerly. Here we had to cross the shoal known as the Stony Binks. On this particular evening the confusion of tide and white water over the Binks was quite manageable, at last allowing us to turn the tip of the point and reach the shelter of the western side.

It was 1835 and after eleven hours' continuous paddling we were weary. South of the modern framework of piers and walkways used by the Humber Pilots and lifeboat crew, we ran our boats ashore on the sands beneath the old lifeboat shed which stands precariously on stilts with a great launching ramp. A brief look at the neighbouring sand dunes was all that was required to eliminate their camping possibilities. Feeling despondent, the sight of someone waving at us from the Coastguard tower gave us immediate hope of avoiding a gritty camp.

When we walked over to the huge tower complex we were treated to mugs of tea, assistance to carry our boats over the dunes and, most welcome of all, the offer of their rest-room to eat and sleep in. Later, when we had showered, put on dry clothes and had a proper meal, we spent an interesting evening absorbing the sophistication of the tower's various observation platforms. The Coastguards shared the tower with the Humber Pilots and had banks of fascinating equipment to monitor shipping movements in and off the Humber. We were particularly struck by the number of "frivolous" phone calls that the evening Coastguard shift had to deal with, ranging from buoy lights being reported as S.O.S. signals to a summons for help to treat a seagull with a broken wing!

After a comfortable night's sleep, we awoke to find the weather had brightened up and by 0915 we had our boats in the water in spite of the long carry. A fresh north-easterly wind had chopped up the sea off the point. During the previous day the sea had grown increasingly dirty and murky as we approached the Humber and now, in the estuary proper, the bright sun accentuated the yellow-brown coloration of the dancing wavetops.

Paddling from the shelter of the haven, we found ourselves in a strong eddy that carried us rapidly off the tip of the point into an area of broken white water, and clearing it we were among the numerous ships at anchor, presumably waiting to go up river on the tide. Our task was to ferry-glide the tide flooding into the river to reach its southern shore in the vicinity of the featureless point known as Donna Nook. Here we would be in another R.A.F. range, so we had made arrangements before leaving the Coastguard tower for them to alert the range officer that we would be calling them on our radio. This we duly did and the bombing stopped to let us through.

This part of the Lincolnshire coast proved very difficult to navigate. From the vantage point of a sea kayak, it appears as mile after mile of the same low terrain and is mostly sand dunes. Attention to detail was what was required, but the surf set up by the fresh wind was forcing us to stay outside the numerous sand banks and shoals. Out at sea we could not see over the dunes to the features which usually provide navigational points of reference. At one stage we grew too casual and allowed ourselves to get too close to an offshore sand-bar. Mick and I were inattentively chatting when we simultaneously noticed a much bigger set of swells bearing down on us. We swung rapidly to seaward and dug in hard to generate sufficient power to burst through the top of the green surf wave, bouncing down heavily on the far side. Two similarly large waves followed, then the danger had passed. But Richard had fared less well. Paddling apart from Mick and myself he had not seen the problem as early. He barely survived the break as he was surfed in backwards until deep inside the normal breakline. Consequently he had to endure several nasty minutes as he shakenly paddled back out to where Mick and I sat laughing at him.

We had left Spurn Head intending to have a short day that would take us to Saltfleet Haven, a tiny creek hidden in the Lincolnshire marshes which is obscured to view from the sea by the sand dunes. The channel that approaches the creek has to dog-leg between sand-bars and so is marked by tall poles or perches that mark the route. Both Richard and I had attempted to memorise the pilotage instructions but now we were on the spot we could not identify a single feature to pinpoint the creek's position with any certainty. We had estimated our arrival time at the perches as around 1230, but by 1300 it was clear to us that somehow we had missed seeing them. We were in no mood to turn back, so settled on plodding on to where we knew the dunes would terminate, at the seaside resort of Mablethorpe.

We were anticipating problems of running in through the surf but by approaching the beach in the lee of a big sewer-outfall that set off the beach at an angle and took the "sting" out of the breaks, we landed without difficulty. Once ashore, we could cross the sea defences extending from the dunes and found the resort set out before us. It was a child's paradise and a sea paddler's nightmare – row upon row of amusement arcades, blaring music and the smell of frying. Uninviting though the scene was, after the 40-mile paddle of the previous day and another 18 miles that morning, moving on again was an even less attractive proposition. We hoped the local inshore lifeboat station might offer secure lodgings in such urban surroundings, but it turned out to be under reconstruction. The tourist information office kindly arranged for us to use a council store-shed on the front but we had to decline the offer when we found we would not have access to our boats outside normal working hours. It was the local Coastguard auxiliary who came to our rescue. He had a garage and store for his Land-Rover and rescue equipment about 250m from the beach. It was a long carry but by far the best option open to us and we thankfully made it our home for the evening.

That afternoon we sauntered around the streets feeling uncomfortably out of place. The people were friendly but the surroundings not to our taste. All we wanted to do was to get away.

Before turning in for the night I phoned the Spurn Head Coastguard to get the latest weather forecast for Saturday. The prognosis was for fair weather and F2–3 variable winds that would become fresh westerlies later. It was as near a perfect forecast as we could hope for, bearing in mind that we were about to undertake our last major open crossing to get across the Wash to Norfolk.

At 0545 we were up and packing. There was a long paddle ahead of us, but before that, 40 minutes of strenuous carrying to put us on the beach. It was therefore 0800 on this clear, sunny morning of gentle easterly breezes before we actually launched into what was now only a very slight surf.

The plan was to paddle against the last of the ebbing tide so that we would get the full run of the flood into the Wash, once the tide had turned. Our next landing was to be Brancaster Staithe, about 30 miles to the south-east. Initially we paddled southwards, keeping close to shore to stay out of the foul tide, but having put the radio masts of Trusthorpe and then the Coastguard look-out tower at Chapel St. Leonards behind us, we began moving out to sea as the tide began to run in our favour. By the time we were abreast of Ingoldmell's Point, we were two miles out and had picked up the buoyage system we would use to monitor our progress on the long crossing. We were now steering a course of 150° M into a rising south-easterly breeze, taking us to seaward of the green cone buoy off Skegness and after another two hours' paddle to the Lyn Knock Buoy, right on schedule. This was where we would cross the main shipping lanes that give access to the Wash ports, but events were not running quite to plan. The breeze had continued to freshen and created a steep, choppy sea that was slopping onto our port bow, giving us regular dousings. So much for our "perfect" weather forecast!

Four miles on we had crossed the shipping lanes and reached the red can buoy of the Woolpack. The detail of the Norfolk coast was becoming clearer but it showed that the rising wind and tide were pushing us further west towards Hunstanton than we wanted to be. To make this good meant paddling straight into the wind, which had backed and become a F5–6 easterly. The paddle had degenerated into a sinew-stretching and back-aching grind and we cursed the Met. Office for their unmentionable forecast. The sand dunes of Scolt Head pinpointed the entrance to Brancaster harbour beautifully, but getting there was a different story. Every metre of progress was very hard work and eight hours from setting out, with the tide now turned and running out of the lagoon against us, we gave up the struggle. We were off the western side of the entrance at Thornham, where the road leading to the Royal Norfolk Golf Club gives access to the beach. Here we came wearily ashore to modify our plans for the evening.

Our reason for making for Brancaster Staithe was that we were assured of a good welcome there. The first headmaster of my teaching career, Bob Dent, had retired to Norfolk and kept a holiday home at Brancaster, so we were under pressure to inform him of our whereabouts. Fortunately, the golf professional at the Royal Norfolk was prepared to let us leave our kayaks near his shop and allowed me to telephone the Dent household. A few minutes later, we had changed into dry clothes and were being bustled into the Dents' car for an evening of relentless spoiling. I had always viewed Bob Dent as an avuncular figure, but he now exceeded my expectations as Mrs Dent kept up a constant stream of food coming our way. Comfortably installed in their cottage, we could ignore the heavy rain that had set in as the wind turned to the west as forecast.

Since leaving Rod Mitchell on the previous Sunday afternoon we had paddled almost 200 miles. We therefore required no persuading to take the next day off which had an indifferent forecast for the morning, so the day began with tea in bed at 0745, to be followed by a cooked breakfast and a walk before Sunday lunch. It was altogether a different sort of day and terribly civilised compared to that to which we had grown accustomed. A drive into the North Norfolk countryside and visit to the nature reserve at Holme-next-the-Sea saw us through the afternoon, then more food and an evening of watching television.

Had it been possible, we would have left Brancaster at 0400 on Monday morning, but that seemed such an inconvenience to our hosts that we could not bring ourselves to suggest it. The problem was that we needed to work the ebb tide along the North Norfolk coast, so our ungracious compromise was to rise at 0500, and grab a bread-and-jam breakfast on the run to be driven back to our boats, pack and launch for 0615. Waving farewell to the Dents, we paddled east beneath an oppressive grey sky that produced a blood-red dawn as the sun rose out of the North Sea.

There was no wind and the sea had settled to an oily swell as we paddled over the bar to clear Scolt. Our view landward was of sandy beaches, dunes and glimpses of conifers, but it hardly matched the impression one gains from landward. For the visitor on foot, this is one of the most beautiful sections of the Norfolk coastline, offering the classic combination of fine sands, dunes and pine forest, backed by salt marsh and a chain of lovely villages of flint cottages that sit at the foot of the low hills. But very little of this can be appreciated from the cockpit of a sea kayak and a view point of less than a metre above sea level.

We had little more than three hours of good tide which took us past the entrance of Wells and eventually to the huge bank of shingle that makes the spit of Blakeney. By the time we were there the wind had freshened from the north-east and the tide was beginning to run against us. The cloud had failed to disperse and it was a cold, grey day with spots of rain on the wind. We wanted a hot drink and about 1115, when off Cley-next-the-Sea (where several commercial fishing-boats are stored on the higher terraces of Blakeney Spit), we ran ashore through an increasingly lumpy sea that broke awkwardly and violently on the steep shingle.

Our idea was to sit out the remainder of the flood tide and wait for it to ebb, but having brewed and drunk our tea in the lee of a car-park shelter, we found it unseasonably cold and decided to push on. To try to stay warm, we put on our buoyancy aids. It was just as well, for when we came to launch, the wind had strengthened to become a F5 north-easterly and the sea state even lumpier than when we landed. The waves were now steep, short and sometimes broke unexpectedly and it was out of the question to move into the deeper water because the tide was running far too hard against us.

In such uncomfortable conditions we battled eastwards to clear the Blakeney Spit and reach the low cliffs which form a coast of different character at Weybourne. Meanwhile, the weather was continuing to worsen, along with the sea state and our prospects of landing in one piece on the steep pebble beaches that form the cliff foot. When the lifeboat station at Sheringham came into view we felt inclined to force the issue and attempt a landing. It looked to be a daunting prospect for the waves were breaking in a single, vicious "dump" the length of the beach. However, just west of the lifeboat turntable and tractor ramp, the shingle was a little less steep, so this had to be the place where we would attempt to get ashore.

As I began the approach, a figure in oilskins appeared on the lifeboat turntable and ran to the water's edge, waving me in. This, we later learned, was the mechanic, Brian Pegg, and very thankful of his assistance I was when I rocketed up the beach in a mess of breaking water to find him hanging on to my bow-loop, preventing me from being pulled out again in the backwash. Scrambling out as best I could, we both dragged my kayak clear, then together rendered similar assistance to Richard and finally Mick.

With the boats safe on the lifeboat ramp we could take better stock of our new friend. Tall, long-limbed and in well-preserved middle years, Brian told us in his broad Norfolk brogue (punctuated by an equally broad smile) that he had been asked by the Coastguard to look out for us, for the Met. Office had just issued a north-easterly gale warning. He went on to tell us that his lifeboat was undergoing a refit on our home waters of the river Medway, so we would be welcome to stay in the station for as long as we liked.

That evening, from the comfort of the look-out tower, we watched a fiery sunset. The full gale that had been forecast did not materialise, but it did blow hard and set up an evil-looking sea. We knew when we bedded down that our prospects of getting away the next morning were poor, but I could not resist the temptation to get up at 0500 to make sure, before turning in again until 0730. We were effectively on the horns of a dilemma. To utilise the powerful tidal stream and avoid fighting it, we needed to get away around high water; either side of high water the seas were breaking on the steep part of the beach to the extent that launching was not possible. We had no choice but to await the abating of the wind and sea state. When Brian arrived for work he concurred with this assessment, although in his unassuming way he was anxious to add that he was not a canoeist himself and therefore did not want to tell us what to do. He had already informed us that he was about to take over as coxswain of the lifeboat (which happened to require beach-launching and landing) so we would have been foolish not to take the advice he offered. So it was that we had a day off in Sheringham.

During the early hours of Wednesday 17th September, the wind finally dropped. We were up at 0500 to catch the tide but found to our dismay that the sea had still not gone down, for plunging breakers were still collapsing on the shingle in a frightening manner. I remember feeling in a particularly ruthless and determined mood to press on so we still breakfasted and got ready to leave, hoping that conditions would improve. The spirit of impatience urged us to carry our loaded boats out onto the turntable.

Sheringham lifeboat station, with a wave breaking on the steep shingle beach on the left.

There was unanimous agreement that it would be impossible to launch off the shingle, but we could not agree on the feasibility of sliding down the lifeboat slip in an extended seal-launch. The problem was that some of the waves were washing across the slip and while I was urging that we could get off this way, Richard blatantly refused. There was no way to resolve such a conflict and we had always agreed that if one of us did not want to attempt something we would respect that wish. All the same, there were a few sour comments as we moodily sat around awaiting some new development. Incidents of this nature place the best of friendships under great strain. I resented the decision and the atmosphere it created and have no doubt that Richard felt the same, but retrospectively we were a very fortunate team in so far as this was one of less than a handful of such incidents in the 21 weeks we had been living in each other's laps.

The "new development", when it materialised, appeared after high water in the form of Brian Pegg's arrival on the scene. The falling tide had just exposed an area of pebbles which had less of a gradient than most of the beach and Brian offered to put on his oilskins, enter the water and hold the boats in position so that we could pick the right wave set to launch into. We in fact committed ourselves to his expert judgement and timing. The extra impetus that he gave to the kayaks was just enough to get us off the beach and by 0830 we were in the clear and off eastwards towards Cromer.

The late getaway had already lost us most of the favourable tide and it had gone slack by the time we had covered the few miles to Overstrand. It was the beginning of a long slog into the powerful stream of a spring tide. We had little choice but to keep going if we were to clear the difficulties of steep beaches and reach an area of sand beach which would give us some chance of launching again on the top of the tide. It meant we had to get at least as far as the natural gas terminal at Bacton and this became our goal.

Every mile was hard won. Having passed the radio mast at Walcott our next significant landmark was the great bulk of the medieval church at Happisburgh where we knew there would be sand beaches. Meanwhile, Richard continued to have a bad day. He was caught inside the breakline of a single, freak wave that surfed him off backwards towards the beach and he barely avoided a reverse-loop.

Just after 1500, the red and white bands of Happisburgh lighthouse came into view and we surfed ashore towards a ramp that climbs the low, sandy cliffs and leads to the inshore lifeboat shed and a portable Coastguard cabin. On this coast, the sea is eroding the cliffs at a very fast rate, so that elaborate wooden sea defences forming a palisade have been built to protect the cliff foot. By so doing, they bar access between the beach and the cliffs, apart from a bridge and gateway at the foot of the ramp. We could see immediately that launching into the surf at the top of the tide would have to be over this bridge (which would be awash) and not without its special problems.

For the time being we were glad enough to get ashore after such a slow and physical 19 miles. It also made a welcome change to find we had a choice of accommodation. The top of the ramp led to a caravan and campsite where we were offered a free night, but when Richard telephoned the local Coastguard, we gladly accepted his offer to stay in the Coastguard Portacabin.

Late in the afternoon, as the time of high tide approached, we kept a careful watch on the water line in relation to the sea defences. Both the palisade and the "bridge" were eventually awash and being battered by the surf. Unless the north-east wind disappeared overnight, we would have major difficulties in getting away the next morning.

During the evening, Richard had been in contact with home. Rob Catchlove and his fiancée Linda were on holiday and were driving to Norfolk to visit us for a couple of days. It gave us something to look forward to, for Rob would no doubt paddle with us and so give us a complete break from our usual routine. The couple arrived just after midnight.

The weather forecast we had taken before Rob's arrival was a good one. Overnight, the wind which had plagued us since Brancaster was due to die away to a F2. In theory, it should allow the surf to drop enough to allow us to get away on the morning tide, when it would still be dark. It was therefore worrying to be woken several times in the night by the noise of high winds shaking the cabin. When the alarm went at 0400 the wind strength was a good F6 and the surf running accordingly. In a spirit of optimism fired by Rob's enthusiasm for a paddle to Great Yarmouth, we packed our boats by moonlight. However, as the minutes ticked by, I was losing confidence that we could launch in such conditions. By 0730, when we had lost the best of the fair tide, we decided the day would have to be written off. For peace of mind I phoned the Coastguard to get their latest forecast. It was still predicting a F2. In the Portacabin was a hand-held anemometer which we took outside to get a reading. It registered a steady 28–30 knots!

Faced by a lost paddling day, the availability of Rob's car at least made it possible to salvage something useful. B.B.C. Radio Norfolk had been in contact with us and now we could drive into Norwich to give them an interview. The visit to Norwich led to one of the more farcical episodes of our expedition.

The young lady who met us at the B.B.C. headquarters was determined to tape an interview in what she described as "authentic, natural surroundings". For us, this conjured up the image of an outside broadcast by the sea shore, with the sound of breaking waves and seagulls. But this was not what she had in mind and we should have become wary at an early stage when she kept using terms like "marooned in Norfolk" and "shipwrecked"!

She led us, like lambs to the slaughter, to an outside broadcast estate car in the car-park. She then took us to a quiet brook in the parkland of the University of East Anglia. I have deliberately avoided using the expression, "drove us", because a "driver" she certainly was not. After hurtling across the studio car-park in reverse (we were expecting to go forwards) we leap-frogged, by stages, into the road. As we looked at each other in nervous apprehension, she light-heartedly assured us that she could drive but could not reach the clutch. At each busy roundabout on the ring-road we careered into the path of oncoming traffic – there was no point in giving way to the right because that would require us to pull away again – only to stall in the middle as furious motorists swerved to avoid us.

None of this appeared to dismay our cheerful radio journalist. As she muddled along she continued to bombard us with questions in preparation for the real interview. She finally asked the inevitable and most pertinent question of all. "What was the most anxious and dangerous moment in your expedition?" I did not hesitate in giving her a direct and honest answer: "This car ride."

There was, of course, a light-hearted aspect to all this but it was not quite so funny for Mick who nearly ended the expedition at this point, a victim of concussion. He had opted to lie across the luggage area. As we entered the university grounds the roadways narrowed and "sleeping policemen" occurred at regular intervals to slow traffic down. They were no deterrent whatsoever to our chauffeur. At each ramp, Mick took off, bouncing his head off the roof before crashing back into the floor. I made a serious offer to drive but it was declined. But then she did need the practice.

To be fair, her journalistic skills were better than her driving. By the time the seaside noises had been dubbed over the babbling brook and bird-song the finished tape would not have sounded out of place on *Desert Island Discs*. Broadcast initially on Radio Norfolk, the tape was forwarded to Radio Kent. Clever editing had produced a result that was sensational in the worst and most embarrassing sense of the word.

Back at Happisburgh that evening, Rob and Linda prepared a barbecue for us. We had just finished eating when the Coastguard arrived to see us. He had just seen the television weather forecast and thought we would like to hear some good news. An anticyclone was establishing itself over the British Isles and was likely to produce fair weather with light winds for several days. If this forecast was correct, then we would be home before the weather deteriorated again.

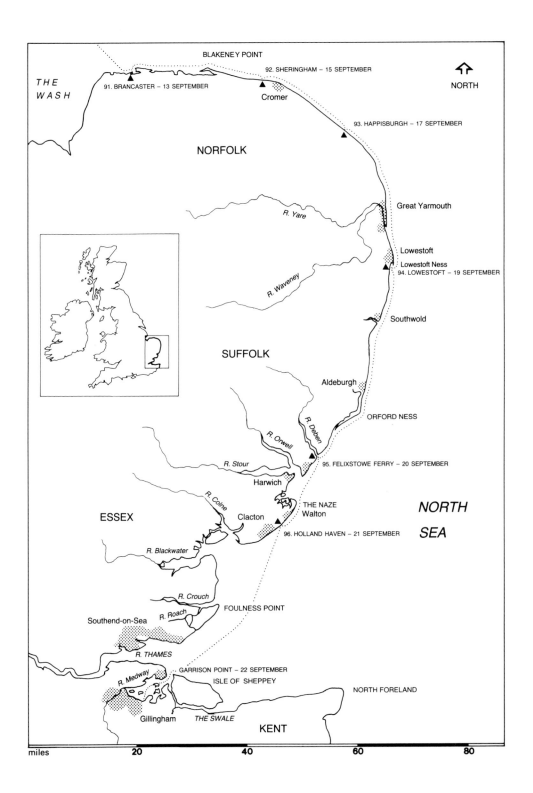

BLAKENEY POINT

92. SHERINGHAM – 15 SEPTEMBER

THE WASH

NORTH

91. BRANCASTER – 13 SEPTEMBER

Cromer

93. HAPPISBURGH – 17 SEPTEMBER

NORFOLK

R. Yare

Great Yarmouth

R. Waveney

Lowestoft
Lowestoft Ness
94. LOWESTOFT – 19 SEPTEMBER

Southwold

SUFFOLK

Aldeburgh

ORFORD NESS

R. Deben

R. Orwell

95. FELIXSTOWE FERRY – 20 SEPTEMBER

R. Stour

Harwich

R. Colne

THE NAZE
Walton

ESSEX

Clacton

96. HOLLAND HAVEN – 21 SEPTEMBER

NORTH SEA

R. Blackwater

R. Crouch

FOULNESS POINT

R. Roach

Southend-on-Sea

R. THAMES

GARRISON POINT – 22 SEPTEMBER

R. Medway

ISLE OF SHEPPEY

NORTH FORELAND

Gillingham   *THE SWALE*

KENT

miles   20   40   60   80

16

The Circle is Closed

Happisburgh – River Medway: 19th – 22nd September

Friday 19th September was the 153rd day of the expedition and exactly five calendar months on from when we set off. We were up for 0415 and within half an hour were out of the Portacabin, moving our kayaks out of its shadow to pack them by the light of a full moon. The air was chill and still, the surf only light and we had launched through it without mishap by 0540. Paddling beyond the groyne ends to clear the danger of any freak breaks, we regrouped, absorbing the memorable qualities of our surroundings. It was a particularly beautiful night. In the west shone the full moon, providing ample light to paddle by; to the east, the barest trace of paling sky was beginning to blossom, heralding the magnificent sunrise that was to follow at about 0630.

The tide picked up in strength very rapidly so that the Happisburgh lighthouse quickly fell astern. In the first two hours we covered over 13 miles to pass the sand dunes at Winterton. Meanwhile, the coast increasingly trended southwards so that the residual oily swell (all that remained of the sea that had been hindering us) was now a positive assistance. South of Caister the tide was running hard enough to set up overfalls and swirls and the 20-mile journey to the entrance of Great Yarmouth harbour was covered in only 3¼ hours.

Linda was due to meet us here with the car, but the tide was too good to waste. While Rob left us to paddle in and honour the rendezvous arrangement, we pushed on in the hot sunshine to Lowestoft. The seven miles took exactly an hour, but our speed was hardly surprising, for when we stopped paddling to observe the tide running off a buoy at Lowestoft Ness (the expedition's furthest east) we were swept by at almost 3 knots.

We were therefore able to paddle into the harbour in time to see Rob and Linda arrive and slipped our boats at the Royal Norfolk and Suffolk Yacht Club. The club bosun had already been contacted by Rob and we were directed to a disused garage where we were told we could leave our boats and spend the night. Even now it was only 1030 as we walked over to the clubhouse for a shower and it was both unusual and satisfying to have put in a reasonable mileage and still have a whole day of fine weather in front of us.

During the afternoon we called in at the offices of the *Eastern Daily Press*, where a photographer wanted pictures to include our boats and so drove us back to the harbour. It was a fortunate move, for on our arrival we were met by a television news cameraman from the B.B.C. (Eastern Region). For his benefit we changed back into paddling clothes

175

and, feeling rather self-conscious, we made an "action replay" of our entry into Lowestoft harbour.

Rob and Linda set off to leave us a little later, taking with them our assurances for all at home that we would be with them within a week. Our proximity to our final goal was to be re-emphasised that evening. Len Thompson, a friend and teaching colleague from school, arrived to buy us a beer. We were in a particularly buoyant mood as we sat in the pub and I could announce with some satisfaction, having checked my arithmetic, that our total distance paddled by dead-reckoning was now 2,500 miles.

It was another early start with a 0415 alarm on Saturday morning to get the best from the tide. Once again we packed by moonlight before beginning a long boat-carry to get afloat. As it was low water, the slip where we had landed was unusable so we carried to the beach on the south side of the harbour. The sea was flat calm as we pushed off, just in time to beat the sunrise. The crystal-clear weather of Friday had given way to hazier conditions, but it still promised to be another hot day.

Here in Suffolk we were on a different type of coast. Low cliffs alternate with stony points and shingle beaches that are occasionally backed by trapped lakes or broads. Thanks to the strong tide, we were travelling very fast again. The lighthouse at Southwold was the first major landmark, followed by a low, wooded and scenic section of coast that leads to Dunwich. Generations of schoolboys have been told of the rapid erosion of this part of the East Anglian coast, leaving several medieval churches under the sea. A less romantic landmark followed, when the ominous bulk of the power station at Sizewell began to emerge through the haze.

At Aldeburgh we began a run of several miles along the famous spit of Orford Ness and still carried the tide as we crossed the expanse of Hollesley Bay, but just after the entrance to Orford Haven we reached the Martello tower at Bawdsey Point and the tide stood on its tail. There was no period of time which we could identify as "the slack". At one moment the tide was with us and a few minutes later it was hammering out against us at about 3 knots. We had hoped to reach the river Deben before this happened but had narrowly lost our race against time and tide. The result was a difficult hour to pull past the radar complex, with our boats just off the beach to escape the worst of the tide. The last few minutes of effort took us across the Deben's mouth to the Felixstowe Ferry Sailing Club on the southern side of the narrows. We were only just in time. Within minutes of our arrival the tide was roaring out at about 6 knots and causing major problems to the yachts attempting to enter the haven of the inner estuary.

The final hour's paddling may have been hard work but the day as a whole had been an easy one considering that we had covered over 40 miles. It was certainly enough to impress the committee members of the sailing club on whose "doorstep" we had arrived and we were offered one of their changing rooms as accommodation, as well as complimentary tickets to their evening social – a plentiful supply of beer to the music of a German band.

Compared to the early starts we had been having, a 0615 alarm seemed a lie-in. We could afford this luxury because we were now on the northern limit of the Thames Estuary, where the tidal sequence gave us more time to get organised in the morning.

The steep beach at Felixstowe Sailing Club.

There was time to treat ourselves to a cheap, cooked breakfast in a nearby café that opened at 0700 to cater for local anglers, leaving plenty of time to launch by 0800, on the last of the tide ebbing from the Deben.

It was another still, hazy morning promising a hot day to come. As it was low water, a great bank of shingle was exposed, almost blocking the entrance to the Deben and accounting for some of the tidal problems of the little estuary. Clear of this obstacle, we set off south-west to pass Felixstowe and the entrance to the river Stour and port of Harwich, although because it was Sunday, most of the sailing traffic was cruising yachts. They were enjoying the benefits of a fresh south-westerly breeze that had sprung up as the sun climbed higher. For us it was an annoying head wind as we swung out to seaward on a compass course for Walton-on-the-Naze, obscured from view by a thick heat haze. As we turned the Naze's promontory, we at last picked up some benefit from the tide that was now flooding into the Thames.

Approaching Clacton I had to make a decision as to how we would make our final run for home. There was enough tide left to carry us further, but this would place us on the estuaries of the Blackwater and Crouch, with their complex configuration of offshore sands, mud flats and tidal creeks. In such terrain it would become problematic to find a campsite that would not demand a long run into a creek, distancing us from the most direct route home and making the tides even more difficult to work. Having talked this problem through, we decided to make an early stop, before reaching the Blackwater, so that we could attempt to enter the Thames (and probably the Medway) in a single, extended hop. So, although it was not yet midday, we came ashore by the Clacton Sailing Club at Holland Haven to beg shelter for the night. The fine weather had ensured that there were plenty of people about. Within a few minutes we had received three offers of accommodation and accepted the invitation to sleep in the club itself, for this would give us the easiest start on Monday.

Having showered, we spent lunchtime in the bar and a relaxing afternoon lounging in the sun. Several times I rechecked the tide tables and calculations before assuring Richard and Mick that we could be into the Medway the next day. As the club members began to leave and their premises became ours for the evening, an air of hushed anticipation descended. Such was the level of suppressed excitement that was beginning to build, none of us were keen to visit a pub that evening. But having telephoned home to explain our whereabouts and plans, I had a very good reason to adopt a sombre mood.

Bev had passed me an awful piece of news. The previous evening, Mick's younger brother David had been killed in a motorcycling accident. Mick's parents did not want him to know this for fear that he would return home immediately and so complicate the conclusion of the expedition. They were also worried that he would pick up the news from a local radio station or simply phone home and detect that something was amiss. It was one burden of responsibility that I had never anticipated. We had to get home fast, but I had to keep the news of David Wibrew's accident away from Mick. I shared the secret with Richard and we conspired to ensure that between us we would not let Mick down on either count.

Entering the Thames Estuary from the North Sea in a kayak is not an easy task. Tides run hard; there are huge areas of offshore sands that can dry out, whilst the shoreline is mostly salt marsh, fronted by mud flats. The biggest of these is the Maplin Sands, which extend north-eastwards from Southend to the point of Foulness and on out to sea for several miles. To add an air of seriousness, the M.O.D. uses the entire area for firing ranges. To avoid getting caught out in this mess, we would have to work the tides with precision and paddle for over 30 miles in the shipping lanes to guarantee getting into the Medway. The resulting plan was simple but the route complex.

We would work along the shoreline against an hour of foul ebb tide, then cross the last hour of the weakening ebb as we put in a dog-leg out to sea to pick up the buoyage of the shipping lanes. This would give us the period of slack water and the full six hours of the flood tide to carry us up the deep-water channels between the sand banks, into the Thames Estuary, across to Kent and so into the estuary of the Medway before high water. When I phoned for a weather forecast for the Thames area it was not ideal. F3–4 westerly winds, occasionally reaching F5, would not only be a head wind but create wind-against-tide conditions. There was also the possibility of fog banks. But now we had to get home. Monday 22nd September therefore started for us at 0500 and the first piece of good fortune was when I looked out to see that the weather was far better than had been forecast. A very gentle breeze was blowing and although the haze was thick, it was certainly not fog.

There was no one around to share our "sense of occasion" as we launched on this special leg of our journey. It was still only 0650 and we headed off south-west, paddling just off the groyne ends to keep out of the tide. Past the pier at Clacton we came to a navigation beacon on the beach and a construction site for an enormous breakwater, where a crane was working in the water. Paddling past an astonished crane driver, we swung the boats to face straight out to sea. I remember thinking that the next time we would be this close to land, we would have achieved the object of our journey. It was a good spur to effort, so having checked the compass, we headed directly off shore on the first dog-leg. This was to last an hour, putting us out of sight of land, and at 0900 we reached the buoys that mark the channel to the river Crouch between Buxey and Foulness Sands.

A fresh westerly head wind had arisen as forecast, but proved to be advantageous in providing us with a "game" to break the monotony of the featureless miles. There were several yachts that appeared to be entering the Thames by a route similar to ours and it amused us to race and beat them along the channel, for the need to tack cancelled out their superior speed. The "race" brought us past the Whitaker Beacon (marking the outer extremity of Foulness Sands) and within earshot of artillery fire. When this became uncomfortably close we decided to move away from the Maplin Sands towards the southern side of the West Swin Channel, delimited here by the shoals of the West Barrow. Since we had to work towards the Kentish coast sooner or later, I decided to cross the western end of this great sand bank, finding there was barely enough water to do so. It makes a strange experience to be many miles from shore, completely out of sight of land but to find one's paddles hitting the bottom. The wind picked this moment to strengthen to a F5, setting up a sloppy chop, but it was short-lived and soon afterwards dropped right away so that the afternoon was spent paddling in a virtual calm with hot sunshine.

Our first sighting of a familiar landmark was when the Red Sands Forts began to emerge out of the haze on our port bow. These forts were anti-aircraft gun platforms constructed as part of a series of defences. I had paddled to them several times and they have always reminded me of the war machines from H. G. Wells's *War of the Worlds*. Miles from shore, the rectangular steel box of each platform is perched about 30 feet above the water on tripod legs, with each platform connected to its neighbours by twisted and corroded cat-walks. On this occasion, these monstrosities were more like old friends welcoming us back to home waters.

Shortly afterwards we sighted the Medway Buoy that marks the beginning of the buoyed channel forking off into this major tributary. Before we reached it an Essex Police launch bore down on us and hailed us, ordering us to stop. My first reaction was to think there was a connection with the accident, but they simply wanted to know what we were doing. I told them where we had come from, where we were going and that the Walton Coastguard had all the details. The tone of the officer's voice gave the distinct impression that he thought we were a group of idiots to be crossing the shipping lanes. We did not argue and I could not be bothered to tell them the full story.

Suitably "chastened", we paddled off on a more southerly heading to show willing in heeding their warning and shortly afterwards the low silhouette of the Isle of Sheppey came into view. It triggered a mixture of emotions. I had lived the moment a hundred times in my imagination and had to assure myself that this was the real thing. The sense of achievement was minimal compared to that which I had anticipated; there was some feeling of relief that the pressure was nearly off; there was some sadness that a major episode in my life was coming to a close, but my main feeling was a growing sense of dread, anticipating the moment when I would have to break the news of David Wibrew's death to his brother. To make matters worse, Mick was clearly on a "high" and I would dearly have loved to shirk my responsibilities in bursting the bubble.

As we closed with the Sheppey shore the moment came when we could pick out the cranes of the port of Sheerness and the squat outline of the blockhouse on Garrison Point. Could it really have been almost half a year before that we had sat beneath it to eat our lunch on an April morning? At precisely 1420 we paddled round the point, just a few metres off the beach. The circle had been closed.

High water was not due until 1600. The tide would therefore continue to pour into the Medway, giving us plenty of time to paddle to Gillingham Strand by the end of the afternoon. The circumnavigation was already complete at the point we crossed our original course and this prompted us to postpone our arrival at Gillingham. We felt we owed it to all those who had supported us to make something special of our finish and, for this reason, we had decided to hold back and make an official arrival on Saturday. Meanwhile we would keep a low profile at home and try to minimise the number of people who knew where we were. Richard's father had been brought into this plot and so was going to meet us a few miles short of Gillingham at Mariner's Farm, a small inlet on the south side of the estuary, where he kept a caravan.

Everywhere we looked as we paddled on up river from Garrison Point was familiar. Swale Ness, Burntwick Island and the jetties of Bee and Oakham Ness (known throughout our club as "Berry Wiggins", after the company that works them); over the flooded mud spit of the Bishop Ooze we entered Half-Acre Creek and the final short paddle to Mariner's Farm. Shortly before we left the main channel, the paddle steamer *Waverley Castle* chugged by, her decks teeming with sightseers. From somewhere among them a voice shouted Mick's name. So much for our secret arrival.

At 1615, on top of the tide, we came to the quiet backwater and slip of Mariner's Farm and Dave Elliott (Richard's dad) was there to meet us. In his typically exuberant style he was more enthusiastic about our homecoming than we were. He was so proud of his "boy". We had agreed to stay in Dave's caravan, parked in a neighbouring orchard, but Mick's bereavement required a change of plan. Mick was still unaware of what had happened and remained unsuspicious even when Richard suggested we leave our gear at the caravan but sleep at his home, where his mother had prepared a meal for us.

Almost two hours later we were in the Elliotts' house, showered and eager to eat, when Mick decided he would telephone home. It was the moment I had been hoping to avoid all day but I could no longer put off. Within half an hour the necessary arrangements had been made and Mick's brother-in-law arrived to take Mick home. As he closed the door behind him it marked the breaking up of our fellowship and to all intents and purposes was the end of the expedition.

We did not come together again until we met at Richard's house on the following Friday evening. But this was more a formality, like a rehearsed performance, rather than a real part of the journey. While Mick had been away, Richard and I had busied ourselves tidying up many loose ends and paving the way towards a return to a normal, land-based existence. There was little doubt that we were glad to be back and were looking forward to the reception that was being prepared for us but of which we were denied details. Our instructions were to finish at 1300 and, know-

As we entered the Medway Estuary we were overtaken by the 'Waverley Castle'.

ing this created problems with the tide, we said we would spend the morning in the estuary at Darnet Fort.

Saturday dawned a splendid day and at first light we left Richard's house to drive to Mariner's Farm and pack our boats for the last time. We had to be out of the creek early to guarantee water over the mud flats and launched at 0700. Half an hour's paddle was all it required to reach Darnet Island. With its western neighbour Hoo Island, it commands the major narrows into the Medway. Both islands have splendid ruins of nineteenth-century forts and it was on a muddy beach below the fort at Darnet that we now disembarked to kill time.

We had a whole morning in front of us and resorted to habit without discussion. Driftwood was collected and we soon had a fire going to sit round. It was not necessary for cooking or keeping warm, for it was sunny and calm; it just seemed the natural thing to do. As the morning wore on it became increasingly difficult to contain a growing excitement. Eyes were frequently drawn towards Gillingham, just a little way up river. Who would come out to meet us?

Shortly before midday we noticed a large number of specks among the moorings up river. A few minutes later the tell-tale flash of paddles identified the specks as an armada of kayaks. Barely containing our excitement, we awaited their arrival. Almost all our club members, along with many paddlers we had never seen before, pulled into the beach on Darnet. They had come to bring us home.

When we joined them on the water, we were treated to a re-enactment of a ceremony first performed for Geoff Hunter's benefit when he paddled home after his solo trip in 1970. We knew something was about to happen when we noticed that Rob Catchlove had suddenly sprouted a bow-tie. Pulling the boats together around us in a great raft he then delved into his cockpit to produce a napkin and a silver tray bearing flutes of champagne. Two bottles were demolished in the space of a few minutes – as if we were not light-headed enough without the alcohol.

Arrival at Gillingham Strand after five months of paddling.

The accompanying fleet fell in behind us just before we reached the Strand. As we turned ashore from the moorings, bunting-decked yachts sounded off horns. The boats ran up the beach next to the slipway and we were back. A host of people were waiting for us. While we looked for the faces we loved among the crowd, we had to suffer the formalities due to local dignitaries and master our emotion and slightly swimming heads to be interviewed by a news team from T.V.S. Then it was hugs and kisses from all directions and our boats were being carried off for us.

The party went on until late that Saturday night.

It is not for us to comment on whether our journey was "significant" in canoeing terms. It was certainly a "first" and it is better to let some of the statistics speak for themselves. Readers can then draw their own conclusions.

By the time we finished we had paddled 2,612 miles. Surprisingly, this is only marginally further than the mileage logged by Nigel Dennis and Paul Caffyn when they made the first trip around the British mainland. The closeness of the figures highlights the extent to which we took a direct line and cut as many corners as possible. We had certainly taken on many long open crossings as a matter of routine in our journey.

The weather was generally poor and statistics would suggest we were unlucky. We ended up paddling on slightly less than two-thirds of our total days away. On the days we did paddle, we therefore had to paddle further and the average length of a paddling day was around 27 miles. The most noteworthy point about the weather amounts to a cruel irony. The research before the expedition suggested that our greatest constraint was the available length of the paddling season. The weather cycle of 1986 showed quite clearly that our April start was too early for that particular year and the best weather sequence began in mid-September, lasting for several weeks after we had finished. Yet, having stated that, Graham Almack (the solo paddler we had encountered at Applecross) had started his journey round the mainland in July but failed to finish in the late autumn.

In terms of publicity, our trip was not publicly acknowledged or acclaimed on any national scale. Local television and local newspapers served us well but no national newspaper was prepared to print a single line of the press release we put out to announce the successful conclusion of our expedition. Even allowing for the vulture-like qualities of a media which generally displays a preference for reporting sensational disaster rather than successful endeavour, I found this disappointing. We had collected a respectable sum of money for charity during the expedition and I would have expected this to have news value, even if the canoeing itself was not deemed worthy of public interest.

The charity we had chosen was the Bob Champion Cancer Trust but the collection of money posed a difficult problem. "Operation Raleigh" had appeared to solve this problem when they offered to organise money collection, using their regional administration to drum up publicity and their "venturers" to do the foot-work as we paddled past each region. The partnership offered considerable potential. Given that I had been treated for a malignant tumour in 1977, the idea had obvious appeal. Unfortunately, the support "Operation Raleigh" had offered was not forthcoming.

Celebrations at the end of a memorable trip.

Handled properly, a great deal of money might have been made. What we collected personally was a tiny fraction of what could have been raised. Whatever the reasoning, the national press ignored us.

The expedition was over as far as most people were concerned by the end of September but for Mick, Richard and myself, resettling into normal life would take many months. Life at work and in personal relationships had moved on while we had been absent and not always for the best. In this sense the expedition would leave some permanent scars. If we had really understood the full cost of the expedition in the widest sense, I have serious doubts if it would have taken place.

Mick seemed to cope the best and from outward appearances he slotted straight back into his old life without hitches. Richard paid dearly. His relationship with Mandy had been a great support to him during the journey and getting back to her was a major motivating factor. Now they split up. He was also dissatisfied with his work and eventually left the avionics industry to work in his father's carpentry business. I went through a long period of insomnia. Having got used to long, physical days and a bare minimum of sleep, I could not cope with the inactivity of school life and rarely slept for more than three or four hours. It did not seem to harm me, but it was an inconvenience until I realised I could use the extra time it created as an ideal "quiet time" that would lend itself to being used for writing up the paperwork generated by the expedition.

The most difficult thing for me was to take my working life with due seriousness. Decisions that had been taken on a daily basis during the expedition had frequently been matters of life and death. Now I was trying to work in a routine where my colleagues became engrossed in long, soul-searching pontification over some child who was not wearing his school uniform properly. Worse than that, many discussions took place only to reach no meaningful conclusions or decision. Sometimes it made me want to shout out for sanity. In a way I resented no longer being my own boss.

The inevitable question to be asked is, "Would you do it again?" The answer from me would undoubtedly be in the negative. It is difficult to wish something "undone" that has taken up such a big chunk of our lives and required so much effort. There were many parts of the journey that were superb and a few that were quite grim, but on the whole, five months of such activity was too much in one go. All of us wanted to carry on canoeing, but the appeal lay in doing something different for a while. Mick and Richard went straight into race training and after a heavy winter schedule, were part of the Gillingham team that finally took the Team Trophy for the Devizes–Westminster Canoe Race of 1987. Although I carried on with some coaching work, I stopped race training to make the time to write up this account.

On balance, one of the best things to come out of the journey was something for which we had never looked or planned. That was the number of friends we made and the hospitality we were asked to share at our numerous stopovers. The memories of this aspect of the expedition deserve an equal place with the host of canoeing experiences which the three of us will no doubt relive in our minds for many a year.

Postscript

By the time this book goes to press, the events described and illustrated in these pages will have slipped four years into the past. What I had written in haste to give some sense of immediacy to the story has now lost its topicality.

Hopefully, however, my sense of early urgency was not entirely wasted. Although the objectivity of long-term hindsight will have suffered, there remains some value in recording events in "hot blood", whilst they are real and vivid memories. Having had ample opportunity to recount the story in parts, I am only too aware of how easy it is to create a myth, enshrined in a cosmetic haze or superficial gloss (whichever best suits the story-teller, the episode and awareness of the audience) – a tendency which becomes easier as the events recede into the distance. Whilst the story-line may benefit from such an approach, the truth does not. By leaning heavily on our three separately kept diaries, it was always my intention to re-create our perception of events as it was at the time. This may not always have been to the personal credit of our team, but for this I make no apologies.

Readers may well be curious to know how some of the long-term consequences of our journey have worked out. My own view is that our characters have continued to run to form. Mick's life has predictably followed its old routine, revolving almost entirely around swapping the seat of his lorry cab for that of a racing kayak. Richard is securely established as a self-employed builder and, as will be explained, has displayed a canoeing potential that may yet peak even higher. My own attempts to seek new challenges have been focused on a career change. Although I continue to work in education, it is for the London Borough of Havering as Head of their Outdoor Education Centre. Sea canoeing remains an important and vital drug in my life and I continue to indulge in dreams of new challenges . . .

Some important characters and aspects of my tale have sadly passed from the scene. Rod Mitchell, who had been my closest friend for so many years and provided such good moral support to us in Northumberland, was to die of the cancer that he was fighting during our stay with his family in Cullercoats. Gillingham Canoe Club is no more. It was strangled into oblivion by the economic pressures of paying commercial rents, with no council subsidy and in spite of members contributing £12.00 per month in an attempt to keep the club alive. The marathon racers of the club then moved as a group to Maidstone Canoe Club, and it is ironic but satisfying to know that they should have been the backbone of the Maidstone team which took the Team Prize in the Devizes–Westminster Canoe Race of 1990. This performance was capped by Richard and Rob Catchlove winning the Senior event, whilst Mick and Richard's old partner Dean took the medal for third place.

Sea kayaking continues to flourish and grow in popularity. This must be viewed against the background of increasing aggravation and frustration over canoeing access to inland rivers – the most irritating and important aspect of the modern paddling scene. I would also guess that this is partly due to the increased awareness of environmental experiences available through sea kayaking, and an expression of the "Green Movement" in paddling terms.

Above all, one should not ignore the recent technical advances in equipment. The rudders which we fitted at a time when they were comparatively rare are now common. The most important new development in my view will prove to be the availability of seaworthy and properly designed double-seat sea kayaks like the Aleut II. With their higher cruising speed, the potential for more demanding journeys (and long open crossings in particular) is greater than ever.

If paddlers can race at 6 knots with portages for 20 hours, then why not cruise at 5 knots and without portages for slightly longer periods? The prospect of kayak crossings in excess of 120 land miles does not seem so unreasonable. Bearing in mind that many white-water rivers which were considered impossible to paddle fifteen years ago are now paddled regularly, what journeys will some intrepid team from the next generation of sea paddlers be prepared to undertake? Who will paddle round Britain and Ireland but taking in the Channel Islands, the Scillies, St. Kilda and the Shetlands? Who will island-hop from the Scottish mainland to the Faeroes? Who will circumnavigate South Georgia, perhaps paddling the difficult west coast as one uninterrupted leg?

No sea paddler worth his salt can have failed to be inspired by the sense of physical space and limitless horizons when paddling out of sight of land. The appreciation of how far these horizons might extend is a realisation I envy the sea paddlers of the twenty-first century.

Appendix A: Tidal Terminology

Some writers on nautical matters and many "boating" people appear to gain perverse pleasure in making the understanding of tides as difficult as possible. They often assume everyone knows as much physical science as they do and sometimes describe their subject with as much jargon as they can muster. Of course, a deep understanding of tides is a science in itself but the rudimentary concept is not really as "magical" as some people would have you believe.

I have generally tried to explain the technical terms I have felt it proper to use within the text or allowed the context to speak for itself. Acknowledging that there will almost certainly be instances when I have failed in this objective, I have therefore put together this appendix as a point of reference. To keep the explanations brief, I have assumed an understanding of the preceding terms in the list.

TIDE   Most commonly, the vertical movement of the sea in relation to the shoreline or sea-bed and caused by the gravitational pull of the moon and sun.

TIDAL STREAM   The horizontal movement of the sea along a shoreline or across the sea-bed as large bodies of sea water are moved in response to the same forces that cause the vertical movement.

SPRING TIDE   Once a fortnight, the gravitational pull of the moon comes into line with the gravitational pull of the sun. This occurs close to the "new" moon and "full" moon. It causes a larger than usual bulge of water to form. Consequently, both the tides and tidal streams are more pronounced at this time, producing a greater "tidal range". This means that the tide comes in further and goes out further than usual. Since greater volumes of water are being moved about, the tidal streams are also swifter. At certain times of the year the moon is closer to the earth than at others. At such times the moon is said to be "in perigee"; it will be exercising a stronger gravitational pull and therefore producing exceptionally big spring tides.

NEAP TIDES   Half-way between each set of spring tides the gravitational pull of the moon is at right angles to that of the sun. This occurs around the time of the "half" moon. It causes a more even distribution of water on the earth's surface so that the tides, tidal streams and tidal range are less pronounced. Therefore the tides do not go out or come in as far as usual. At certain times of the year the moon is further from the earth and is said to be "in apogee". Therefore the associated tides are particularly small.

TIDAL SET   The direction towards which a tidal stream is moving.

TIDAL DRIFT   The rate at which a tidal stream is moving. This is usually expressed in knots – one knot being a speed of one nautical mile in one hour and one nautical mile being one minute of latitude. This all sounds terribly nautical. As a rule of thumb, think of a nautical mile as being a little less than two kilometres.

FLOOD TIDE   A rising tide.

EBB TIDE   A falling tide.

TIDAL BEHAVIOUR PATTERNS   The movements of the moon are the single most important factor influencing the tides. The moon takes about 24 hours and 50 minutes to circle the earth. This is called a "lunar day". During the course of a lunar day there will be two complete tidal sequences – every 12 hours and 25 minutes the tide will go through a complete sequence of high water to low water to high water. This half-daily cycle is properly described as "semi-diurnal". In open water, away from major obstacles to movement such as headlands and estuaries, the tide will

187

flood for half a sequence and ebb for the other half. Accordingly, tidal streams move in one direction for half the cycle and reverse their flow for the other half. Thus far the pattern seems simple but a study of tidal movements on many parts of the coast will soon reveal a complication – the time at which the tide stops rising and begins to fall does not always coincide with the time that the tidal stream reverses its direction of flow. The extent to which this anomaly occurs depends on the configuration of the coastline in question. In my experience, this idea is not readily grasped.

I found it easier to form an understanding by trying to visualise the tidal movements in three dimensions. Imagine the tide as an elongated bulge of water of huge proportions, like some enormous, rounded wave or ripple that rolls along the coast. As the wave begins to arrive at any given point on the shore, so the tide begins to rise up the beach while the wave face continues to move on. High water at our given point will coincide with the arrival of the crest of the wave, which is still moving in the same direction (perhaps for another couple of hours) while the back of the wave passes by. During this time the tide is dropping down the beach but the tidal stream has not yet reversed.

The period of maximum tidal movement is usually about half-way through the flood and again half-way through the ebb. Around the time when the tidal stream changes direction there is relatively no movement and this part of the tidal sequence is often described as "the slack" or "slack water". Therefore one should end up with a picture of the tide building up in strength from slack to mid-tide and then lessening again as it approaches the next slack.

Unfortunately, there are numerous exceptions to these generalisations, which is why mariners pay such careful attention to collecting tidal information from charts, tidal stream atlases and from pilotage publications. The most common complication is the way that the inshore tides tend to turn before the offshore tides that are shown on the tidal stream atlases. This difference in timing can be as much as a couple of hours, underlining the importance of trying to gather local knowledge as well. However, it is the permutations of these variables that make navigation on the sea so challenging and interesting. The forces of nature involved can be on an immense scale. The experienced sea canoeist will usually be looking to plan an expedition to use these forces to his advantage rather than fight them.

TIDE RACE   Where a fast-flowing tidal stream is constricted – as off a headland or between islands – the constriction causes acceleration and the associated water movements can be exceptionally violent. This is particularly so when the wind blows against the direction of flow, so that the increased friction between the water surface and the air moving over it causes particularly large waves. The tide race may be an area of sea that paddlers wish to avoid or a white-water playground, according to the weather conditions (the wind being the main factor) and the ability and inclination of the party.

OVERFALL   Where a fast-flowing tidal stream meets a shoaling bottom, then upward-moving water currents can occur to create a disturbed water surface. Such a disturbance can manifest itself as an oily-looking upwelling "mushroom" or "boil" of water, or can cause irregular, unpredictable, steep-sided, pyramidal waves that are sometimes called "stacks". They may have crests that appear to be bursting upwards and in extreme cases the scale and violence can be an area for the kayak paddler to avoid or play in. Just to confuse issues, overfalls often form in conjunction with tide races and consequently sea paddlers tend to be rather loose in their application of these terms.

TIDE RIP   Most commonly, the violent horizontal movement of water along a surf beach, caused by the scouring action of the surf inside a sand-bar, so that water drains along channels running parallel to the shoreline. There will usually be a point where such channels turn to flow back out to sea. They are particularly dangerous to swimmers and capsized kayaks but will also provide a route out to sea through the surf. It can also be a particularly swift flow of tidal water, as along the edge of a breakwater, and is sometimes used to describe the area where two or more differing tidal streams come together.

Appendix B: Wave Terminology

Whole books have been written on the subject of waves but the technical terms used in this text have been kept to a minimum.

Only two methods of wave formation are relevant to an understanding of our journey. The first of these occurs when waves are being caused by upward-moving water currents where a fast-moving tidal stream meets a shoaling bottom. This is the classic "overfall", as explained in Appendix A. However, most of the waves encountered on the sea have been generated by the wind – where the movement of air disturbs the water surface because of friction. The result is ripple patterns of varying size, according to the forces generating the disturbance and the distance over which the wind is travelling, more properly called the "fetch". Many terms are relevant to describing the physical appearance of waves or an area of waves.

WAVE CREST   The highest part of the wave.

WAVE TROUGH   The lowest part of the wave.

WAVE HEIGHT   The vertical distance from trough to adjacent crest.

WAVE LENGTH   The horizontal distance from one crest to the next.

WAVE FACE   The steep side of the wave.

WIND WAVE   A wave generated by the wind blowing over it at that particular moment.

BREAKING WAVE   When the wave face becomes so steep that the crest begins to tumble down it. Where the crest is spilling down the wave face fairly gently, it is called a "spilling break" but sometimes the whole wave suddenly collapses and this is a "plunging breaker" which is said to be "dumping". This latter type of wave is usually formed on steeply shelving beaches.

SURF   An area of breaking waves, usually close to the shoreline but also over reefs and shoals.

"SOUP"   The area of white and foaming water that forms to shoreward after the surf has already broken and dissipated most of its energy.

GREEN WAVE   A wave that is not breaking.

SWELL or GROUNDSWELL   Waves may continue to travel long distances from the point on the ocean's surface where they are first generated and they become more regular in form as they do so. Such waves are called the swell or groundswell.

A "SEA"   Where several wave patterns combine it can cause a complicated and confused pattern, usually called a "sea".

CLAPOTIS   When two wave patterns are moving in near-opposite directions (as when they are reflected from a cliff-face or breakwater) they may momentarily combine to form particularly big waves with tall, pyramidal crests and steep sides. They are difficult to predict and can be extremely violent, sometimes throwing many tons of water high in the air in a great, vertical explosion. Such conditions are described as clapotis.

BACKWASH   The seaward movement of a spent wave as it retreats back down the beach. Where this water is moving down the beach beneath the oncoming waves the backwash is sometimes called the "undertow".

Appendix C: Wind Strength

The sea canoeist can always add layers of extra clothing to protect himself against the cold; he can remove clothing, increase fluid intake or wear protective headgear to shield himself from the debilitating effects of the sun and excessive heat; he invariably expects to get wet; tight navigation can allow him to venture out in the thickest fog; but he is relatively helpless when it comes to delimiting the effects of strong winds. On open water, the canoeist's main concern is the wind.

During the course of the expedition I became obsessed by my concern for what the wind was going to do. It could make a long leg of the journey easy or make a short leg impossible. It could give us an easy day or a physically exhausting one. At worst, it could turn our enjoyment into a nightmare.

In the text, I have sometimes referred to the wind strength in terms of knots, I have used technical, descriptive terms (such as "fresh breeze") and often used the number system of Admiral Beaufort's Wind Scale, used by mariners since 1808. While such terminology means a great deal to those who regularly use the outdoors, it will be useful for those less familiar to have a point of reference so that all these methods can be seen in relation to each other, with some idea of what effects this will have on the state of the sea. The table set out here has leant heavily on that set out in John Ramwell's *Sea Touring*, a manual for sea canoeists that is presently out of print; the table is reproduced here with his kind permission. For more detail, in the standard reference which presents Admiral Beaufort's observations in full, one should consult the Meteorological Office's publication, *Meteorology for Mariners* (H.M.S.O., London 1979).

Beaufort Wind Force	Mean Wind Speed (Knots)	Met. Office Descriptive Terms	Sea State in the Open Ocean	Likely Wave Height in Feet
0	0	Calm	Sea like a mirror	---
1	2	Light air	Scale-like ripples form	---
2	5	Light breeze	Small wavelets. Crests have a glassy look but do not break.	½
3	9	Gentle breeze	Large wavelets. Crests begin to break. Scattered "white horses".	2
4	13	Moderate breeze	Small waves with larger wave length, Frequent "white horses".	3½
5	18	Fresh breeze	Moderate waves. Many "white horses". Possibly some spray.	6
6	24	Strong breeze	Large waves begin to form. Extensive foam crests. Probably some spray.	9½
7	30	Moderate gale	Sea heaps up. Wind-blown foam. Some spindrift.	13½
8	37	Fresh gale	Moderately high waves. Long streaks of foam. Crests breaking into spindrift.	18
9	44	Strong gale	High waves. Dense foam. Tumbling crests. Extensive spray.	23
10	52	Storm	} Not relevant to sane paddlers!	29
11	60	Violent Storm		37
12	68	Hurricane		

Index

Italic page numbers refer to black-and-white illustrations.